Friendship
IN CONTEXT

Friendship
IN CONTEXT

Edited by

HELENA ZNANIECKA LOPATA
Center for the Comparative Study
of Social Roles
Loyola University

DAVID R. MAINES
The Pennsylvania State University

 JAI PRESS INC.

Greenwich, Connecticut   London, England

Library of Congress Cataloging-in-Publication Data

Friendship in context / edited by Helena Z. Lopata, David R. Maines.
    p. cm.
    ISBN 1-55938-325-9
    1. Friendship.   I. Lopata, Helena Znaniecka, 1925–
II. Maines, David R.
BF575.F66F75   1990
158'.25--dc20   90-23155
                                                            CIP

Copyright © 1990 JAI PRESS INC.
55 Old Post Road, No. 2
Greenwich, Connecticut 06836

JAI PRESS LTD.
118 Pentonville Road
London N1 9JN
England

Manufactured in the United States of America

ISBN: 1-55938-325-9

CONTENTS

PREFACE

A book devoted to FRIENDSHIP—the minute I mention to anyone, whether it be colleague, friend or acquaintance that we are putting together a book on friendship, I'm greeted with instant response. People, it seems, are willing to talk for hours about their own friends or about their theories of friendship. Europeans, South Americans, in fact most peoples of societies other than American, stress the significance of their relation with same-gender friends and comment on the incidental nature friendship seems to have in the lives of members of American society.

Yet, friendship is one of the most emphatically idealized relations in America. It is described in popular culture and pop sociology, "serious" sociology and related literature as one of only two social relations (the other being that of erotic love) developed and maintained with freedom of choice, unpolluted by ulterior motives and free from the crass demands of "secondary" or more instrumental relations. It is the *par excellance* of the primary relations described by Cooley and positively evaluated by social scientists; the term "primary" implying not only an order of appearance but also of "bestness." Primary relations are seen as purer, nicer, more "human" and humanity-maintaining than their counterparts, secondary relations. Friendship as a primary relation is visualized as even closer than that of blood brothers, without the competitiveness that mars biological relationships. It is able to "hang loose" from other relations, the love manipulating or obedience enforced association with a mother or father, the attention demanding connection with a child or spouse, the status maintaining regimentation of the military or executive office. It is ideally multi-faceted, involving each partner in interaction scenes supplying in kaleidoscope manner opportunities for all self-feelings and sentiments, showing the total human being, freely trusting and self-disclosed through confidant exchanges. Friendship ideally supports positive self-images, the view of a social person who is respected and accepted, whose trespasses are forgiven without an aftermath of diminished worth. It offers a "looking-glass" image of attractiveness, wit, wisdom, tenderness, strength, loyalty, braveness and kindness. Friends are people of equal status and equal power, who do not coerce the relationship or take advantage of it in order to reach external goals. Friends help each other when needed, dropping other obligations if the need is strong. Friends stay with each other on the battlefield, in societal or private wars protecting and taking care of each other's wounds. Friends provide a feeling of warmth and serve as security even when they are not physically present, a reference group for testing ideas and team back-up for performances in front of audiences.

As people talk to me about this beautiful relationship, and when the social scientists, including our authors in this volume write about it, they tend, however, to move easily into a discussion of the constraints that make friendship impossible to accomplish, at this stage of life, or in their real situations. The constraints appear from many sources. The men who speak of close friends often lodge them in European knightly legends, the spirit of pioneer men fraternally bonded together in conquering the elements, buddy relations of emotionally charged battles, in retrospect and film idealized wars (see Little, chapter 10). And, they explain, life is now very different. Men, and sometimes women, lodge this relation in masculine terms, á la Tiger. Women do not "bond" or form similar friendships by nature of their roles and their socialization which leads to competition and a lack of trust. Women have cliques, coffee klatching and the exchange of recipes and confidences in an "other directed" world of suburban bedroom communities—as caricatured in cartoon and, sometimes, in sociological works. Although much of America's media emphasis is now on the changing roles of women as they leave *en masse* fulltime homemaking, the stereotypes of the past persist. A major emphasis of the feminist movement is to "teach women how to be friends," according to Acker, Barry and Esseveld (Chapter 5), although several male sociologists also claim their gender cannot develop really close friendships because of fear of consequences of disclosure.

The constraints on friendships reported by Americans come not only from gender identity but also from age related status. Friendships are the province of the young or the very old—of those who do not need to be involved in important roles which could be interfered with by the demands of such a strong relation. Traditionally, the woman in patriarchal families, at least, had to hang loose, never developing too demanding relations because she had to leave her home and territory to enter the territory dominated by hostile women, her mother- and sisters-in-law. The man, recently freed from patriarchal control, is taught to remain free from many self-selected entanglements. As close and exciting was the gang or the war, man has to "grow up" and establish his own household, with his own family which he is responsible for maintaining through his job. If he marries a "modern" woman, he must not return to help former friends in their gang "rumbles," as did Tony in *West Side Story*. If he has middle class values, he is not supposed to retain pre-marriage friendships unless they can be turned into couple-companionate ones, and sitting in neighborhood bars is no longer an acceptable way of spending free time (even in England). His obligations to his family are, or should be, much more important than his obligations to his friends. The same holds true of the wife, whose closest friend is ideally her husband—not a girlfriend chum—and whose major role focus is supposed to be within the house.

It is not just the family which places constraints on the friendship of adults, but also the job, particularly the "career" of the man. American culture demands strong job commitments of men, even if the occupation is in itself not very rewarding. Men are expected to shed inconvenient friends and even relatives who might interfere with the career, and not divulge, or "give off" information about themselves and their families which may be used against them later by today's friends. Upward mobility requires frequent changes in friendship cliques; changes made easier by geographical mobility. Even wives are taught by certain work organizations, especially the military, how to "cool the mark out" when dropping friends and how to develop new relations within companionate circles of the appropriate rank. Both are freed from obligations to blood brothers and sisters in the man's upward climb by the American emphasis on the economic institutions, but the couple must learn that devotion to a career, with which the man's ego and self-identity are tied, also means not insisting on life-long, demanding friendships.

Employers are often unwilling to allow the formation of friendships on the job. The purely bureaucratic mentality of the formal organization assumes that personal feelings may interfere with logical decision making in assigning a task or position. Ever since the Hawthorne studies, management has been wary of the informal support system among workers which prevent "rate busting" or "efficient" production. Loyalty toward the organization, not to friends, is what makes for efficient work. Since friendships are known to develop under conditions of stress, particularly in the face of a common enemy, which work organization wants strong cliques operating among the workers? Who else but management would be perceived as the enemy against which ranks must be closed?

Constraints on friendship can be lodged in the very location of the job or the home and size of the unit, be it an organization or a community (see Baker and Hertz, Chapter 11). Even when purposeful interference with friendship formation is absent, jobs vary considerably in the ease of social interaction during work hours and of the carry over into non-working times that are away from the work space. They also vary as to the kinds of people they offer as a pool for the conversion of vocationally associated contacts with peers, customers and people of a variety of roles. Thus, external and internal factors impinge on relations within any social group, affecting what happens among its members as they proceed toward the goals which brought them together in the first place. It has demonstrated how important household location is for contacts and friendships among the elderly.

Another very important source of constraints on friendship in adulthood is culture, and evidence from several societies, but mainly from the United States, indicates that the sub-cultures of lower social classes often lack the pre-conditions necessary for the conversion of acquaintances into friends. Fear, lack of trust, lack of self-confidence, the presence of a negative self-image and the lack of familiarity with norms outlining steps in friendship formation combine with the inability to protect privacy and the wish to hide past or present events so as to hinder the development and maintenance of achieved and voluntary relations aside from relatives and life-long associates.

People differ in whether they feel that friendship is part of normal life or not—that mutual trust, empathy, are possible or limited only to certain others. Many do not know the ceremonies of exchange and etiquette needed for the maintenance of interaction of "polite companionship" without invasion of privacy. Besides, as several people have explained to me, "I could never be friends with those people."

In spite of all the talk about friendship and references to "my friends" in common conversation, there has been surprisingly little sociological examination of this relation, except in specific situations or locales. It is possible that historical or cultural reasons for the weakness of friendship in America—if we are to believe our informants—have created a gap between definitions and expectations on the one side, and actuality of friendship on the other. We must, therefore, examine the historical and theoretical aspects of friendship, before turning to the chapters written especially for this volume.

We have been fortunate to find among our friends, sociologists who have studied various social relations in a variety of contexts, and we thank them for pulling out those aspects of research findings which deal with friendship. We are proud to be part of this much needed effort, which brings to social scientists and related folk such solid and well-written reports of new research.

Helena Znaniecka Lopata
David Maines

FRIENDSHIP:
HISTORICAL AND THEORETICAL
INTRODUCTION

Helena Z. Lopata

This chapter lays some of the foundation for Volume II of the *Research in the Interweave of Social Roles,* but this time the focus is on *Friendship.* After presenting a dictionary definition of the concept of friends, it moves to a brief historical overview of friendship in Western Europe and America during the last two to three centuries; a brief summary of studies including this relation; and a brief "social psychology of friendship" summarizing knowledge gained from these sources, the other chapters of this volume and my own research.

Americans appear to hold contradictory attitudes, sentiments and even definitions of friendship. At one extreme there is the idealization of friendship as a totally involving relation of great closeness, able to meet most, if not all, of the emotional and social needs of the partners. At the other extreme Americans explain, as I discussed informally in the preface, that such a relation cannot really exist in modern society, except during youth and among the elderly, because of the constraining measures on adults in their middle years of life and certainly not in their own circumstances. Philblad and Rozencranz (1968) found elderly people in small towns of Missouri who reported that "everyone in town is my friend," while others claimed not to have any friendships. Some Chicago area widows claimed to have had close friends before the husband's fatal illness or death, friends they never see now. They have made no new friends since widowhood although it occurred many years ago (Lopata, 1975, 1979). Other widows list many friends who enter only their social support system, as people with whom they engage in social activities outside of the home, but do not list them in the emotional support system, even when given over 30 chances to do so.

The wide range of use of the concept of friend by Americans is reflected in the definitions enclosed in a standard English dictionary. *The Oxford Universal Dictionary* (1955:752) offers several related definitions of friendship: "1. The state of being a friend; association of persons as friends; a friendly intimacy. 2. Friendly feeling or disposition felt or shown; friendliness." None of these definitions deal with a relation so we turn to definitions of "friend" in the hope of a more sociological emphasis, and find the following:

1. One joined to another in mutual benevolence and intimacy (J.). Not ordinarily used to lovers or relatives.
2. Applied loosely, e.g., to a mere acquaintance, or to a stranger; also, used by members of the 'Society of Friends' as the ordinary mode of address. Also often ironically.
3. A kinsman or near relation. Now only in pl.
4. A lover or paramour of either sex-1765.
5. One who wishes (another, a cause, etc.) well; a sympathizer, patron or supporter.
   b. transf. Anything helpful.
6. One not an enemy; one who is on good terms with another, not hostile or at variance, one who is on the same side in warfare, politics, etc.

The above certainly includes a variety of uses of the term friend in the English language. Our contributions to this volume do not include analyses of the "Society of Friends" or of behavior guaranteeing protection from the hostility of a mere acquaintance, but even then they contain great variations in what is expected of friendship.

The difficulties sociologists have in dealing with friendship as a social relation stem not only from the popular uses of this concept, but also from some of our own conceptual frameworks. The sociological division of the relational world into "primary" and "secondary," with all the implied biases toward the primary, pushes us into the idealized version of friendship as a total relation, so that many relations we study within specific situations become defined as limited in form or depth (Cooley, 1915).[1] A similar problem occurs when we try to polarize relations into "expressive," with friendship considered the perfect example, and "instrumental," with exploitive translated as the example. Parsons and Bales (1955) set the sociology of the family back into the nineteenth century of "true womanhood" and the "public man" with their view of the division of labor in this unit (Lopata, 1965; see also Sennett, 1977 and Welter, 1966).

The contributors to this volume refrain from such simplistic polarization of social relationship, instead they show how varied friendship is—ranging from a specific social role to a set of friendly sentiments. Most of the authors analyze the interweave of friendship with other relational features of such roles as priest, member of the armed forces, student (post-doctoral or re-entry), member of a community or a voluntary association, etc. They indicate that the compartmentalization of life in modern society makes it very difficult to involve the same individual in all of one's roles so that friendship often becomes a set of sentiments and actions which can develop in relations within social roles having other functions or purposes, rather than being an encompassing role of itself. That does not mean that all friendship relations are so embedded, but that many of those described in this volume appear to be so. A second main theme is that friendship has become—maybe always was—a conditional relationship, made so by the fact that Americans consider other social roles more important and assume that friendship in its fullest bloom would be competitive with these roles. In its ideal form it is often defined as potentially interfering with the primary roles, while some other societies appear to grant it a position of greater significance. If this conclusion is correct, then we will find Americans mainly developing friendly relations within the context of the job, the role of neighbor, the priesthood, etc., rather than pulling youthfully developed "chumships" into adult life as roles apart from other social roles (see Brown, chapter 2).

In order to examine this tentative conclusion as a hypothesis, we must look back historically, toward Western Europe and earlier America to see how observers have pictured the interweave of friendship with other social roles at other times.

SOME VIEWS OF FRIENDSHIP IN HISTORY

Human beings have spent most of their historical time in hunting, gathering or agricultural societies, usually organized along patriarchal lines

(Boserup, 1970; O'Kelly, 1980). Women in home economy societies joined the husband's family work group and were guaranteed numerous social contacts. Men and children were born into such groups. Most families traveled or lived with larger social units, providing an expanded pool of intimates. As late as the seventeenth century of Europe, the nuclear family of husband and wife with their children were embedded in an extended set of relations, making its members less dependent upon each other for social and emotional gratification than currently apparent. (Rosaldo & Lamphere, 1974; Ryan, 1979).

"A great place was given to friendship in the whole of the seventeenth century literature; a friendship which was a social relationship carried even further than most," writes Philippe Aries (1965:376) in his charming *Centuries of Childhood*. Examining the literature and art, including iconography, of Western Europe from the Middle Ages through the 18th century, he concludes that until the second part of the seventeenth century much of social life combined all aged and all ranked people into a round of constant contact. "No one was ever left alone" (399) and sociability was a purposely developed skill, with great emphasis on etiquette, games and amusements. The streets and the "big houses" of the upper classes afforded numerous opportunities for social contact. The streets were "the setting for commercial and professional activity, as also for gossiping, conversation, entertainments, and games" (341). In societies lacking the cafe or the English public house or pub where men spent hours in each others company "the only place where friends, clients, relatives and proteges could meet and talk" (393) were the manor homes. There was an interweave between friendships and other social relations, as the constant flow of visitors at all hours of day and night had numerous functions. "These visits were not simply friendly or social; they were also professional; but little or no distinction was made between these categories (393)." The societies of Europe were expanding dramatically, urbanizing and engaging in commerce with an increasing emphasis on personal success. Daily contacts and a great deal of sociability were identified as important sources for such success.

> "To make a success of life was not only to make a fortune, or at least that was of secondary importance; it was above all to win a more honorable standing in a society whose members all saw one another, heard one another and met one another nearly every day (376)."

The expansion of the society's middle class and the diffusion downwardly of upperclass behavior, particularly of norms and activities such as games, required training and books of etiquette specified how people should interact with each other and which behaviors they should refrain from in public.

However, changes occurred in these relations during the seventeenth century:

> The story outlined here strikes one as that of the triumph of the modern family over other types of human relations which hindered its development. The more man lived in the streets or in communities dedicated to work, pleasure or prayer, the more these communities monopolized not only his time but his mind. If, on the other hand, his relations with fellow workers, neighbors and relatives did not weigh so heavily on him, then the concept of family feeling took the place of the other concepts of loyalty and service and became predominant or even exclusive (375).

Thus, Aries claims that social life was removed from the streets. Social relations other than those involving the two spouses and their pre-adolescent children were pushed into the background of importance with the evolution of the very concept of family as opposed to "line," meaning patriarchal descent line, or household, which encompassed many people not related by marriage, descent, or the village community for peasants. According to Aries, the trends creating a family as a unique unit were accompanied by its privatization, "the family began to hold society at a distance, to push it back beyond a steadily expanding zone of private life (399)." Servants were removed to separate quarters; the common room within which all activity—eating, sleeping, playing, visiting, working and so forth, took place vanished. The halls were replaced by separate rooms for each activity; childhood was invented and children acquired a new importance; and "it was no longer good form in the late eighteenth century to call on a friend or acquaintance at any time of day and without warning (399)." Thus, "professional and family life have stifled that other activity which once invaded the whole of life; the activity of social relations. One is tempted to conclude that sociability and the concept of the family were incompatible, and could develop only at each other's expense (407)."

Interestingly, however, the privatization of the family did not improve the status of women, which had been going downhill for a few centuries, merely decreased their opportunities for social contact in shared complex households and public places. Aries does not explain the reasons for this loss of status, but the life of the family at the beginning and during the eighteenth century which he does describe is very constricted. In prior centuries, friendships of both children and adults were formed across sex, age and class lines, the children very early in life taking part in the play and work of adults. A family's own children were often apprenticed to other families to learn adult life under a discipline felt to be absent in parent-child relations, and were replaced by "little strangers" from other families. Adults in societies lacking the all-male cafes or pubs, and even those which drew sex lines in such places, afforded cross-sex contact not just casually in the street or through visits in the home, but in the highly institutionalized habit of the "promenade" in fashionable streets and parks, and village thoroughfares. The cutting off of street life and the privatization of the family limited each type of person in interest groups to the company of similar types by age, sex, class and family. Servants could no longer relate personally with masters; the village folk had to keep their distance from the landed gentry; business transactions took place in buildings isolated from other forms of human intercourse, and so forth.

Aries did not deal with the other factors changing society prior to the twentieth century in his concentration on the thesis of the alleged competition between the nuclear family and other forms of sociability and the consequences of gain of power by the former. Societal changes starting with the seventeenth century were dramatic and observed by other thinkers. Max Weber (1930) attributed these changes mainly to the prior Protestant revolution (it was more of a revolution than a reformation) which shifted the institutional focus toward the economic sphere of life, concentrating a man's effort upon the creation and accumulation of economic goods as proof of God's blessing. Other revolutions were taking place in the scientific, technological, industrial, navigational, commercial and political spheres of life, thus transforming the structure and social life of European societies. These were the factors (rather than the voluntary creation of the nuclear family) which freed the man from major dependence upon his patriarchal line at all times and in all places. Once able to gain training, tools and an income from sources other than the father or other relatives, he could set up and maintain his own household.

Simultaneously, the loss of power and status by his wife, as described but not explained in *Centuries of Childhood,* was an inevitable consequence of the shift of local values to the economic institution away from the home and the restrictions placed on the home vis-à-vis the public sphere of life. The nuclearization of the family supported economically by the husband working outside of its province, the separation of most of the productive work from the home, and the importance assigned to roles contributing directly to economic production rather than to other institutions made multileveled contact with people outside of the home difficult for the woman. The man became increasingly identified with his own marketability in the economic sector of social life, in competition with peers and with the self, as Erich Fromm (1947) pointed out a long time ago. Thus, while the woman's social world narrowed to the home based, private sphere, the man's world expanded to various aspects of the public sphere but became competitive and individualistic (see also Touba, 1980).

American society, supposedly depending heavily on friendships during the colonial and western expansion eras, adopted some of the European value systems, adding complications of its own which had inevitable consequences on the role of friend for women, for men, and between the genders. According to Dulles (1965) and Davidson (1974), pre-nineteenth century life in the colonies, particularly among the upper classes, included many leisure-time activities offering repeated contacts and opportunities for friendship of same sex and cross-sex types outside of the work or neighborhood interaction. Although life was varied in the different locations of settlement—ranging from summer resort play at Newport, Rhode Island to cowboy and miner, same-sex daily sharing of lunchtime and campfires interrupted by wild weekends in town—leisuretime and friendships were positively valued until clamped down upon by Puritanism in the 19th century. The Puritan ideology compounded the effects of the focus of work and monetary success with religious "detestation of idleness." Women were removed from the public lives of men and Dulles (1965) quotes many European travelers in America in their shock over the dullness of life on this side of the ocean. Lunchtime meals were eaten rapidly and often devoted to work; streets were quiet and lacked the games and amusements of the European streets; men and women could not enjoy outdoor activities together; theaters and horse races were the only major amusements available, and they were attended mainly by males (see also Davidson, 1974). Dulles concludes that "The status of women in the social life of the nineteenth century also had a very definite bearing on recreation. . . . It was a man's world with its tremendous emphasis on work and getting ahead (95)."

Actually, the pushing back of friendship when connected with leisure time or work (so from most of life) to the level of a "nice" but insufficiently important relation to warrant interference with family and the man's occupational life was functional to the rapidly and dramatically industrializing and immigrant absorbing American society. Within such a system, friendship becomes an unnecessary luxury for the man who must devote all his energies to success outside of personal relationships, and it continues to be difficult for those women who do not have the village street, the large household, or long known associates as pools from which to draw at least partial friendships. This does not mean, however, that "relations of polite companionship" have ceased (Znaniecki 1965). In fact, the opposite has developed. Rules of etiquette and occasions for organized social contact have spread from the "leisure classes" down the social pyramid, which has in the meantime, changed shape—bulging in the middle class, as "Americanization" and upward mobility siphons off those members of the lower or working classes which are not kept down by the vicious circle of prejudice-discrimination-limited life chances, and so forth (Veblen, 1899).[2] Carnegie (1936) and other experts have been teaching people how to win friends. Wives and husbands are now expected to be friends and companions involved in both comradeship and platonic relations while mutually engaged in couple companionate relations devoted to leisure time activities (Burgess, Locke and Thomes, 1971; Lopata, 1971, 1973, 1975, 1979). Work organizations expect friendly relations among their managers, although they are still concerned with too much friendliness among their workers (Fawles 1980; Kanter, 1977; Seidenberg, 1973; Vandervelde, 1979; Whyte, 1956).[3] Other complex organizations, such as the military, a university, or the church vary as to whether they consider friendship among their members, between some categories of their members, or with non-members "functional" or "dysfunctional" to their goals (see Janowitz, 1960; and Little, Maines, Gannon in this volume). Even the kibbutzim movement appears to be suspicious of personal or exclusive friendships (Baker and Hertz, chapter 11). Yet many people warn you in American society never to borrow money or a major tool from a friend, hire one to work for you or work for them and even the *Oxford Dictionary* previously quoted in the first definition notes that relatives and lovers are not friends. Like incest taboos, some of the norms of American society imply a need to segregate the role of friend from that of other social roles while allowing "friendly relations," if they are non-interfering, with goals of these other roles.

STUDIES OF HUMAN INTERACTION TOUCHING ON FRIENDSHIP

The main body of friendship literature focuses on its formation in the early years of life, or, at least, in the "pre-adult" period. Much of the research falls back on the work of J. L. Moreno, and other authors in the early issues of *Sociometry,* of Theodore M. Newcomb's (1961) *The Acquaintance Process* and on the small-group studies of Hare, Borgatta and Bales 1965. Both Suelzle (chapter 3) and Brown (chapter 2) summarize this literature in their chapters. Weinberg (1970) focused upon adolescent friendships of the same sex.

A second set of studies of friendship locates its significance and components in the life cycle although there is usually a limitation of stages such as to adulthood and old age. Friendship in later life has a rich recent literature. Most books on aging devote some attention to the meaning of this relation or to the ways in which people voluntarily or forcibly disengage and re-engage in it, as well as to factors influencing variations in such interaction (see Blau, 1951; Cumming and Henry, 1961; Havighurst and Albrecht, 1953; Hochschild, 1973; Lopata, 1973, 1975, 1979;

Philblad and Rosencranz, 1968; Williams and Loeb, 1960).[4] Friendship in middle years of life is usually described in connection with other social roles, as competing with family or work roles or as part of situational interaction. This includes the whole set of studies influenced by Elizabeth Bott's (1957) *Family and Social Network,* including Young and Wilmott's (1957) and Wilmott and Young's (1960) analysis of social relations in London, England; Joel Nelson's (1966) study of cliques in New Haven; and DeHoyos and DeHoyos' (1966) description of "The Amigo System and Alienation of the Wife in the Conjugal Mexican Family." These, and my own *Occupation: Housewife* (1971) as well as Bernice Neugarten's *Middle Age and Aging* (1968) relate friendship to family roles, as does the work of Babchuk and Bates (1961, 1963) and Blood (1969), and Blood and Wolf (1960). The new network research falls into this classification (see also Brown, chapter 2; Acker, et al., chapter 4; Bankoff, chapter 5).

Role strain or conflict produced by friendship relations in work roles or in certain types of organizations are described vividly by Vance Packard in *The Pyramid Climbers* (1962) and *The Status Seekers* (1961); William Whyte, Jr. in *The Organization Man* (1956); and Peter Blau (1957) in his discussion of the upwardly mobile business executive. George Homans (1951) in *The Human Group* summarized some of the research conducted over the decades in economic complex organizations which operate on the assumption that the informal communication, interaction and loyalty system would inevitably interfere with the formal structure's goals. David Maines, has an extensive bibliography of references to friendships in work and total institution situations in his dissertation "Encounters and Careers of Post-Doctoral Students" (1973): see also Maines, chapter 8; Levy, chapter 6; Gannon, chapter 8).

Other research in which friendship was examined, at least as part of a larger design, deals with total institutions such as the military, prisons or mental hospitals. Roger Little (see chapter 9) summarizes the work of Stauffer and his associates (1949), Janowitz (1959, 1960) and Moscos (1970), on the military. Friendships among male prisoners have been studied by Gresham Sykes (1958/1966) and others and reported in Cressey's (1961) *The Prison: Studies in Institutional Organization and Change.* Rose Giallombando (1966) discusses such relations in her study of a women's prison.

Friendship has also been studied within selected types of social groups, often those engaged in deviant behavior or at least in action which does not belong to the mainstream of American middle class behavior. This includes the literature on boy's adolescent gangs by Thrasher (1927), Short and Strodbeck (1965), or Miller (1973). Much of Becker's (1963) work has been focused on the *Outsiders* and some of it has dealt with friendships. Ned Polsky (1969) studied *Hustlers, Beats and Others* and

Gregory P. Stone (1972) combined several of these studies of different human activities in which friendship, or its manipulation, form part of the interaction scenes in *Games, Sports and Power*.

Baker and Hertz's chapter 11 contains a summary of the literature on friendship in various types of more or less open communities as part of their analysis of the factors that facilitate and constrain friendship in a kibbutz. The classic William Foote Whyte's (1955) *Street Corner Society* and the more recent, but equally insightful, Elliot Liebow's (1967) *Tally's Corner* focus on loose networks of relations among men who use a geographical locus within a neighborhood for repeated interaction. Gerald Suttles (1968) does the same in his *Social Order of the Slum*, showing how different ethnic groups vary in the form of their social integration. Many of the studies of urban and suburban life also deal with friendships, as exemplified by Bennett Berger's (1960) *Working Class Suburb* or Spectorsky's (1955) *The Exurbanites*. I (Lopata, 1971) studied various levels of friendliness and neighboring, both within the city and suburb. The classic analysis, albeit a rather biased one, is Riesman, Glaser and Denny's *The Lonely Crowd*, while Packard (1972) claimed an absence of deep friendships in his *A Nation of Strangers*. Studies which also covered friendship within ethnic communities include Gans' (1962) *The Urban Villagers*, Lopata's (1976) *The Polish Americans* or the famous *The Ghetto* by Louis Wirth (1928). Hochschild (1973), Rosow (1967) and Stephens (1976) studied levels of friendship interaction among people living in special housing centers (see Gusfield et al., chapter 10 and Baker and Hertz chapter 11).

A major contribution to our understanding of friendship per se, rather than friendship located situationally, comes from the symbolic interactionists. Dating as far back as Adam Smith, Georg Simmel, William James, George Herbert Mead and Charles H. Cooley this, "in retrospect formed" school has focused on the self, identity, human sentiments, significant symbols and the contribution of intimates to their development. Various levels of significant others and reference groups have been analyzed in their relation to the person from role taking, social interaction, relations and roles. Such concepts are interwoven in the theories of Herbert Blumer, Everett Hughes, Ralph Turner, Sheldon Stryker, Manford Kuhn, S. Kirson Weinberg, Gregory Stone, Howard S. Becker, Erving Goffman, Anselm Strauss, George McCall, Norman Denzin, Tamatsu Shibutani, Irwin Deutscher, and both of the editors as well as most of the authors contributing to this volume. Their work is also included in Arnold Rose's (1962) *Human Behavior and Social Processes*, and the various collections put together by Alfred Lindesmith, Anselm Strauss and Norman Denzin (1969, 1975), Norman Denzin (1978, 1979), Stone and Farberman (1981), and Gordon and Gergen (1968).

A SOCIAL PSYCHOLOGY OF FRIENDSHIP

The remaining section of this chapter will be devoted to a brief, highly exploratory analysis of various types of social relations, the directions in which they can develop, the facilitating and constraining factors in the development of friendships, situational locations, and the consequences of friendship for all those involved.[5]

Friendship between two or more persons can develop from the gradual transformation of a stranger non-relationship, through acquaintanceship to deepening intensity, to any combination of relational components defined by those involved and, though not necessarily, by observers as being a friendship. Strangers can be accidentally thrown together and friendship can emerge—purposely or in serendipity—among persons interacting under facilitating conditions in other relations or roles. It is important to note that the relation of friendship is one between individuals, since it involves individuated personalities, no matter how much each dyad or triad is immersed in a friendship network (Simmel, 1917/ 1950; Blau, 1961). A friendship relation can hang loose from other relations, but only if no one knows of it and no one else is involved in the exchanges of rights and duties associated with it. Thus, most friendships are immersed in the role of friend, if we use the Znaniecki (1965) concept of a social role as a set of patterned, interdependent relations between a social person and a social circle encompassing rights and duties on both sides. The function of the social circle may simply be to support, or even to interfere with the friendship, but it forms part of the role as long as there are definite duties and rights tying together more than two persons into patterned interaction revolving around the friendship relation. Relations between the friends or within the friendship core are usually tighter than their relations to the rest of the social circle which is supporting or constraining the partners.

A partial model of relations among people which can develop into different kinds of friendships would look something like Figure 1, although the conversion of friendship-developing lines would differ, depending on the starting point of the interaction and there is no inevitability of movement into any one of the different social relations.

The problem of creating a model of friendship paths, as indicated before, is the presence of so many images of friendship among Americans. The concept of stranger is easier to pinpoint; most people differentiate between non-person interaction as with a servant or waiter (Goffman, 1959), acquaintanceship and friendship. Formal role relationships within larger settings contain constraints or facilitators, which we will presently summarize. At this point, I would like to express disagreement with Simmel's (1950:317–329) thesis concerning the impossibility of role-

Figure 1. A Model of Social Relations by Degree of Personal Involvement and Paths of Movement to Friendships.

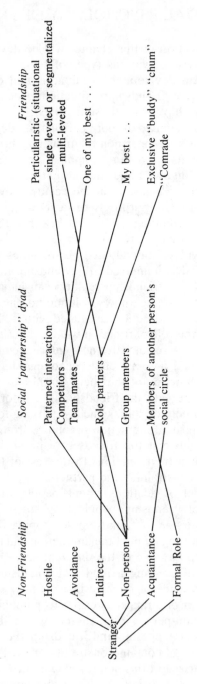

contingent or segmentalized relations becoming intimate friendships. Human beings can learn of each other's total lives indirectly, without having to be involved in each others whole role complex. They are freed from dependence on concrete interaction; they can live vicariously through the communication of past, present and future lives with each other. As Little (chapter 10) points out, "buddies" in the combat zone can become intimately familiar with each other as total personalities through confidences and shared correspondence, without having been woven into the familial, neighborhood, associational, play and work areas of each other's lives when these become activated. Our view of friendship should not be affected by "gemeinschaft" biases against changes in modern society that make direct involvement in our friends' total lives frequently impossible.

Thus, accepting the compartmentalization and confinement of friendship to the situational, we can classify the locus within which such relations can develop and be maintained as follows: (see also Brown, chapter 2) geographical situs of frequent contact, informal such as corridors or parks, formal devoted to leisure time activities or places devoted mainly to other functions but enabling repeated interaction; social role performance locations such as the club, the work place; larger social systems or spaces such as communities, military bases and multi-leveled settings in which the persons shift from one role to another while still in contact. The facilitating factors or conditions enabling friendship to develop include repeated interpersonal interaction (preferably face-to-face at least at the beginning), allowing pleasurable interchange using norms of "sociability" (Simmel, 1917, 1950) among social or situational equals, sharing a common culture and able to "take the role of the other" and to communicate significant symbols. The future friends must be willing to take the relation through one of the paths leading to different kinds of friendship.

Constraining conditions include the absence of facilitating conditions strong enough to help move the relation toward friendship, strain or role conflict, personal characteristics or emotional mismatch, and so forth. The components of friendship relations would include total personality involvement, with the help of communications showing elements of the person not brought out by the situation, symmetry of involvement, sharing of the definition of the situation and of power in interaction determination, intimacy, "transparency" (Jourdan, 1964), positive judgement of each other, affection, loyalty, shared activity and "team performance."

The consequences of friendship relations, in terms of benefits affect each friend individually in providing positive self- and other-feelings, sentiments of closeness, comfort, pleasure, anticipatory pleasure, empathy, trust and so forth; practical benefits such as gifts, services, protection, sociability, training, in skills, testing behaviors, partnership, team cooperation; inclusion in a network of friends; protection from unpleasant sentiments and activities, such as loneliness.[6] On the other hand, costs may include ostracism, isolation when the friend is absent, role conflict or strain in other roles, demands on time, energy, loyalty, sentiment, and self-disclosure, fear of, and actual future misuse of the former friendship. Consequences for other people because of the relation may be beneficial because of cooperative action, positive ambiance and services. Or, consequences may be negative because of the exclusiveness of the relation, jealousy, neglect, failure to meet emotional needs of the nonfriends, and so forth. Consequences upon the larger social system in which the friendship is lodged vary, depending on the nature of the system and whether the friendship contributes to its morale, esprit de corps, other interpersonal relations, meeting of the unit's goals, reinforcement of culture and internal status division, distribution of authority and power, or the opposite.

We can now turn to the chapters describing friendship in specific locations, or over the life course, keeping in mind the above outline and adding to it as we move into greater detail of the different kinds of friendships.

NOTES

1. Cooley (1915), who introduced the concepts of "primary" and "secondary" groups and relations was actually less restrictive in his division than are many of his followers, stating that the "we feeling," though developed in the primary group, was able under democracy to extend to the brotherhood of mankind. "Everything that tends to bring mankind together enlarges the reach of kindly feeling" (191). He was very much interested in the "enlargement of consciousness" and the "broadening of sentiment in all directions," and would not have endorsed the assumptions of many sociologists that it is impossible to feel friendly toward, or interact comfortably with, a variety and larger numbers of people. The bias against "secondary relations" is evident in much of the literature on "crowding" or the city, failing to take account of the mechanisms by which human beings can insure privacy (see Strauss, 1961; and Smith, Form and Stone, 1954 for discussions of this bias).

2. Much of the literature on lower or working class American life discusses strong cultural constraints on intimacy with nonrelatives (Komarovsky, 1967; Lopata, 1973, 1979; Rubin, 1976). Yet, friendship relations of a different time sequence and different obligations are available, in spite of these constraints, among certain categories of "under-class" men and women who are not involved in strong competing roles. This is one of the conclusions Elliot Liebow (1967) drew of the black adult men he studied in *Tally's Corner*. In spite of the fact that "Attitudes toward friends and friendships are . . . always shifting, frequently ambivalent, and sometimes contradictory" (181), such relations are an important part of the life-style of the men who, according to Hylan Lewis' introduction, are living under "unrelenting stress and catastrophic conditions (x)." Liebow's explanation for the great importance of friendships to the men meeting at Tally's Corner is as follows: "Unlike other areas in our society, where a large portion of the individual's energies, concerns and

time are invested in self-improvement, career and job development, family and community activities, religious and cultural pursuits, or even in broad, impersonal social and political issues, these resources in the streetcorner world are almost entirely given to the construction and maintenance of personal relationships (161)." One feature of these relations, however, is their short-lived and open-break availability. ". . . the easy quickness with which a casual encounter can ripen into an intense man-man or man-woman relationship, and the equal ease with which these relationships break down under stress (182). Such relations are then of a different nature than cause concern in other parts of American society, concern over too many demands, too often made, and invading the privacy of an anxiety-filled man or woman.

3. Since the classic Hawthorne studies, management has been leary of informal relations among workers, because of proven restriction of production and consensual alienation from the goals of the organization. Discussions of these attitudes are contained in any book on industrial relations, or occupations, including George Ritzer's (1977) and the earlier Edward Gross's (1958) *Work and Society*. See also summaries of the studies in George Homans' (1951) *The Human Group*.

4. And yet Havighurst and Albrecht (1953:191) found out that, among the older people they studied . . . "Only 7 percent have close-knit clique relations, such as giving and receiving invitations to dinner or to parties. By far the majority, 71 percent, have only scattered social contracts in loosely assembled groups such as the greetings to acquaintances at weekly church services, or the casual conversations with people in taverns or cigar stores, or on the courthouse lawn in summertime. Another 4 percent are quite solitary." A similar dependence upon casual outdoor contact can be found among many Chicago area widows (Lopata, 1975; 1979). In both studies, the older women tend to have been socialized into lower class culture so that it is likely that future generations of older people, having more education and more of an at least lower middle class life-style in younger years will be more inclined to developing friendships.

5. I am borrowing the concept of constraint from Zena Blau's (1961) classic "Structural Constraints on Friendship in Old Age."

6. The study of older widows which I conducted in the late 1960s found few of the sample of 301 women aged 50 and over still relating to, or receiving assistance from, their in-laws once the connecting link died. Unfortunately, we did not ask whose choice was the release of the tie (Lopata, 1973).

REFERENCES

Aries, Philippe
1965 Centuries of Childhood. New York: Random House, Vintage Books.
Becker, Howard S.
1963 Outsiders. New York: The Free Press.
Berger, Bennett
1960 Working Class Suburb. Berkeley, Calif.: University of California Press.
Blau, Peter
1957 "Social mobility and interpersonal relations." American Sociological Review 21:290–295.
Blau, Zena
1961 "Structural constraints of friendship in age." American Sociological Review 26:429–439.
Blood, Robert O., Jr.
1969 Marriage. New York: The Free Press.
Blood, Robert O., Jr. and Donald M. Wolfe
1960 Husbands and wives. New York: The Free Press.

Boserup, Ester
1970   Woman's Role in Économic Development. New York: St. Martin's Press.
Bott, Elizabeth
1957   Family and Social Network. London: Tavistock Publications.
Burgess, E. W., and H. J. Locke, and M. M. Thomas
1963   The Family: From Traditional to Companionship. New York: D. VanNostrand,
       4th ed.
Carnegie, Dale
1936   How to Win Friends and Influence People. New York: Simon and Schuster.
Cooley, Charles H.
1909   Social Organization. New York: Charles Scribner's Sons.
Cressey, Donald
1961   The Prison: Studies in Institutional Organization and Change. New York: Holt,
       Rinehart and Winston.
Cumming, E. and Henry William
1961   Growing Old. New York: Basic Books.
Davidson, Marshall
1974   Life in America: Bicentennial Edition. Boston, Mass.: Houghton Mifflin Company.
       2 Vols.
Dulles, Foster Rhea
1965   A History of Recreation: America Learns to Play. New York: Appleton Century
       Crofts.
Fowlkes, Martha R.
1980   Behind Every Successful Man. New York: Columbia University Press.
Fromm, Erich
1947   Escape from Freedom. New York: Rinehart and Co.
Gans, Herbert
1962   The Urban Villagers: Group and Class in the Life of Italian-Americans. New
       York: The Free Press.
Giallombando, Rose
1966   "Social roles in a prison for women," Social Problems 13 (Winter):268–288.
Glazer-Malbin, Nona (ed.)
1975   Old Family/New Family. New York: D. Van Nostrand Company.
Gordon, Chadd, and Kenneth J. Gergen (eds.)
1968   The Self in Social Interaction. New York: Wiley.
Gross, Edward
1958   Work and Society. New York: Thomas Y. Crowell.
Hare, A. P., E. F. Borgatta, R. F. Bales
1955   Small Groups. New York: Alfred Knopf, 2nd ed., (1965).
Havighurst, R. J., and Ruth Albrecht
1953   Older People. New York: Longmans, Green.
Hochschild, Arlie R.
1973   The Unexpected Community. Englewood Cliffs, N.J.: Prentice-Hall, Inc.
Homans, George
1950   The Human Group. New York: Harcourt Brace.
Janowitz, Morris
1960   The Professional Soldier. Glencoe, Ill.: The Free Press.
Kanter, Rosabeth Moss
1977   Men and Women of the Corporation. New York: Basic Books.
Komarovsky, Mirra
1967   Blue-Collar Marriage. New York: Random House.

Liebow, Elliot
   1967   Tally's Corner. Boston: Little, Brown and Co.
Lopata, Helena Z.
   1971   Occupation: Housewife. New York: Oxford University Press.
Lopata, Helena Z.
   1973   Widowhood in an American City. Cambridge, Mass.: Schenkman Publishing Company, General Learning Press.
Lopata, Helena Z.
   1975   "Couple-companionate relationships in marriage and widowhood." In Nona Glazer-Malbin (ed.), Old Families/New Families. New York: D. Van Nostrand Company.
Lopata, Helena Z.
   1976   Polish Americans: Status Competition in an Ethnic Community. Englewood Cliffs, New Jersey: Prentice-Hall, Inc.
Lopata, Helena Z.
   1979   Women as Widows: Support Systems. New York: Elsevier North Holland, Inc.
Moscos, Charles C.
   1970   The American Enlisted Men. New York: Russell Sage Foundation.
Nelson, Joel J.
   1966   "Clique contacts and family orientation in the nuclear family." American Sociological Review 31 (October): 663–672.
Neugarten, Bernice L. (ed.)
   1973   Middle Age and Aging. Chicago, Ill.: University of Chicago Press.
Newcomb, Theodore
   1961   The Acquaintance Process. New York: Holt, Rinehart and Winston.
O'Kelly, Charlotte G.
   1980   Women and Men in Society. New York: D. Van Nostrand.
(The) Oxford University Dictionary
   1955   Oxford: Clarendon Press, 3rd. ed.
Packard, Vance
   1959   The Status Seekers. New York: Cardinal Pocket Books.
Packard, Vance
   1962   The Pyramid Climbers. Greenwich, Connecticut: A Fawcett Crest Book.
Packard, Vance
   1972   A Nation of Strangers. New York: David McKay Company, Inc.
Parsons, Talcott, and Robert F. Bales
   1955   Family, Socialization and Interaction Process. New York: The Free Press.
Philblad, Terence, and Howard Rosencranz
   1968   Old People in the Small Town. Columbia, Mo: University of Missouri report.
Pleck, Joseph
   1975   "Man to man: is brotherhood possible." Pp. 229–244 in Nona Glazer-Malbin, Old Family/New Family. New York: D. Van Nostrand.
Polsky, Ned
   1969   Hustlers, Beats and Others. Garden City, N.Y.: Doubleday. Anchor Books.
Rainwater, Lee, Richard Coleman, and Gerald Handel
   1959   Workingman's Wife. New York: Oceana Publications, Inc.
Riesman, David, Nathan Glaser, and Reuel Denney
   1950   The Lonely Crowd. New Haven: Yale University Press (also in Doubleday Anchor Books. 1956).
Rosaldo, Michelle Zimbalist, and Louise Lamphere (eds.)
   1974   Women, Culture and Society. Stanford, California: Stanford University Press.

Ritzer, George
    1977   Working: Conflict and Change. Englewood Cliffs, N.J.: Prentice-Hall.
Rose, Arnold M. (ed.)
    1962   Human Behavior and Social Processes. Boston: Houghton Mifflin Co.
Rosow, Irving
    1967   The Social Integration of the Aged. New York: The Free Press of Macmillan.
Rubin, Lillian Breslow
    1976   Worlds of Pain: Life in the Working-Class Family. New York: Basic Books.
Ryan, Mary P.
    1979   Womanhood in America: From Colonial Times to the Present. New York: New
           Viewpoints, 2nd. ed.
Seidenberg, Robert
    1973   Corporate Wives—Corporate Casualties. New York: American Management
           Association.
Sennett, Richard
    1977   The Fall of Public Man. New York: Alfred A. Knopf.
Shea, Nancy
    1941   The Army Wife. New York: Harper and Brothers, Publishers.
Simmel, Georg
    [1915] The Sociology of Georg Simmel. Trans. and Ed. by Kurt H. Wolff. New
    1950   York: The Free Press.
Spectorsky, A. C.
    1955   The Exurbanites. Philadelphia: J. B. Lippincott Co.
Stauffer, Samuel, et al. (eds.)
    [1949] The American Soldier. Princeton, New Jersey: Princeton University Press.
    1950
Stevens, Joyce
    1976   Loners, Losers and Lovers: Elderly Tenants in a Slum Hotel. Seattle: University
           of Washington Press.
Stone, Gregory P. (ed.)
    1973   Sports, Games and Power. New Brunswick, N.J.: E. P. Dutton.
Stone, Gregory P., and Harvey Faberman (eds.)
    1970   Social Psychology Through Symbolic Interaction. New York: Wiley.
Suttles, Gerald
    1968   The Social Order of the Slum. Chicago, Ill.: University of Chicago Press.
Sykes, Gresham
    [1958] The Society of Captives: A Study of Maximum Security Prison. New York: Ath-
    1966   eneum Press.
Touba, Jacquiline R.
    1980   "Sex segregation and the woman's roles in the economic system: the case of
           Iran." Pp. 51–98 in Helena Z. Lopata (ed.), Research in the Interweave of Social
           Roles: Women and Men. Greenwich, Conn.: JAI Press.
Welter, Barbara
    1966   "The cult of true womanhood: 1820–1860." American Quarterly 18, 2 part 1
           (Summer): 151–160.
Whyte, William F.
    1955   Street Corner Society: The Social Structure of an Italian Slum. Chicago, Ill.:
           University of Chicago Press.
Whyte, William H. Jr.
    1956   The Organization Man. New York: Simon and Schuster.

Williams, Richard H.
  1960 "Changing status, roles and relationship." In Clark Tibbitts (ed.), Handbook of Social Gerontology. Chicago, Ill.: University of Chicago Press.
Wilmott, Peter, and Michael Young
  1960 Family and Class in a London Suburb. London: Routledge and Keagan Paul, Ltd.
Young, Michael, and Peter Wilmott
  1957 Family and Kinship in East London. New York: The Free Press of Macmillan.
Vandervelde, Maryanne
  1979 The Changing Life of the Corporate Wife. New York: Mecox Publishing.
Veblen, Thorsten
  1899 The Theory of the Lecture Class. New York: B. W. Heubsch.
Wirth, Louis
  1928 The Ghetto. Chicago, Ill.: University of Chicago Press.
Znaniecki, Florian
  1965 Social Relations and Social Roles. San Francisco, Calif.: Chandler Publishing Company.

PART I
FRIENDSHIP IN THE LIFE COURSE

A LIFE-SPAN APPROACH TO FRIENDSHIP

AGE-RELATED DIMENSIONS OF AN AGELESS RELATIONSHIP

B. Bradford Brown

There is an ageless quality to friendship. We can make friends at virtually any age, keep them for as many years as we like, and disavow them whenever it seems necessary or convenient. Friends differ from parents, children, siblings and other kinfolk, whom we inherit at birth (ours or theirs). They aren't like a spouse, for whom we have to wait two decades and then must promise to love and live with for the rest of our life. Nor are they like neighbors and co-workers, who "come with the territory" or the job, and who, by definition, are lost as soon as we move to a new home, a new position. Unlike the other close associates of one's life, friendship is a relationship for all seasons—or for none, as we so choose.

It is perhaps this "agelessness" that has induced most researchers to ignore age as a crucial variable in friendship. To many investigators, friendship is friendship, regardless of when it occurs or how long it lasts. Yet, there are three ways in which age enters into the fabric of friendship. It is, first of all, a *relational* characteristic of the partners, representing the difference in age between oneself and one's friend. Although we commonly conceive of friends as age mates, there is nothing in the definition of friendship (at least as I define it in this essay) that requires them to be so. But as relational age expands, the inherent similarity between individuals diminishes. It seems likely that individuals who share the same life stage and who have lived through the same historical events would forge a different relationship than two people from separate generations.

Age can also be viewed as a *temporal* characteristic of the relationship. That is, friendships are formed, deepened and sustained across time. One cannot expect two individuals who have been friends for decades to relate in the same fashion as they did during the first months of their acquaintance, just as one cannot expect the "honeymoon phase" to be maintained over the entire course of marriage.

Beyond this, of course, is the *individual* age of each partner. As people progress across the life course, they witness changes in their abilities, experiences and developmental needs, as well as in the expectations and opportunities they have for close interpersonal attachments. Both the form and function of friendships must adjust to these developmental changes.

Each of these age-related characteristics adds to the complexity of friendship. Each, in a sense, undermines its "agelessness." The purpose of this essay is to examine how the relational, temporal and individual facets of age affect the nature of friendship.

DISTINGUISHING FRIENDSHIP FROM POPULARITY AND CONNECTEDNESS

In our society, friendship is a relatively flexible relationship. It isn't circumscribed by legal sanctions the way most blood ties are. Nor is it governed by status (position or title) or location, as are work and neighborhood ties. As a result, compared to other interpersonal relationships, friendship is not well defined. Just what it takes to be a friend, what it means to be a friend is a matter for research, not a matter of course. And neither researchers nor their respondents seemed to have reached any consensus on a definition of friendship.

One consequence of our inability to settle on a definition is that numerous phenomena have been studied under the guise of friendship. Moreno's (1934) introduction of sociometric analysis spawned several decades of studies investigating the characteristics of the members of a given classroom, club or other group whom peers most often wanted to sit by, work with, play with, go to the movies with, lead their athletic team or any of a host of other activity-oriented criteria. Invariably, the data revealed a few individuals with many "friends" (that is, a few who received many nominations), a few with no friends (no nominations), and everyone else somewhere in-between. Researchers concentrating on the first group attempted to identify determinants of popularity. Their findings emphasized both personal characteristics—name, gender, attractiveness, intelligence—and social skills, the ability to communicate effectively, "savvy" in making friends (Asher, Oden and Gottman, 1977; Coleman, 1961; Gottman, Gonso and Rasmussen, 1975). In nearly all cases, however, investigators treated friendship in very superficial terms. Despite liberal use of the word, "friend," in both title and text, their articles focused on determinants of status among one's peers. "Friendship" was merely a vehicle for measuring popularity.

Researchers concerned with respondents in the second group, those who received no nominations, seemed to concentrate on "connectedness," the degree to which an individual was accepted by peers and tied into a social network. In addition to identifying characteristics of isolates, investigators assessed various techniques (largely through coaching people in social skills) to improve an isolate's sociometric ratings (Asher, et al., 1977; Oden and Asher, 1977). Here again, however, friendship has been presented in superficial terms, as if the important thing is to be connected to others, regardless of the content of such connections.

These studies are valuable as long as they are labeled properly. There is a difference between factors determining friendship and factors associated with popularity or connectedness. In this chapter my concern is not with one's position within a social network, but with the complex characteristics, the form, function and meaning of a specific subset of one's social connections. This subset subsumes relationships which are voluntary, mutual, flexible and terminable; relationships that emphasize equality and reciprocity, and require from each partner an affective involvement in the total personality of the other. These are the basic, defining characteristics of friendship.

AGE AS A RELATIONAL CHARACTERISTIC: AGE HOMOGENEITY IN FRIENDSHIP

A primary interest of investigators concerned with friendship has been to identify its "ageless" features. Their findings emphasize two factors that characterize most friendship dyads at all ages. First is proximity: people tend to make friends with individuals living nearby (Pellettieri[1];

Dimock, 1937; Priest and Sawyer, 1967; Riley and Foner, 1968). Second is similarity on a variety of characteristics, including gender (Booth and Hess, 1974; Lowenthal, Thurnher and Chiraboga, 1975), socio-economic status (Hollingshead, 1949; Laumann, 1966; Riley and Foner, 1968), and attitudes (Newcomb, 1961). But the similarity most relevant to this essay is age itself. Most friendships, at all life stages, are "age-homogeneous," that is, they involve partners who are virtually the same age (Booth, 1972; Evans and Wilson, 1949; Furfey, 1927; Lowenthal, et al., 1975; Riley and Foner, 1968).

What accounts for the predominance of age homogeneity in friendship? One factor, certainly, is social norms: we expect individuals to draw friends from age peers, and we are surprised, if not concerned, when someone violates this expectation. Hess (1972) suggests that children who befriend younger companions may be seen as excessively dominant or immature, while those who prefer to play with older associates may strike us as unduly dependent or precocious.

More important, however, are the consequences of age being a major mechanism for structuring society. Age similarity connotes common membership in a given generation or "cohort." Members of the same cohort not only occupy the same life stage but also share a common history. They face similar challenges and constraints; they have lived through the same historical events. Since people prefer to have friends who are similar to themselves, these commonalities clearly facilitate friendship.

The preponderance of age-homogeneous friendships also reflects people's limited opportunities to interact with older or younger persons who could become friends. From the first through the eighteenth year of life, the bulk of our associates outside the immediate family are within a year of our own age. Adulthood exposes us to a more age-heterogeneous mix of associates. But since the progression through career and family events is associated strongly with age (Neugarten and Moore, 1968), those who share our role statuses and with whom we have the most frequent contact are, by and large, age peers. Even older adults may encounter a remarkably age-constricted environment, especially those who rely on public programs—senior citizen housing, senior centers, "Golden Agers" clubs, and so on—to provide housing and social activities.

The apparent preponderance of age-homogeneous friendships, however, is partially an artifact of researchers' assumptions and expectations. Many investigators *define* friendship in terms of age parity, either explicitly by casting their questions about friends in terms of "people close to your own age," or implicitly by limiting respondents to discussing the people they feel closest to in a given classroom, dormitory, elderly housing project or other age-homogeneous research setting. Granted, it may be difficult to distinguish relationships that, aside from age, meet all the requirements of friendship (equality, reciprocity, mutuality and so on) from those which do not. Yet, this seems preferable to reinforcing the dubious assumption that age parity is prerequisite to friendship.

Although evidence is scanty, it appears that an appreciable portion of friendships, particularly in later adulthood, do involve partners with notably different ages. Twelve percent of Lowenthal, *et al.*'s (1975) preretirement sample named a considerably younger person as their closest friend. In Powers and Bultena's (1976) study of individuals aged 70 and older, one-fourth of the women's friendships and two-fifths of the men's were with partners sixteen or more years younger. If researchers encouraged respondents to ignore age as a criterion for determining which of their associates to classify as friends, they might discover a surprising number of age-heterogeneous friendships in all stages of adulthood. Indeed, "age similarity" is a rather subjective and variable notion: two years may strike someone as a significant separation in childhood and adolescence, whereas a difference of five years or more may be considered roughly equivalent in middle age. And there is probably as much inter-individual variation as there is life-stage variation in the subjective meaning of "age peer." Lewis, *et al.* (1975, p. 58), condemn the common tendency to use "peer" and "age mate" synonymously:

> the meaning of peer—from the point of view of the infant—may be quite different from the currently used age-mate criterion. We maintain that peer should have a meaning related to *function* rather than *age*. That is, a peer would be on one occasion all the children who could climb a tree, while on another occasion it would be those able to sing songs.

The general point, then, is that despite the normative and structural constraints on doing so, people can and do carry on friendships with individuals appreciably older or younger than themselves. Indeed, such partners can fulfill a variety of functions that cannot be met through relationships with age peers.

Heckel (1964), for example, reports that relationships in adolescence with opposite-sex adults often serve as an intermediary step in the transfer of emotional ties from parents to spouse. These "transitional figures" are perceived by the adolescent not only as mother- or father-surrogates but also as love objects. They are drawn from the immediate social environment to maximize interaction, but are typically considerably older so as to impede the adolescent from acting on sexual inclinations.

An adolescent may also turn to a teacher, coach, minister, older sibling, or parent of a close friend as a counselor or parental surrogate. In one sample of college students, 60 percent acknowledged having this type of friendship during their teenage years.[2] These relationships allow adolescents to receive adult feedback on their attitudes and behaviors without maintaining the parental dependence they typically wish to disavow, and without having to divulge information to parents that could exacerbate an already tenuous parent-child relationship. Short of this, an adult friend may simply supply an impartial "second opinion" to complement parental advice. Such relationships, of course, are meaningful to the adult as well as the adolescent. In one sample, middle-aged women who acknowledged having such a relationship found it rewarding not only because of the honor of being chosen as an advisor-confidant, but also as compensation for the sudden estrangement in their relationship with their own teenage daughter.[3]

Children and adolescents who are temporarily "out of phase" in their cognitive and physical development may look beyond age peers for close companionship. A physically late maturer, for example, who has not summoned sufficient self-confidence and interpersonal expertise to move into heterosexual networks may instigate what Sullivan (1953) called a "chumship" with a younger partner until maturing enough physically and interpersonally to be able to reestablish effective age-peer relationships.

During adulthood individuals may strike up activity-oriented friendships with age-heterogeneous partners. A junior executive may team up with a senior vice-president to form a fierce doubles tennis team. An older person will join a young adult in the park each Saturday for some friendly conversation over a game of chess. These common interests serve as a base from which the relationship can be expanded toward the more "total personality" orientation characteristic of friendship. In other words, the partners use shared activities in the same fashion that other budding friendships appeal to age similarity.

Relationships initiated through the Big Brother, Big Sister, and Foster Grandparent/Grandchild programs are intended initially to compensate for missing kinship ties at various points in the life course. Partners fulfill each other's needs for nurturance, succorance or simple companionship. But however closely they attempt to mimic blood relationships, the voluntary, terminable basis upon which they are built casts them into the arena of friendship. And because they are contracted by choice rather than by force, they are endowed with special significance.

Of course, just as there are unusual assets in age-heterogeneous friendships, there are also special costs. For one thing, they must combat the common tendency to cast the elder member in the role of socializer of the partner from a younger generation (Parsons and Platt, 1972). To preserve the equality characteristic of friendship, partners must acknowledge and accept reciprocal socialization roles. American society also discourages friendship between individuals who differ in both age and sex—especially between an adult male and younger female—because of its seductive, sexual potential. Even if the partners resolve the sexual issue to their own satisfaction, they may have to conceal the intensity of their bond to avoid disparaging frowns from doubting associates. Furthermore, for better or worse, members of adjacent generations are competitors for favored social roles and statuses: the younger person's task, in a broad sense, is to supplant the older while the older struggles against being replaced. Even unconscious awareness of this struggle can strain an age-heterogeneous friendship.

I do not mean to doubt the preponderance of or even the preference for age homogeneity between pairs of friends. The social-structural similarities and normative sanctions they provide are compelling advantages. Yet, despite their difficulties, friendships that transcend the typical boundary of relational age address some needs which cannot be met by associations with age peers. Clearly, as the relational age between partners expands it alters the nature of friendship, but without necessarily destroying the fabric of friendship.

AGE AS A TEMPORAL CHARACTERISTIC: THE CAREER OF A FRIENDSHIP

Up to this point, I have endorsed the implicit assumption of most researchers that, once formed, a friendship retains a relatively fixed and stable set of characteristics. In fact, however, friendship is a *dynamic* relationship, drawing partners through a progression of emotions and levels of involvement: from friendly feelings through positive regard to genuine, lasting caring or loving (Rangell, 1963). Just as individuals age, so do their relationships. The "temporal age" of the bond contributes to its character in significant ways. Suttles (1970, p. 127–128) reminds us that: "Friends do not simply live 'happily ever after' and certainly there is more to [friendship] than its primary and terminal junctures." It is unfortunate, then, that most studies only measure friendships as they exist at a particular moment.

In order to understand how the temporal facet of age affects friendships, we must first examine what it entails. Numerous authors have attempted to model the "career" of a relationship. Although their theories usually are intended to describe interpersonal relationships in general or marital dyads in particular, several seem applicable to friendship. Newcomb (1961) applied Heider's (1958) "balance theory" to friendship, proposing that individuals make adjustments over time so as to maintain an equilibrium between attitudes and attraction. Individuals are attracted to those who share their attitudes. When one component in this system is altered—self's attitude toward an object, other's attitude toward the object, or self's attraction to other—one of the remaining components also must shift in order to restore balance. Friendship, therefore, involves a systematic exploration of one another's attitudes; the relationship will grow as long as attitudes appear to be shared.

Drawing upon Homans' (1956) "social exchange" theory, Altman and Taylor (1973) argue that the basic developmental process in interpersonal relationships is "social penetration." Partners engage in a systematic, mutual exploration of progressively more extensive and intimate aspects of each other's personality and past history. The rate of penetration varies across time and among individuals, generally decelerating as partners reach deeper levels of their personalities or as they encounter fewer rewards in the relationship. The deterioration of a relationship involves a systematic retreat from extensive and intimate to increasingly superficial and constricted levels of interaction.

McCall and Simmons (1966) postulated that interpersonal relationships serve as arenas for enacting one's various "role identities"—preferred ways of performing in social roles so as to allow expression of one's individual "identity." Over time, the "strain towards totality" (Simmel, 1950) encourages partners to incorporate an increasing number of their role-identities into the relationship and to invest increasing amounts of time and resources in its maintenance. They also suggest that relationships gather their own inertia: even as opportunities to perform various role identities diminish, the relationship may continue because of the levels of commitment, involvement and attachment that have developed over time, and the high cost involved in building an equivalent new relationship.

There is a tendency over time, McCall and Simmons argue, to incorporate increasing dimensions of self into a friendship. But there is also a tendency to maintain relationships in which one has invested considerable time, effort, self-disclosure and so forth, as long as rewards outweigh liabilities or until the cost of maintaining the bond exceeds the cost of replacing it. In other words, we initially cultivate associations which allow us to express and reaffirm our superficial "self," we deepen bonds with those with whom we can share our more intimate and extensive selfs, and we maintain friendships which permit continued sharing or which have elicited considerable caring.

Longitudinal data on pairs of friends are too scarce to indicate conclusively how accurately these theories describe the dynamic features of friendship. But because the theories address the entire range of close relationships (spousal, parent-child, and so on), they probably provide only a set of general principles from which to develop a model aimed more specifically at explaining the career of friendship per se. I propose that such a model can be derived from the defining characteristics of friendship. Each characteristic represents a separate dimension along which friendships develop. The salience of each dimension rises and falls over the course of the relationship. Initially, partners concentrate on establishing a base of superficial similarity and *equality*, guided by the principles of balance theory. After this base is cemented, social penetration intensifies (through mechanisms outlined in social exchange theory), leading to an emphasis on *mutuality*. As partners incorporate more numerous and intimate role-identities into the relationship they become oriented toward each other's total personality. Consequently, *reciprocity* rises to the fore. Because of these shifting saliencies a friendship can serve different functions at each phase. By varying the extensiveness and intimacy of one's friendships, a person can assign different primary functions to each friendship. What emerges, then, is a complex and dynamic network of friendships that differ in duration, diffuseness, functions and focal concern.

This, of course, is only a rough outline of how friendships evolve over time. There is some evidence, however, to support a multi-dimensional, phase-oriented approach to modeling the career of friendship. Heilbronn (1976) examined the friendship choices of college students at the beginning and end of their first year in a dormitory and again one year later. She found that the most effective predictors of final friendship status shifted across time, from an expression of interest in furthering the relationship (at the outset) to the number of mutual activities and rewards exchanged (at the end of the first year) to the equity of give and take (at the end of the second year).

Among the college students Newcomb (1961) studied over the course of their first year together in a small dormitory, attraction seemed to be governed primarily by perceived and actual similarity of attitudes. He concluded that people are more likely to abandon acquaintanceship than alter their attitudes or behavior. Had he continued to monitor his sample, however, Newcomb might have uncovered a shift in emphasis toward mutuality. This dimension is reflected in findings of longitudinal studies of more firmly-established relationships. Kandel (1978), for example, reported that a substantial portion of the pairs of adolescent friends she studied over the course of one year showed shifts toward consensus on attitudes about drug use, educational aspirations and political ideology. Pairs with relatively similar attitudes at the first testing showed even stronger attitude agreement nine months later. In another fascinating study of college women, McClintock (1971) discovered a highly significant increase over the space of a year in the synchronization of menstrual cycles between both roommates and close friends. Surprisingly, the synchronization was higher between best friends than between roommates.

Both the models and the findings reflect two important features of friendship which researchers should bear in mind. First, the factors underlying the selection of friends may differ from the criteria for sustaining or deepening relationships. Investigators who fail to control for the length of relationship among their respondents (as is the case in most studies) decrease their chances of finding common characteristics among the friendships under study. This helps explain the weak statistical relationships and inconsistent findings among the numerous attempts to identify behavioral, attitudinal and background similarities in friendship dyads.·

Second, the temporal age of a friendship varies directly with individual age (age of the participants). Nominations of closest associate are progressively more stable across the life span (Skorepa, Horrocks and Thompson, 1963; Shulman, 1975), indicating that the best friends of older persons are more long-standing companions than the best friends of younger persons. Cross-sectional studies attempting to compare friendship at different life stages are therefore likely to mistake career-related differences for life-stage differences unless there is some control for the length (or level) of the relationship.

EFFECTS OF INDIVIDUAL AGE: LIFE-SPAN CHANGES IN THE SALIENCY AND FUNCTIONS OF FRIENDSHIP

Researchers attentive to the effects of age on friendship have focused their attention on individual age. That is, they have looked for changes across life stages (or differences at various points in adulthood) in various features of friendship. Most studies of friendship, however, deal with age-homogeneous samples, so that efforts to chart changes across the life span in the character of friendship must rely upon connecting findings from studies whose samples and methods are not always wholly comparable. This limits the confidence that can be placed in any patterns that emerge. Nevertheless, it does appear that individual age exerts considerable influence on the saliency and functions of friendship. What follows is a selective but illustrative review of evidence from each major life stage.

INFANCY

How early in life do friendships form? Most people discount their existence during the first two years of life because of certain presumptions about the nature of infancy. They picture the infant as preoccupied with the mother-child relationship. They point to deficiencies in cognitive capacities whose development seems prerequisite to friendship: the sense of object permanency, or the ability to see the world accurately from another's point of view. They doubt friendships can exist in the absence of such social skills as language or cooperative behavior, which are largely absent during the first two years of life. They argue that peers have little to contribute to the major goal of this stage, mastery of the environment, and suggest that infants therefore turn to adults, who can help them explore the environment through direct contact and useful feedback (Bronson, 1975).

Yet, part of the environment to be mastered involves interactions with peers. And those who have studied infant interactions have found that "[e]ven by one year of age, the fabric of the social network is rich and varied" (Lewis, *et al., 1975*, p. 30). There is ample evidence to suggest that infancy serves as a stage of *orientation* to friendship, a time to become acquainted with peers not only as objects to observe but as partners in explorations of the environment.

Infants are cautious in their initial interpersonal encounters. They generally do not approach and touch strange peers, but they do devote considerable time to looking them over (Bronson, 1975; Lewis, *et al.,* 1975). Given opportunities for repeated interactions, such staring at a distance will give way to proximal, mutual play (Lewis, *et al.,* 1975). Companions are more than interesting playthings to infants. Eckerman and Whatley (1977) found that, contrary to popular belief, toys did not distract infants from peers but served instead as vehicles for mutual interaction.

Infants also display the ability to discriminate among peers or between peers and adults in ways that foreshadow later differentiation of friends and acquaintances. In Lewis, *et al.*'s (1975) study, twelve- to eighteen-month-olds offered a toy to an unacquainted peer about as often as to their own mothers, and twice as often as to strange adults (mothers of the other infants). Although data are limited and individual variation is extensive, Hartup (1975) notes that some infants' reactions to separation from familiar peers is similar to their reactions to separation from parents. It also appears that differentiation among peers can occur at a very early age. Lee's (1973) observations of day-care infants demonstrated that preferences for proximity to and play with certain peers appeared as early as ten months of age.[4]

One reason these rudimentary friendships may seem so rare is that few infants are given opportunities to interact with peers. Studies indicate that only 20 percent of one-year-olds have contact with age mates on a regular basis, and only 30 percent of two-year-olds participate in formal or informal peer play groups (Lewis, *et al.,* 1975). Mothers, by and large, do not regard this as a pressing need of infants. The growth of day-care centers in response to the swelling participation of young mothers in the labor force should accelerate infants' opportunities to become oriented toward peers and accelerate their development of the interpersonal skills necessary to form friendship. It also will expand researchers' opportunities to explore the functions these rudimentary friendships can serve in individual development during the first several years of life.

CHILDHOOD

Friendship is not only a type of interpersonal relationship but also a social role, replete with normative expectations and rules of conduct into which people must be socialized. Most youngsters have acquired the cognitive and social skills prerequisite to friendship by the time they enter grade school. Childhood, thus, serves as the stage for *socialization* into the friendship role. This is reflected in the sizeable number of studies concerned with how well children seem to have mastered the role (sociometric analyses of peer popularity) or with how to enhance their mastery (evaluations of methods aimed at increasing their connectedness). These studies leave the impression that childhood friendships are superficial bonds. The relative instability of these relationships reinforces that impression. It is not uncommon for youngsters to alter the nominations of one or more of their best friends over intervals as short as one month (Hallinan, 1978; Horrocks and Buker, 1949; Thompson and Horrocks, 1947). Yet, it is dangerous to equate ephemerality with superficiality. In fact, Lewis, *et al.* (1975, p. 28) claim that "[c]hildren establish contacts that have all the aspects of personal and intense friendship." At the same time, however, it is unlikely that childhood friendships are simply inchoate versions of adult relationships.

Researchers are beginning to chart the complex and developmental nature of friendship in childhood. Bigelow's content analysis of essays first through eighth graders wrote about their best, same-sex friend revealed twenty-one dimensions along which children describe their closest friendships (Bigelow and LaGaipa, 1975; Bigelow, 1977). Some dimensions were important characteristics across age: reciprocity of liking and ego reinforcement. But based on the age at which certain dimensions appeared and their frequency in the essays of each grade level, Bigelow has proposed a three-stage development in what children regard as important criteria of close friendship. Paralleling Kohlberg's (1969) three levels of morality, there is a shift across childhood from concern with the rewards and costs of the relationship to an emphasis on normative expectations and finally to expectations of empathy and understanding from close friends. Friendship expectations also increase in complexity, as measured by the number of dimensions children use in describing their closest associate. Bigelow (1977) acknowledged that, to a certain extent, age differences may be artifactual: younger respondents may have comprehended and considered certain dimensions important but lacked the skills necessary to express them in an essay. Reisman and

Shorr (1978) applied Bigelow's system to essays from another sample of second through eighth graders. While the 21 dimensions did not behave identically to Bigelow's samples, the more general patterns were similar. With age, the importance of best friend as playmate diminished while expectations of intimacy, shared interests, loyalty and commitment increased.

Based on interviews with 250 individuals aged three to 45, Selman and Selman (1979) have formulated a five-stage developmental model describing changes across childhood in conceptions of friendship. From the momentary playmate orientation of the pre-schooler, they found that children progress to regarding friends as more stable companions, but still oriented toward self's interests. At about the commencement of primary school, this gives way to a "fair weather" partnership, in which children expect reciprocal cooperation for each person's self-interests. Intimacy and mutuality as well as a protective exclusivity characterize expectations in the fourth stage, followed, in adolescence, by "autonomous, interdependent" friendships which maintain the intimacy and emotional support of stage four, but with added respect for each partner's individuality.

ADOLESCENCE

As children move into adolescence, friendship seems to become a dominant component of their lives. At no other life stage are conditions so ripe for extensive, intensive friendship ties. Adolescents encounter growing autonomy from adult constraints on attitudes and behavior. They are allowed more freedom to move about on their own and to select and interact with associates, even in the face of objections from parents or other adults. As teenagers relinquish the close family dependencies and attachments of childhood, and until they assume the responsibilities of major adult roles such as worker, spouse or parent, they have fewer role-related obligations competing with their commitments to friends. Further, the hours they spend at home or alone diminish as they devote more time to school, sports, social activities and part-time jobs. Since these environments all are dominated by age and status peers—that is, by those best able to offer the equality and similarity crucial to forming friendships—they enhance the growth of friendship bonds. Most important, however, is the degree of social approbation accorded friendship at this stage of life. In childhood, society expects youngsters to learn to get along with others; in adolescence society expects individuals to become close to others. We worry about teenagers who fail to form close friendships.

The confluence of societal norms, environmental conditions and lessened role obligations creates in adolescence an unprecedented and un-equaled set of conditions in which friendships can flourish. Adolescence emerges as the primary life stage for *investment* in friendship. Findings from several studies reflect the importance teenagers attach to these investments. When asked which would be hardest to accept, disapproval of parents, teacher or close friend, nearly as many respondents in Cole-man's (1961) survey of high school students chose friend's disapproval (43 percent) as parents' disapproval (53 percent). "The balance between parents and friends," Coleman (p. 5) concludes, "indicates the extent of the state of transition that adolescents experience—leaving one family but not yet in another, they consequently look both forward to their peers and backward to their parents." A group of college students, when asked to think back to high school and rate the importance of various factors to their life then, named "having close friendships" as more important than any other factor.[5] It outranked having a good social life or sex life, having a "boyfriend"/"girlfriend," being popular, getting along with parents, getting good grades, even having control over their own life. When the same sample was asked how important various people had been to their personal well-being and development during the teenage years, their closest friend ranked second only to their mother (ahead of father, sibling, other relatives, teachers, coaches and schoolmates in general). Adolescents anticipate that friends will remain important com-ponents of their adult life. A national sample of high school seniors ranked close friendship second only to a good marriage and family life as a major life goal (Bachman and Johnston, 1979).

Despite the importance adolescents attach to friendships, researchers have ignored specific relationships in favor of analyzing the effects on adolescent development of the larger, more nebulous peer group (e.g., Brittain, 1963; Coleman, 1961; Sherif and Sherif, 1964). But the clinical insights of psychoanalytically-oriented investigators do provide some in-dications of how friendships facilitate individual development in adolescence.

Sullivan (1953) contends that "chumships," intimate same-sex friend-ships which form just prior to adolescence, are used as stepping stones into heterosexual relationships. Chumships are the first relationships in which a young person demonstrates genuine, altruistic concern for the other person. They are vehicles for developing a sense of accepting and being accepted, trusting and being trusted, of reciprocal commitment and mutual ability to understand, support and satisfy one another's inter-personal needs. The confidence achieved through chumships helps propel adolescents into opposite-sex, "romantic" relationships.

The importance of friendship, however, does not necessarily wane once heterosexual attachments have been established. They continue to be a significant source of emotional support as well as a vehicle for achieving a stable self-concept or "sense of identity" (Erikson, 1963). Douvan and Adelson (1966) contend that adolescents need to cultivate friends who can help them interpret and control the bodily changes and frightening sexual impulses they are experiencing. Friends serve as models, mirrors and judges in the young person's attempts to crystallize an identity, and as empathic associates who will tolerate occasional retreats from efforts to master sexuality and identity when these tasks become overwhelming. Douvan and Adelson also argue that a teenager often seeks associates who are quite unlike him/herself. Such friends allow the adolescent to experience vicariously secret impulses (s)he is unwilling to express directly; or they may be an object of identification, an ego-ideal whom the adolescent strives to equal.

If these perceptions are accurate, then the efforts of many researchers to chart personality and value similarity in adolescent friendship pairs seem misguided. The friends of adolescents are not necessarily people with whom they share values. They are individuals with whom they can bare their soul, share their secret dreams and terrors, analyze their aspirations, dissect their failures. They are close compatriots in the effort to achieve both adulthood and personhood. Future studies should concentrate on the intensity and individuality of friendships in this stage, the degree to which they saturate all facets of an adolescent's life. By extending Bigelow's (1977) approach or Selman and Selman's (1979) stage model to adolescence, we may be able to appreciate better both the complex dimensionality and the individuality of friendships during the teenage and college years.

YOUNG ADULTHOOD

Beth Hess (1972, p. 361) points out that:

> the number and type of friendships open to an individual at particular stages of his life course depend less upon explicit age criteria for the friendship role itself than upon the *other* roles that he plays. As his total cluster of roles changes over his lifetime, so do his friendship relations undergo change.

For most individuals, young adulthood signals a dramatic reorganization of roles, with the resumption of major family responsibilities through marriage and parenthood, and the beginning of additional responsibilities in the occupational sphere. Each new role cuts into the time available to devote to relationships with friends. But marriage seems to provide the greatest impetus to the changes in friendship that seem to typify the transition to young adulthood.

At marriage, many of a middle-class person's individual friendships are terminated, and those that survive generally become less intense, joint friendships of the conjugal pair: "joint acquaintanceship succeeds individual friendship" (Bott, 1971, p. 301). These joint relationships often evolve into "couple-coordinate friendships" so that, for example, not only does a wife's friend become a friend of her husband, but the friend's spouse becomes a friend of both husband and wife as well (Babchuk and Bates, 1963; Lopata, 1973; Davis, Gardner and Gardner, 1941). Couple-coordinate friendships form the basic unit of middle-class social life (Hess, 1972; Lopata, 1973), although spouses typically maintain additional friendships independently of each other (Babchuk and Bates, 1963; Lopata, 1973).

The autonomy of friendship choice enjoyed in adolescence deteriorates as one moves into marriage and confronts the preferences and appraisals of one's spouse. In middle-class couples, the husband appears to dominate the selection of joint conjugal friendships (Babchuk, 1965; Babchuk and Bates, 1963), probably because of the importance of "business" friendships to middle-class life. The current growth of dual-career marriages threatens the male's superordinance as it becomes equally important for the wife to develop social relationships with her business associates. Whether this will encourage more equality in spouses' selection of couple-coordinate friendships or will encourage spouses to develop more independent social networks has yet to be determined.

Marriage also alters the social networks of working-class young adults. Joint conjugal participation, however, is usually confined to kin and acquaintance relationships, while spouses typically maintain separate friendship networks (Dotson, 1951; Komarovsky, 1964). Parenthood draws working-class husbands and especially wives further into the extended family circle (Bott, 1971; Lopata, 1973), making friendships subordinate to kinship interactions (Adams, 1968; Gans, 1962; Komarovsky, 1964). Middle-class young marrieds, on the other hand, devote as much if not more time to neighbors and friends as to relatives (Axelrod, 1956).

One reason for these class differences is that working-class individuals tend to grow up in stable, "close-knit" networks, while middle-class youngsters are exposed to a more "loose-knit" social environment (Bott, 1971). That is, compared to the middleclass, blue-collar youngsters grow up around more relatives, interact with them more frequently and, because they are more likely to remain in the same area as adults, maintain more frequent kin associations through adulthood. Given the relative stability of their communities, it is not surprising that most adult friendships of the working class are derived from childhood associates (Bott, 1971; Dotson, 1951; Gans, 1962).

All of this ignores the growing proportion of young adults who have delayed or decided against marriage or who have again become single after a brief, unsuccessful marriage. How does the transition to adulthood affect friendships in this group? Single adults, especially those who have never married, report more numerous intimate friendships and more frequent interaction with friends (Shulman, 1975) than do married individuals. And Bott (1971) suggests that the shocking absence of shared confidences among middle-class friends in Babchuk's (1965) sample is largely an artifact of marriage. Cross-sex friendships are more frequent and more intimate among single adults, who don't have to confront the social sanctions and spousal jealousies that discourage young marrieds from initiating or maintaining more than casual acquaintanceships with the opposite sex (Booth and Hess, 1974). It is as if the intensity and autonomy of adolescent friendships continue unabated until marriage. Yet, without the protective institutions of adolescence (e.g., the school) and with the additional demands of being a worker, a lover and/or a parent, it is unlikely that single adults can sustain the saliency they accorded to friendships during the previous life stage. Furthermore, to the extent they have achieved a sense of identity, they are likely to redirect friendships to serve more pressing developmental needs: adjustment to adult roles, substitution for the intimacy and sexual gratifications offered by a spouse, and so on.

Since the repertoire of roles varies among young adults more than among individuals in earlier life stages, and since the content of roles differs dramatically according to gender and socio-economic status, it is not surprising to see less consistency in the character of friendship at this life stage. Young adulthood is a time of *adjustment* for friendship, a period in which these bonds are redefined and redirected to become better coordinated with the demands of an expanding role set. Friendships retain their importance, although their functions are more diverse and dependent upon the other roles an individual occupies. Those who are married transfer the intimacy and emotional support so crucial to friendship in adolescence to their spousal relationship. Friends become more important as partners in social and leisure pursuits. Friendship continues to be an important vehicle for peer socialization: just as "chums" help prepare young adolescents for heterosexual roles, friends assist young couples in adjusting to marital and parental roles. The friends of single adults can provide a means of joining in couple-oriented social activities, can serve as confidants, can socialize individuals into work or "swinging single" roles, or can do all three.

These various functions are often served better by new relationships than by the associates who figured so centrally in the search for identity during adolescence. Yet, in the face of the major life changes characteristic of adulthood, it is important to maintain some long-standing friendships as a link to the past, a means of preserving some continuity in one's sense of identity across life stages (Fallding, 1961). Such relationships do not require the proximity and frequent contact that seemed to be inherent to the friendship role at earlier life stages.

MIDDLE AGE

As individuals settle into middle age the intense friendships of earlier life stages begin to fade (Williams, 1959). Most people in their forties and fifties have pared their friendships to a small but stable network of associates (Lowenthal, *et al.,* 1975; Shulman, 1975). Confidants are more likely to be drawn from relatives than friends (Shulman, 1975), although interactions with friends who remain close appear to occur more frequently than in young adulthood (Lowenthal, *et al.,* 1975). In short, the middle-aged seem more *selective* about their friendships, relinquishing the sense of obligation they felt in earlier adulthood to maintain ties with a larger number of associates (Shulman, 1975).

The diminished importance of friendship in middle age stems partially from competing obligations in other social roles. In this stage, working individuals typically are struggling to reach or retain a hold on the top rung of their career ladder. The family demands a considerable portion of a person's time. And much of what is left must be given to voluntary organizations and church or community activities. The burdens of middle age leave little time for friendship. Financial demands of maintaining a household, paying for children's education and preparing a "nestegg" for retirement take precedence over enjoying good times with good friends (Lowenthal, *et al.,* 1975). In other respects, it is imprudent to be too close to individuals outside the family. The battles for career success and community status discourage people from baring their weaknesses to close associates, who are not only their prime candidates for close friendship but also, in many cases, their major competitors for prized positions (Bensman and Lilienfeld, 1979).

Furthermore, as children depart for college, marriage and/or careers, the commonality that has cemented many friendships of earlier adult years disappears. Associates whose only basis for friendship was the shared activities of their children begin to drift apart (Brown[6]; Hess, 1972). Other friendships suffer from having been too close over the years. Many middle-aged women report that their friends have become so familiar, so predictable that they are boring (Hagestad[7]).

This collage of pressing demands from other social roles and diminishing bases for close attachments outside the family leads many middle-aged people to form a collectively diverse but individually specific set of attachments. Friendships are compartmentalized, each one gratifying a particular interest or need (Cumming and Henry, 1961; Lowenthal, *et al.*, 1975). They offer satisfactions without committing their partners to the obligations accompanying the diffuse friendships of adolescence (Parsons, 1951).

OLD AGE

By the late fifties or early sixties, many of the pressures that occupy such a central position in middle age begin to subside. Children have departed and assumed responsibility for their own lives; one's career is winding down; leadership roles in community organizations are being handed to the next generation. With health still intact and sufficient savings to pursue leisure activities, individuals find themselves with resources, time and energy to reinvest in friendships. It is not surprising, then, that in the twilight of middle age people transform their selective, compartmentalized set of relationships into a larger and more diffuse friendship network (Lowenthal, *et al.*, 1975). Small cliques of middle-class couples who have maintained friendships through middle age may even arrange to build or purchase "retirement homes" adjacent to each other so they can maintain their social network through the remaining decades of life. In many respects, old age appears to be a stage of *reinvestment* in friendship.

But this upsurge of friendship activity is short-lived. Withdrawal from occupational and marital roles poses new barriers to friendship. Retirement deprives individuals of daily contact with familiar associates and, among lower income groups, places financial constraints on socializing with friends (Townsend, 1957; Shanas, *et al.*, 1968). Widowhood can prove even more devastating, particularly to the first few in a given social network to whom it occurs (Blau, 1961). Considering the couple orientation that dominates the social life of middle-class adults, Lopata (1973, p. 216) concludes that:

> Unless she is able to find a male escort acceptable to friends the [widow] finds herself a fifth wheel in the interactional scenes involving couples. Attempting to continue the same round of activities becomes impossible, or in any case difficult, and the initiating widow finally reorganizes her friendships. If she continues contact with former friends, it tends to be on a sex-segregated basis during the week and daytime hours. Often missing male companionship, such a woman at least avoids the jealousy from wives and sexual advances from husbands.

The effects on friendship of widowhood and retirement vary as a function of socio-economic status, gender and personality (Blau, 1961, 1973; Booth, 1972; Lopata, 1973), but most widows and retirees seem to have difficulty maintaining the customary friendship styles of their early and middle adult years. Their withdrawal from friends may occur as much by choice as by force. Yet others who have recently experienced the role loss often prove to be the most proficient at helping the initiate weather the crisis and adjust successfully to life without a spouse and/ or a career (Silverman, 1970). New friendships blossom out of such encounters, and old ones, temporarily suspended while the partners' role statuses were not equivalent, are reaffirmed (Aldridge, 1959).

As health and finances deteriorate, friendships recede. The infirmities that often accompany old age create obstacles to maintaining contact with close associates, thus diminishing both the number of friends (Arth, 1962; Lopata, 1973; Rose, 1965; Rosow, 1967) and the amount of contact with those who remain (Blau, 1961; Rose, 1965; Shanas, et al., 1968; Tomeh, 1964; Townsend, 1957). As in earlier life stages, proximity is an important determinant of friendship choices (Nahemow and Lawton, 1975); but in contrast to adolescence and young adulthood its significance is not diminished by length of acquaintance (Lawton and Simon, 1968). For most old people, contact with relatives clearly exceeds interaction with friends (Riley and Foner, 1968), and the elderly are more likely to turn to family when they need help (Rosow, 1967; Townsend, 1957). The desire to make new friends, to replace those lost through death or infirmity, or even to maintain frequent contact with surviving intimate associates all diminish with age (Cumming and Henry, 1961; Rose, 1965; Rosen and Neugarten, 1960). Those with comparatively few relatives nearby do not characteristically look to friends to fulfill functions usually assumed by family members (Riley and Foner, 1968; Rosow, 1967).

In spite of all this, friendship clearly remains significant to older people. In one sample of individuals over 70, three-fifths of the women and two-fifths of the males reported at least one intimate friendship (Powers and Bultena, 1976). Lopata (1973) discovered that although the sheer number of widowed women's friendships decreased steadily with age, the importance they assigned to the friendship role steadily rose, to the point that in the oldest group it supplanted the roles of neighbor and sibling. The most compelling evidence, however, is the consistently significant association between friendship and morale among the aged (Arling, 1976; Carp, 1966; Hochschild, 1973; Lebo, 1953; Lemon, et al., 1972; Philblad and MacNamara, 1965; Phillips, 1961; Phillips, 1973; Rosow, 1967; Wood and Robinson, 1978). This is particularly impressive since involvement with family does not correlate with morale (Arling, 1976; Wood and Robertson, 1978). It is not clear why friends contribute to the old person's sense of well-being while relatives do not, although frequency of interaction is not the critical factor (Arling, 1976). Some have suggested that the obligatory nature of family roles and the dependent position old people must assume vis-à-vis their relatives create unspoken hostilities and ambivalences (Wood and Robertson, 1978). The equity of friendship allows older persons to maintain their self-respect, even when appealing for help. And because friends offer assistance and association voluntarily, their services may seem more significant.

LIFE-SPAN PATTERNS

In each major life stage the focal concern of friendship seems to shift. Infancy is a stage for *orientation* to friendship, a time when individuals come to grips with the unique characteristics of age-mates that distinguish peers from other "objects" in the environment. Childhood is primarily a period of *socialization,* when individuals are instructed in the rules of conduct, the normative attitudes and obligations that characterize friendship as a social role. During adolescence, the stage of *investment,* individuals build stable, intimate, diffuse, affectively-oriented ties. Many of these will be dropped or de-emphasized in young adulthood, the stage of *adjustment,* in order to meet the demands of new social roles (spouse, worker, parent, etc.). *Selective maintenance* allows middle-aged persons to retain some friendship bonds in the face of waning interests in nurturing intimate relationships and growing competition from the pressures of other social roles. The early phases of old age provide opportunities for *reinvestment* in friendships, although waning physical and cognitive capacities may subsequently force older persons into a stage of *retrenchment,* in which one's network shrinks to a few "good, old friends."

In part, these shifts reinforce Beth Hess's (1972) argument that the friendship role must be integrated with changes in other social roles across the life span. In some respects, other roles inhibit friendship: the constricted, compartmentalized friendships of middle age grow more diffuse only when the pressures of parental and occupational responsibilities recede. But roles can also foster relationships: workmates, for example, provide a pool of candidates for friendship who may be particularly important to single young adults who lack the close family attachments and social contacts that marriage provides.

The shifts also reflect developmental changes in social skills and physical capacities to make and maintain friends. Attachments to peers in infancy, for example, are constricted as much by the child's limited mobility and marginal language skills as by infrequent exposure to age mates.

Finally, and most importantly in my opinion, as the needs or "developmental tasks" (Havighurst, 1972) confronting an individual shift across age, so do the primary functions friends serve. And, in turn, the structure of friendship adjusts to accommodate changes in function. The intense self-exploration of adolescence demands a set of relatively stable, intimate and diffuse ties with peers who are willing to engage in empathic listening, frank evaluation and occasional forgiveness. Old age, by contrast, is a time to put one's life in order and to maintain some dignity in the face of fading cognitive and physical capacities. At this stage the best friends are old friends, who can rekindle memories of the past, who respect us for what we were as well as what we are, and who can offer assistance without demanding dependence.

In sum, while friendship remains a relationship for all seasons, it must accommodate to age-related shifts in interpersonal abilities, individual (developmental) needs, and the competing obligations or facilitating opportunities of other social roles and relationships.

AGE AND AGELESSNESS IN FRIENDSHIP

There are certain "truths" about friendship which most people hold to be self-evident: that friends live near each other, that they share common attitudes and interests, that their relationship is subordinate to the partners' kin ties, and that they are likely to value their relationship considerably if they are adolescents, but only marginally if they are adults. In each case, however, these great truths are only partially valid. Most pairs of close friends do live near each other. But Peters and Kennedy (1970) report that between 30 and 50 percent of the friends named by one residential college group lived off campus (usually in other towns); and Babchuk and Bates (1963) found an extensive network of non-local friends among middle-class couples. Newcomb (1961) argues that attitudes dictate attraction; yet Werner and Parmelee (1979) found only marginal similarity in pairs of friends. Shared activities are usually the basis for instigating a friendship; but few adults refer to common activities in their descriptions of actual or even ideal friendships (Lowenthal, *et al.*, 1975), and the proportion of individuals assessing common interests as very important or essential to friendship declines with age.[8] Most individuals—especially working-class adults—interact with relatives more frequently than with kin; but friendship ties are a significant component of morale among the elderly, whereas kin relations are not. The friendship networks of adolescents are typically more diffuse and intimate than those of adults; but friends remain a significant source of emotional support throughout life, and the complexity of friendships among individuals in later adulthood often rivals the relationships of adolescents (Lowenthal, *et al.*, 1975). In short, although most people take these "truths" for granted, none of them is truly a hallmark of friendship.

In the same manner, the "agelessness" of friendship, however appealing a notion, is only partially accurate, for age alters the form and content of friendship as well as people's commitment to the friendship role. Just as researchers have exposed the inaccuracies of other great truths about friendship, so too we must dispel certain age-related mis-conceptions. Many believe that friendships are basically stable, stagnant interpersonal relationships, contracted between age peers, and fulfilling roughly the same functions at all life stages. The arguments and evidence presented in preceding sections challenge each of these assumptions, suggesting that age affects friendship significantly in three ways. The nature of friendship depends upon the partners' individual ages, the difference in their respective ages, and the amount of time over which their relationship has endured.

These three facets of age are not independent dimensions (Hess, 1972): the chances of having a long-standing friendship increase with age; cross-generation friendships occur more frequently at certain life stages than at others. The effects of age upon friendship, furthermore, are interactive: the long-standing friendships of middle-aged persons are likely to differ not only from their recently initiated relationships but also from the equally long-term associations between young adult or elderly dyads.

Certainly, there is an agelessness to friendship, in its potential significance to personal development and social organization at all stages of life. To understand and appreciate its significance more clearly, however, researchers must replace the implicit, age-related assumptions that have dominated previous studies with a more systematic and controlled exploration of how the multiple dimensions of age affect the nature of friendship across the life span.

NOTES

1. Pellettieri, A. *Factors involved in Friendship Making among Adolescent Boys*. Unpublished doctoral dissertation, George Peabody College, Nashville, TN, 1935.
2. Unpublished findings from a questionnaire survey by the author of 100 students in an undergraduate psychology course at the University of Wisconsin-Madison, 1980.
3. Gunhild O. Hagestad, unpublished data.
4. Lee, L. C. *Social Encounters in Infants: The Beginnings of Popularity*. Paper presented at the Biennial Meetings of the International Society for the Study of Behavioral Development, Ann Arbor, MI, 1973.
5. See note 2.
6. Edna Mae Brown, personal communication.
7. Gunhild O. Hagestad, personal communication.
8. Loeb, Rita. *Disengagement, Activity or Maturity?* Paper presented at the annual meetings of the Gerontological Society, San Juan, Puerto Rico, 1972.

REFERENCES

Adams, Bert
1968   Kinship in an Urban Setting. Chicago: Markham.
Aldridge, G.
1959   "Informal social relationships in a retirement community." Marriage and Family Living 21:70–72.

Altman, Irwin, and D. Taylor
  1973 Social Penetration: The Development of Interpersonal Relationships. N.Y.: Holt, Rinehart and Winston.
Arling, Greg
  1976 "The elderly widow and her family, neighbors and friends." Journal of Marriage and the Family 38(4): 757–768.
Arth, Malcolm
  1962 "American culture and the phenomenon of friendship in the aged." In C. Tibbitts and W. Donahue (eds.), Social and Psychological Aspects of Aging. N.Y.: Columbia University Press.
Asher, S. R., S. L. Oden, and J. M. Gottman
  1977 "Children's friendships in school settings." In L. G. Katz (ed.), Current Topics in Early Childhood Education. Hillside, N.J.: Earlbaum.
Axelrod, Morris
  1956 "Urban structure and social participation." American Sociological Review, 21:13–18.
Babchuk, Nicholas
  1965 "Primary friends and kin: A study of the associations of middle-class couples." Social Forces 43:483–493.
Babchuk, Nicholas, and Alan Bates
  1963 "The primary relations of middle-class couples: A study in male dominance." American Social Review, 28:377–384.
Bachman, Jerald G., and L. D. Johnston
  1979 The freshmen. 1979. Psychology Today, September, 1979, 79–87.
Bensman, Joseph, and Robert Lilienfeld
  1979 Friendship and Alienation. Psychology Today, October.
Bigelow, Brian
  1977 "Children's friendship expectations: A cognitive-developmental study." Child Development 48:246–253.
Bigelow, Brian, and J. J. LaGaipa
  1975 "Children's written descriptions of friendship: A multi-dimensional analysis." Developmental Psychology 11(1):857–858.
Blau, Zena
  1961 "Structural constraints on friendship in old age." American Sociological Review 26:429–439.
Booth, Alan
  1972 "Sex and social participation." American Sociological Review, 37:183–192.
Booth, Alan, and E. Hess
  1974 "Cross-sex friendship." Journal of Marriage and the Family 36:38–47.
Bott, Elizabeth
  1971 Family and Social Network. London: Tavistock.
Brittain, C. V.
  1963 "Adolescent choices and parent-peer cross-pressures." American Sociological Review 28:385–391.
Bronson, Wanda C.
  1975 "Developments in behavior with age mates during the second year of life." In M. Lewis and L. Rosenblum (eds.), Friendship and Peer Relations. New York: Wiley.
Carp, Frances M.
  1966 The Future of the Aged: Victoria Plaza and its Residents. Austin, Texas: University of Texas Press.

Coleman, James S.
1961 The Adolescent Society. New York: Free Press.
Cumming, Elaine, and W. E. Henry
1961 Growing Old. N.Y.: Basic Books.
Davis, Allison, B. Gardner, and M. Gardner
1941 Deep South. Chicago: University of Chicago Press.
Dimock, H.
1937 Rediscovering the Adolescent. New York: Association Press.
Dotson, Floyd
1951 "Patterns of voluntary associations among urban working-class families." American Sociological Review 16:687–693.
Douvan, Elizabeth, and Joseph Adelson
1966 The Adolescent Experience. New York: Wiley.
Eckerman, Carol, and J. L. Whatley
1977 "Toys and social interaction between infant peers." Child Development 48:1645–1656.
Erikson, Erik
1963 Childhood and Society (2nd. ed.). N.Y.: Norton.
Evans, M., and M. Wilson
1949 "Friendship choices of university women students." Education and Psychological Measurement 9:307–312.
Fallding, H.
1961 "The family and the idea of a cardinal role." Human Relations 14:329–350.
Furfey, P.
1927 "Some factors influencing the selection of boys' chums." Journal of Applied Psychology 11:47–51.
Gans, Herbert
1962 The Urban Villagers. N.Y.: Free Press of Glencoe.
Gottman, John M., M. Gonso, and B. Rasmussen
1975 "Social competence, social interaction and friendship in children." Child Development 46:709–718.
Hallinan, Maureen
1978 "The process of friendship formation." Social Networks 1(2):193–210.
Hartup, Willard
1975 "The origins of friendship." In M. Lewis and L. Rosenblum (eds.), Friendship and Peer Relations. New York: Wiley.
Havighurst, R. J.
1972 Developmental Tasks and Education (3rd. Ed.). New York: David McKay Co.
Heckel, R.
1964 "Shifting patterns of affection: Transitional figures." Mental Hygiene 48:451–454.
Heider, Fritz
1958 The Psychology of Interpersonal Relations. N.Y.: Wiley.
Heilbronn, Marybeth
1976 "A longitudinal study of the development and dissolution of friendship." Dissertation Abstracts 36(9-13):4754–4755.
Hess, Beth
1972 Friendship. In M. W. Riley, M. Johnson and A. Foner (eds.), Aging and Society 3 New York: Russell Sage.
Hochschild, Arlie R.
1973 The Unexpected Community. Englewood Cliffs, N.J.: Prentice-Hall.

Hollingshead, August
    1949 Elmtown's Youth. N.Y.: Wiley.
Homans, George
    1956 "Social behavior as exchange." American Sociological Review 63:597–606.
Horrocks, John, and M. Buker
    1949 "A study of the friendship fluctuations of preadolescents." Journal of Genetic
          Psychology 78:131–144.
Kandel, Denise
    1978 "Homophily, selection and socialization in adolescent friendships." American
          Sociological Review 84(2):427–436.
Kohlberg, Lawrence
    1969 "Stage and sequence: The cognitive-developmental approach to socialization."
          In D. A. Goslin (ed.), Handbook of Socialization Theory and Research. Chicago:
          Rand McNally.
Komarovsky, Mirra
    1964 Blue Collar Marriage. N.Y.: Random House.
Lawton, M. P., and B. Simon
    1968 "The ecology of social relationships in housing for the elderly." The Gerontologist
          8:108–115.
Laumann, Edward
    1966 Prestige and Association in an Urban Community. Indianapolis, In: Bobbs-Merrill.
Lebo, D.
    1953 "Some factors said to make for happiness in old age." Journal of Clinical Psy-
          chology 9:384–390.
Lemon, B. W., V. Bengtson, and J. Peterson
    1972 "An exploration of the activity theory of aging." Journal of Gerontology 27:511–523.
Lewis, Michael, G. Young, J. Brooks, and L. Michalson
    1975 "The beginning of friendship." In M. Lewis and L. Rosenblum (eds.), Friendship
          and Peer Relations. New York: Wiley Interscience.
Lopata, Helena
    1973 Widowhood in an American City. Cambridge, Mass.: Schenkman.
Lowenthal, M. F., M. Thurnher, and D. Chiraboga
    1975 Four Stages of Life. San Francisco: Jossey-Bass.
McCall, George, and J. L. Simmons
    1966 Identities and Interactions. New York: Free Press.
McClintock, Martha
    1971 "Menstrual synchrony and suppression." Nature, 229:244–245.
Moreno, Jacob
    1934 Who Shall Survive? Washington, D.C.: Nervous and Mental Disease Publishing
          Co.
Nahemow, Lucille, and M. P. Lawton
    1975 "Similarity and propinquity in friendship formation." Journal Personal Social
          Psychology 32:205–213.
Neugarten, Bernice, and J. W. Moore
    1968 "The changing age-status system." In B. L. Neugarten (ed.), Middle Age and
          Aging. Chicago, Il: University of Chicago Press.
Newcomb, Theodore
    1961 The Acquaintance Process. New York: Holt, Rinehart and Winston.
Oden, Sherri, and S. R. Asher
    1977 "Coaching children in social skills of friendship making." Child Development
          48:495–506.

Parsons, Talcott
1951 The Social System. Glencoe, Ill.: Free Press.
Parsons, Talcott, and G. Platt
1972 "Higher education and changing socialization." In M. W. Riley, M. Johnson and A. Foner (eds.), Aging and Society 3 New York: Russell Sage.
Peters, George, and C. Kennedy
1970 "Close friendships in the college community." Journal of College Student Personnel 11:449–456.
Philblad, C. T., and R. McNamara
1965 "Social adjustment of elderly people in three small towns." In A. Rose and W. Peterson (eds.), Older People and Their Social World. Philadelphia, Pa.: F. A. Davis.
Phillips, Bernard S.
1961 "Role change, subjective age and adjustment: A correlational analysis." Journal of Gerontology 16:347–352.
Phillips, Derek L.
1973 "Social participation and happiness." In J. N. Edwards and A. Booth (eds.), Social Participation in Urban Society. Cambridge, Mass.: Schenkman.
Piaget, Jean, and B. Inhelder
1969 The Psychology of the Child. New York: Basic Books.
Powers, Edward A., and G. L. Bultena
1976 "Sex differences in intimate friendships of old age." Journal of Marriage and the Family 38(4):739–747.
Priest, R., and J. Sawyer
1967 "Proximity and peership: Bases of balance and interpersonal attraction." American Journal of Sociology 72:633–649.
Rangell, Leo
1963 "On friendship." Journal of the American Psychoanalytic Assoc., 11:3–54.
Reisman, John M., and S. I. Shorr
1978 "Friendship claims and expectations among children and adults." Child Development, 49:913–916.
Riley, Matilda W., and A. Foner
1968 "An inventory of Research Findings." Aging and Society 1: New York: Russell Sage.
Rose, Arnold
1965 "Age and social integration among the lower classes in Rome." Journal of Gerontology 20:250–253.
Rosen, Jacqueline, and B. L. Neugarten
1960 "Ego functions in the middle and later years." Journal of Gerontology 15:62–67.
Rosow, Irving
1967 Social Integration of the Aged. New York: Free Press.
Selman, Robert L., and A. P. Selman
1979 "Children's ideas about friendship: A new theory." Psychology Today, October.
Shanas, Ethel, P. Townsend, D. Wedderburn, H. Fritis, P. Milhoj, and J. Stehouser
1968 Old People in Three Industrial Societies. New York: Atherton.
Sherif, Muzafer, and C. W. Sherif
1964 Reference Groups. Chicago: Regnery.
Shulman, Norman
1975 "Life-cycle variations in patterns of close relationships." Journal of Marriage and the Family 37:813–821.

Silverman, Phyllis R.
1970   "The widow as caregiver in a program of preventive intervention with other widows." Mental Hygiene 54(4):540–547.
Simmel, Georg
1950   The Sociology of Georg Simmel. New York: Free Press.
Skorepa, C., J. Horrocks, and G. Thompson
1963   "A study of friendship fluctuations of college students." Journal of Genetic Psychology 102:151–157.
Sullivan, Harry S.
1953   The Interpersonal Theory of Psychology. N.Y.: Norton.
Suttles, Gerald
1970   "Friendship as a social institution." In G. McCall and M. McCall (eds.), Social Relationships Chicago: Aldine.
Thompson, G. G., and J. E. Horrocks
1947   "A study of friendship fluctuations of urban boys and girls." Journal of Genetic Psychology 70:53–63.
Tomeh, A.
1964   "Informal group participation and residential patterns." American Journal of Sociology, 70:28–35.
Townsend, Peter
1957   The Family Life of Old People. London: Routledge and Kegan Paul.
Werner, Carol, and P. Parmelee
1979   "Similarity of activity preferences among friends: Those who play together stay together." Sociology Psychology Quarterly 42(1):62–66.
Williams, Robin M.
1959   "Friendship and social values in a suburban community: An exploratory study." Pacific Sociology Review 2:3–10.
Wood, Vivian, and Joan Robertson
1978   "Friendship and kinship interaction: Differential effect on the morale of the elderly." Journal of Marriage and the Family 40:267–375.

THE STRUCTURING OF FRIENDSHIP FORMATION AMONG TWO- TO FIVE-YEAR-OLD CHILDREN ENROLLED IN FULL DAY CARE

Marijean Ferguson (Suelzle)

The structuring of friendship formation is significantly different for very young children than for older children and adults (Denzin 1977:58). Friendships can only come into existence when there is an opportunity to meet others with similar interests and skills, to interact with these others over a period of time, and to develop affective preferences (Duck, 1973). Older children and adults can seek out situations in which they are likely to meet similar others (Berger, *et al.*, 1977). Very young children are constrained by their lack of physical and cognitive competences. They cannot go across the street, out of the yard, or even out of the house without adult supervision. If parents do not take the initiative

51

to provide their young children with the opportunity to meet others, then young children cannot form friendships.

Parents do care about their children's social and emotional development. Mothers do get together with their own friends who have young children, so that their children can socialize at the same time the mothers do. Mothers form play groups and take their children to the park. When middle-class children reach the age of about three years, companionship is purchased for many through enrollment in nursery schools (Isaacs, 1929:40–41, 122–123). A part-time nursery school experience is a luxury limited to families with high enough incomes to purchase this peer-group socialization experience for their preschool children, and a mother available to provide transportation to and from a program lasting only two or three hours a few times a week. Informal encounters between young children, playgroups, and nursery schools all provide only a few hours a week during which children can be with their peers. The structuring of friendship formation between young children, therefore has not been taken too seriously by parents, educators, or researchers (Denzin, 1977:59, 69–71, 132–135; Maier, 1969:56; Rubin, 1980). Descriptive labeling has been sufficient. The terms "playmate," "classmate" and "friend" are often used as synonyms. Johnny's "little friend" is simply any other child that he sees on a regular basis, no matter how limited the time spent together may be.

Understanding the structuring of friendship formation for very young children will become increasingly important as more children are enrolled in full day care.

LABOR FORCE PARTICIPATION AND CHILD CARE ARRANGEMENTS

The 1970s represented a period of change for American families (Snapper and Ohms, 1978). The increase in labor force participation rates for women reflects a change of life style. Despite the recession and continued high overall unemployment, rates of employment have increased steadily for women, including those who are married and have children. The increase for wives with children under three years, has been from 19 percent in 1963 to 32 percent in 1976; for wives with children under six years, from 22 to 37 percent over the same period. Child care arrangements do depend upon mothers' labor force participation. Enrollments in day care facilities (centers and homes) have risen from an enrollment rate of nine percent in 1964 to 31 percent in 1976 for children three to four years of age. For the one-third of preschool children who spend several years in group care with adults who are not kin, two environments—family and day care—share the responsibility for those children's socialization and development.

The 1960s and 1970s saw widespread publicity given to the expansion of programs aimed at counteracting the effects of poverty on development. Head Start has been the most extensive and prominent of these programs. But, most working wives with young children do not fit the poverty stereotype (Levitan and Alderman, 1975). Correspondingly, the increase in enrollments in day care facilities over the past two decades is not accounted for by Head Start and other remedial programs alone. As more middle-income mothers of young children become employed outside the home, cultural norms regarding the type of group day care considered acceptable also changed. Liberal educators, trained in the nursery school tradition of valuing play activities, challenged the "obvious" solution of providing direct instruction to preschool children. To them the "obvious" solution was quite different. They maintained that cultural and racial differences should be respected, not remediated to white middle-class normative expectations for older children. If supportive teachers provided a materially enriched group environment, and if economic, racial and ethnic differences were respected, then they maintained that readiness for specific academic learning would develop spontaneously in all children. Day care programs evolved as expansions of the traditional nursery school ideology. They emphasized unstructured play activities which allowed self-expression and creativity. School-like routines were avoided or minimized. Opportunities for children to interact with peers were maximized.

As children from the ages of two and one-half onward are brought together into a relatively unstructured group setting for up to nine to eleven hours, five days per week, then they have the opportunity to form friendships selectively. Children do differentiate between classmates, playmates, allies and friends. As has been the case with older children and adults, it becomes important to understand the bases on which the differentiations are made. The day care center provides the situational context for friendship formation. It is no longer appropriate to simply label children as friends because parents arrange for them to spend time together. When access to other children can be taken for granted for most of the child's waking hours, then the children's ability to form friendships is more clearly a question of the children's capabilities and of how opportunities to express preferences are structured within the center.

THE DAY CARE CENTER AS A SITUATIONAL CONTEXT FOR FRIENDSHIP FORMATION

The vast majority of day care programs have evolved an interactionist or eclectic approach somewhere along the continuum from remediation through instruction to free expression through play. Since they tend to be community-based rather than national in scope, day care programs attract little academic or research interest. Their lack of a federal policy mandate makes funds for, or interest in, evaluation almost nonexistent, except in the most global sense of setting safety and staffing standards. The idiosyncrasies of the programs make large-scale comparisons difficult. Findings from a single center, however, can illuminate the impact of a group care environment on children's friendships.

No group environment for young children can be truly unstructured (Roedell, *et al.*, 1977:61). All group environments have teachers, space, and equipment which imply opportunities and restrictions (Chein, 1954). It is the way in which the components are combined that constitute the program (Fein and Clarke-Stewart, 1973). The program sets the parameters within which social exchanges between children can occur.

Four types of social exchanges can be identified and hierarchically ordered in terms of complexity. (1) At the most basic stage situational *relationships* occur by definition simply because children are aggregated in a group as classmates. Each child's behavior has ramifications for others. Teachers communicate behavioral expectations about each child's deportment. Any child's actions should not encroach upon the rights of the others. For example, children must play quietly, must clean up after themselves, cannot throw materials and cannot run within the center. (2) At the second stage *interactions* occur when children engage in ongoing verbal dialogues and joint activities as playmates. Teachers communicate behavioral expectations for the children relative to each other. For example, children are expected to share, to take turns, not to yell at each other, and not to hit each other. (3) At the third stage, *allyships* occur when children identify with each other on the basis of their mutual recognition of similarities in interests or skills. The similarities may be age- or sex-related, result from similarities in family background such as race, or be associated with competencies in a particular activity such as art. Teachers communicate their perceptions of similarities and differences among children by grouping them according to ability for instructional purposes. For example, children might be grouped according to attention span (on the combined basis of age and development) for storytime. (4) At the most complex stage, *friendships* occur solely on the basis of the children's initiative. Teachers do not have any additional behavioral expectations for the children at this stage. While teachers remain basically task-oriented and affectively neutral, it is the children, themselves, who add emotional involvement selectively to some of their interactions with others. These affectively salient interactions with preferred others are labeled as friendships by the children. In this paper, these four types of social exchanges are derived from an empirically-based theoretical account of the structuring of friendship formation among children in a full day care center.

THE RESEARCH SETTING

The data for this study were collected over a three-year period of participant observation in a community-based full day care center in the midwest. There were approximately twenty-five children enrolled at any one time, with an average attendance of fifteen to eighteen. The center was racially mixed with a majority of the children being black. About half were two-year-olds, with the remainder split about equally between three-, four-, and five-year-olds. The center was open fifty-one weeks per year from 7:00 a.m. to 5:30 p.m., although all the observations were conducted during a six-month period, October through March, in each of the three years. In addition to the director, there were four teachers, all with college degrees, three aides, and a number of occasional volunteers.

The center was begun in the early 1970s by a group of parents who wanted their children cared for during the day. During the first three years it was located in a single-room in the basement of a church. In the fourth year, the director and all but one of the original teachers left. A state licensing representative found multiple building code violations and ordered the center closed in that location. In the latter half of the fourth year, a new director was hired and a new multi-room location, also in a church basement, was found several blocks away. With the move, community support dwindled. One-half of the children, one teacher, and two out of sixteen board members made the transition, providing the nucleus for reconstituting a community-based center. Our participant observation began during the fifth year.

The setting consisted of four small classrooms plus adjoining hallways. A kitchen was shared with a nursery school class which met in an adjoining large room in the mornings. In the afternoons that large room was available to the center for large motor activities such as climbing, riding wheeled toys, and playing with balls. Of the four classrooms, one which was physically set apart from the others by the hallways was designated as the art room. The art room was accessible through a single door. The other three rooms were grouped together. The two end rooms each had two doorways, one onto the hall and one into the adjoining room; the middle room thus had three doorways. Activities and supplies within these three rooms overlapped, or travelled with the children as the case might be, except for a stationary climbing loft in the largest of the three small rooms. Thus, it was relatively easy for children to choose to congregate with others.

A typical daily schedule allowed children a great deal of discretionary time:

7:00 a.m.	Self-selected activities: Puzzles, waterplay, record room
8:00	Records and body movement—climbing area; clean-up
8:30	Breakfast snack in art room; clean-up
9:00	Art room; clean-up
9:30	Outside play
10:30	Toileting, wash hands
10:45	Story, drama; clean-up
11:00	Lunch; clean-up
11:45	Toileting, wash hands
12:00-2:00 p.m.	Naps
2:15	Toileting, wash hands
2:30	Snack; clean-up
2:45	Bike room, body movement
3:30-5:30	Small motor activity, records, TV

The schedule was followed by the teachers to make activities available to the children, but there was no set policy concerning where the children spent their time. They could basically go wherever they wanted to go and do whatever they wanted to do. There were usually four to six children per room at any one time. On the other hand, one or two children's obvious enjoyment of an activity—jumping from the loft, rolling cars down an incline, dancing to a record—could result in up to 15 children present in the same room for a short period of time. Ample opportunities were provided for children to engage in activities individually, in small groupings, or in bunches (Stone and Church, 1973:264).

THE RESEARCH PROCEDURES

Participant observation data were collected by nine upper division undergraduate students selected on the basis of previous related coursework and experience with young children. Four were male, five female. One (a male) was black. They were known to be observers working on a research project and were permitted to make jotted notes while essentially serving as aides in the center. Observations were made on a weekly basis during the fall and winter of three consecutive years from fall 1976 through winter 1979. Observers participated in the center for a four-hour period once a week for eight consecutive weeks during the fall and again in the winter. Full field notes, defined as an equivalent amount of time spent recording to that spent observing, at a rate of roughly four pages of typewritten notes per hour, were required for all observational sessions in the fall and on alternate weeks during the winter. (In the winter every other week was devoted to conceptualization and exploring analytic frameworks in short working papers.) Even with the inevitable absences due to observer illnesses or center closings for holidays, observational records were collected on fifty-five sessions for a total of 220 hours of observational time.

Data were recorded from the perspective of the participant observer. Systematic sampling of time frames with check lists was not feasible. Occasionally, observers had the latitude to determine who or what they would observe, but for the most part they were assigned by the center staff to work with particular children or in a particular area. Consequently, it was thought desirable to err on the side of collecting redundant information rather than risk distorting the characterization of a center by the unknown biases of a smaller number of observers over a shorter period of time.

The observers were part of a research team studying the actual practices in a variety of nursery and day care centers serving both normal and handicapped children from a range of socioeconomic backgrounds. Instruction was provided in how to conduct participant observation research and in how to write field notes but not in what was to be observed. The research team, varying in size from ten to twenty observers, met weekly in a two-hour seminar to exchange experiences and findings. The project was defined as exploratory, to detail the parameters of the mundane practices of group care for children as distinct from stated philosophies.

The center selected for discussion in this paper was chosen because it is believed representative of the eclectic community-based approach which characterizes most full day care at least in the midwest. In particular, the center is small, serves children from economically and racially diverse backgrounds, does not have age-segregated classrooms, and places little emphasis on formal instruction. All behavioral incidents recorded involving two or more children were selected as the data for analysis.

RELATIONSHIPS

Situational relationships occur by definition simply because children are aggregated as classmates within the same physical space (see Figure 1). Each child is aware of the presence of classmates even if the child is not communicating, verbally or nonverbally, with another. By virtue of

Figure 1. Taxonomy of the Stages of Friendship Formation Among
Children.

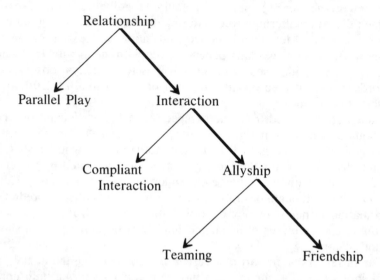

sharing the same physical space, each child's actions are constrained by
the classmates as objects within the environment. Children do not walk
into each other at random any more than they walk into walls, tables
or other inanimate objects at random.

Knowledge of the physical environment is derived by children primarily from the regularity or consistency with which concrete objects
respond when manipulated. Knowledge of the social environment, however, is arbitrary in the sense that it is based upon consensual agreements
among people, comes only from people, and is learned only through
feedback from people (Evans, 1975:232; Shipman, 1972:28–34). The degree of consensus concerning certain aspects of the social environment
varies.

The teachers in the center had behavioral expectations, some of which
all staff agreed upon in ideology and in practice, and instilled in the
children. For example, the doors to the kitchen and to adjacent areas
of the church building were left open, but the children knew they were
not allowed to leave the center classrooms and hallways unless they had
to use the bathroom and then only if they asked permission first. The
rule was seldom violated. Occasionally, one of the younger children
would wander over to a doorway, but readily return when a staff member
called. Also, after eating breakfast, lunch or snack each child was held
responsible for cleaning up his or her place at the table, putting reusable
dishes and cutlery in the sink, and throwing disposable paper products

away in a trash barrel. Over the three-year observational period there was never an example of a child being exempted from this requirement.

In other situations involving expectations for individual deportment, teachers varied concerning the range of behaviors which would be tolerated and concerning their responses when their levels of tolerance were exceeded. For example, if one child pushed another, whether the act would be ignored or reprimanded was contingent upon the teachers' subjective interpretation of the intentionality and seriousness of the act.

If children kept their individual behaviors within the tolerable range of teachers' expectations, then they were free to keep themselves apart from classmates. They could remain as parallel players, involved in separate activities (Rowen 1973:141). Since no child ever withdrew totally from interactions with classmates for a sustained period of time, the limit to which teachers would permit a child to remain solely in parallel play was not established. Typically, a new arrival at the center might reject the advances of other children for the first few hours or days. For example, during her first morning a four-year-old girl would not speak to the other children when they spoke to her. Instead she looked away. As the morning progressed, she spoke more to the others, but when one of the boys asked her how old she was she again turned away. He tickled her. She told him to stop. He stuck out his tongue and walked away. Similar incidents occurred with children who had been at the center for longer periods of time but simply wanted to be left alone at a particular moment.

Sometimes a younger child or a child who lacked previous group experience might remain simply in a situational relationship to a small group of classmates involved in an activity (Rowen, 1973:151–153). For example, a happy-go-lucky, two-year-old boy enjoyed playing catch. However, when older children were playing catch he was also content to observe them in their games. He tried to imitate them but did not seem to mind when the ball was not thrown to him. Younger children may not be able to recognize the complexity of the difference between observing and fully participating.

Expectations for situational relationships are imposed by the social structure of group day care because of the need for order among a peer group of classmates (Bossard and Boll, 1966:406–409). Children must develop competency at the basic level of situational relationships before they can enter into sustained interactions with others (Mead, 1934; Hale and Delia, 1976). A child who is unable to comply with expectations for individual deportment will be avoided by the other children and therefore isolated from on-going interactions. The child who makes a great deal of noise at inappropriate times, who is consistently destructive of materials, and who runs about the classroom uncontrollably may be tolerated for a short period of time by teachers for various reasons (the newcomer who is expected to settle down after a while, the child who is suspected of having a behavioral disorder and is awaiting diagnosis and assessment, the child who is having a bad day). Teachers have to maintain order and be supportive of all children as long as they remain in the classroom. Children are not so constrained. They are not required to interact with a child who is not accepting responsibility for behaving as a classmate should.

Children develop communicative competence, learning the rules vis-à-vis the situation (Rodnick and Wood, 1973; Weber, 1977). Children understand the difference between incompetence based on age, mental retardation, emotional disturbance and deviance. Given guidance from teachers, they will instruct the younger child or the mentally retarded child in developmentally appropriate interactions (Roedell, *et al.*, 1977:46–47). They will show compassion and understanding, adapting their own conversation or activities to a simpler level. They will collude with the deviant to test the limits of behavioral expectations. But they will not voluntarily interact with a child at the time that child is unable to control his or her deportment. The child who is totally unable to engage in appropriate parallel play will be required to leave the center.

INTERACTIONS

From the group of classmates, children have the freedom to interact with each other in smaller voluntary groupings. For example, if two children were playing at the water table, each totally engrossed with his or her separate pouring containers and essentially ignoring each other, they would be in a situational relationship to each other. If they were talking to each other while playing at the table, handing containers back and forth, and fitting their actions together, then they would be involved in an interaction.

More experienced or older children do inform newcomers and younger children about how to move from situational relationships to involvement in interactions. That is, they incorporate an individual's behavior into group activities. For example, a new four-year-old gave a teacher a stuffed animal to hold for him. Another four-year-old said, "It can't be only yours; it belongs to all of us." The message was communicated that materials belonging to the center have to be shared. On another occasion Debbie,[1] a new two-year-old girl, was playing on her own at the water table in a situational relationship to three older girls interacting while playing together at the other end. Every now and then the older girls would turn to the newcomer and direct her to do something. Susan asked her for the blue bowl. Debbie looked at Susan and handed her a pot.

Susan said, "No, the blue bowl!" and pointed. Debbie handed it to Susan this time.

At this center, since new children were readily welcomed by others, teachers did not provide instruction about how to move from situational relationships to involvement in interactions. Teachers were more likely to intervene when they desired the opposite result, to halt a negative interaction and direct the participants back into parallel play (Ilg and Ames, 1955:245). For example, Kimberly went over to Danny and pretended to saw off his leg with a small sharp saw from the art room. Danny immediately began crying. The teacher consoled Danny, and directed Kimberly back into the art room to cut up some cardboard. The teacher was more concerned with maintaining order and keeping the noise level manageable than with providing instruction. In this particular instance, Kimberly was four years old and Danny only two. Danny may not have understood the difference between fantasy play and reality. If this teacher had been oriented towards providing instruction fostering social development, the scenario would have been quite different. The teacher might have first told Danny that Kimberly was only pretending and had Danny take a turn at pretending to cut off Kimberly's leg. This kind of exchange is typical of children developing fantasy play around the themes of accidents and hospitals. But, since the saw was indeed sharp and fantasy play does not usually involve a real saw, the teacher could have then directed both Kimberly and Danny into the art room to take turns cutting up cardboard.

In fact, teachers sometimes intervene to direct negative interactions into positive ones. Where this strategy is consistently followed, a series of positive interactions are more likely to develop and the groundwork for emergent friendships better established than when negative interactions are channeled into parallel play or back into a situational relationship. The latter would occur when, for example, a misbehaving child was given a "time out," sitting on a chair facing the wall.

In the day care center there were behavioral expectations that a child would share and take turns if another child was interested in the same piece of equipment or activity. Such expectations are task oriented and compliance does not require similarity of interests or skills.

Teachers structure possibilities for activities by their introduction of materials. An interaction may occur when two or more children act in unison to respond to a teacher-initiated opportunity. The interaction will be of short duration if the activity will require individual children to listen to or follow the directions of the teacher. For example, if the teacher tells two or more children to work with puzzles the request may result in compliant interaction (Smart and Smart, 1967:246). The children talk to each other and pass puzzles or pieces around. When the teacher signals clean-up time or a new activity the children disperse. The interaction was based upon compliance with authority and continues only as long as required.

Just because an activity is teacher-directed or initiated does not mean children will not wholeheartedly participate. For example, if the teacher makes a general offer to read a story to anyone who is interested, the children who choose to participate may interact as they move to join the teacher. They may talk to each other, communicating their enjoyment of being read a story. The children are oriented toward the teacher reading the story and also toward each other (Newcomb, 1961). The children have been provided an opportunity to recognize similar interests in each other (Byrne and Griffitt, 1969; Duck and Spencer, 1972). They have been rewarded for these similar interests by adult attention when a story is read. Temperamental or personality congruence has been encouraged.

The interaction will be of longer duration when the children cooperate more actively in an activity. This occurs when the teacher acts as a facilitator or participant rather than as an instructor or authority. For example, when blocks are the materials introduced by the teacher, two or more children can participate in building structures. The activity can be repeated over and over, such as building structures as high as possible until they fall over. Children delight in seeing the structure fall and in the loud noise which results as the blocks scatter everywhere. The children excitedly scramble around to gather up blocks in order to rebuild the structure again, fitting their actions together. Through play, they learn what is permissible within different types of activities (Erikson, 1972:152). They develop communication skills that are important prerequisites to the formation of allyships and friendships (Rubin, 1980:56).

ALLYSHIPS

As children learn what is considered appropriate behavior in different situations, they become confident enough to ally themselves together to initiate activities (Isaacs, 1933:394–395). Allyships are based upon an initial recognition of similar interests and skills which is extended over time by the children. The similarities may result from attributes of the children such as age, sex, or race, or may be associated with activity-related interests and competencies (Douvan and Gold, 1966:491–494; Herron and Sutton-Smith, 1971:95). Teachers permit children to interact more frequently with some playmates than with others because the interactions foster a harmonious group environment.

Two or more children will decide they want to engage in the same activity and ask the teacher to facilitate their interest by providing materials. They will ask the teacher to read them a book, to play a record, to build block towers, or to play cards with them. Children also learn that teachers are resources in the sense of providing ideas. If they are bored, they look to the teacher to provide guidance as to what is appropriate. After failing to decide on a mutually acceptable activity, they will approach the teacher to give them something to do. These types of allyships between classmates have their direct counterparts in individual requests. The teacher could read a story or build a block tower with one child. An individual child could approach the teacher and ask for something to do. The fact that the children are in a group setting makes it possible for a child to join with other children to make requests. The same resources are acquired as when a child makes the request individually, and peer group interactions are learned as an additional component of the transaction.

In centers such as this one, which place a high value on self-control, voluntary sharing, cooperation and maintenance of harmonious interactions, teachers do facilitate the formation of allyships (Campbell, 1964:314). Teachers direct two or more children into activities which they know the children enjoy. Teachers group children by ability for instructional purposes. To the extent that the teachers' perceptions are accurate, the imposed groupings structure children's recognition of similar interests or abilities. By contrast, in a more authoritarian center, where obedience and maintenance of harmonious relationships were valued, groupings would more often either be made solely to convenience teachers, or arbitrarily.

When groupings are based upon teachers' perceptions of children's similar interests or skills, inappropriate allyships are sometimes a byproduct. That is, two or more children cooperate within the activity but violate expectations held for the entire group of classmates. For example, taking a mixed-age grouping of children to the park two blocks from the center clearly reveals differences in physical ability. The teachers want to keep the children together for safety reasons, but the older children become frustrated at having to walk at the younger children's slower pace. Such walks typically involve break-aways by the older children. The teachers constantly threaten to return the whole group to the center if the break-aways do not return to the group. At the same time, the older children realize that the teachers' primary concern is getting the whole group the park and believe it unlikely that a transgression will result in more than a verbal reprimand. On one trip, Ralph and Joe ran ahead turning corners before the rest of the group so that the teachers could not see them. They were told to come back, but did not. When the whole group stopped to watch a moving van load up, the teacher told Ralph and Joe that they would be taken back to the center unless they would cooperate. They said they would not go back to the center, they would not get lost, and they did not want to wait for the others. The teacher then made a contingency that more probably would be enforced. Ralph and Joe were told that they would not get snack when they got to the park. They slowed down their pace. Children, such as Ralph and Joe, may be allies during a particular activity without the allyship necessarily carrying over to other activities. Quite the opposite is true for teachers reinforcing allyships; when the children form an allyship to challenge behavioral expectations, teachers may take steps to ensure that carry-over to further activities does not occur. For example, Ralph and Joe could be separated into different groups for subsequent trips to the park. Inappropriate allyships are directed by the teachers into compliant interactions.

The children may inappropriately act as allies to commit an act of deviance, such as breaking away, but they do not form gangs or become junior juvenile delinquents. Their size, developmental abilities, and the degree of teacher supervision preclude the opportunity for secrecy, required in juvenile delinquency (Bossard and Boll, 1966:412–415). Acts of deviance by children in child care are committed in relationship to classmates and in a highly constrained physical space. Thus, teachers can consistently thwart inappropriate activities, thereby preventing the participants from forming ongoing inappropriate allyships. Aggressive children may be accepted as leaders in many activities, but not ultimately chosen as friends (Clausen, 1968:168–169; Campbell, 1964:313).

When teachers are involved, children's allyships are likely to be a means towards some other ends. The content of the allyship centers on getting the teacher to provide materials or attention. In contrast, when children's allyships are self-directed, such as in fantasy play, means and ends coincide (Maier, 1969:45, 51–52). Younger or less experienced children take their cues from those who are older or more experienced. In a typical example, one of the older boys, Brian, encouraged four other children to play "doghouse." Brian said he was the "master" and everyone else was a dog. He would take them out of the cage (the jungle gym) for a walk. The "dogs" would crawl on all-fours howling and growling, a noisy game thoroughly enjoyed by all.

In fantasy play leadership roles are assumed through the demonstration of competence and possession of knowledge superior to peers (Aronson, 1960). In a typical example, one of the older girls, Kimberly, initiated a game of playing house for herself and three others. Kimberly ordered Anne to pour the milk, Joy to set the table and Bobbi to wash the dishes. Kimberly cooked the food. She told a staff member that the "hamburgers" had to cook for five minutes. She checked the "temperature control" and the staff member asked her the temperature at which the hamburgers should be cooked. Kimberly replied, "This temperature!" She made up the rules, and the answers, as she went along. She was the leader because she always had a rule and an answer.

If the children are evenly matched, so that no one child dominates, conflict may arise. For example, when four-year-old Kimberly asserted that the doll who was asleep was "My baby!" Brian, also four, exclaimed, "No! My baby!" A teacher whispered to them not to forget "their baby" was sleeping. They quieted down and continued to play together. In this instance, the adult mediator channeled possessiveness into cooperation by getting the children to take the role of another, "their baby." The teacher also unobtrusively reminded the children that objects, even babies, were for sharing. Learning about personal interests shared by others, the positions of leader and subordinate, conflict management, and cooperative endeavors are competencies acquired through allyships. These competencies are initial steps through which friendships may develop.

Learning to give service is also facilitated in a group environment where children can become experts about the daily routines. Children act as authorities to instruct new arrivals and observers about center activities. They teach newcomers the words and actions to classroom songs, how to work with materials, and how games are played. When adults permit themselves to be taught, the quality of giving service is reinforced. If adults invoke authority to correct the children's explanations, an opportunity for children to give service is lost and the allyship is inhibited. For example, Tanya, Bunny and Brian instructed a new observer on how to play a game. The observer judgmentally recorded that the children did not know the rules. After showing them the "proper" way, he reported that the children lost interest and dissipated to other activities. An allyship was directed back into interactions and situational relationships (Herron and Sutton-Smith, 1971:56).

The formation of allyships is a behavioral prerequisite to friendships. Allyship is a necessary but not sufficient condition. As the same two or three children work and play together with greater frequency and over a wider variety of activities, groupings based upon allyships can become groupings based upon affective preferences. Friendships additionally involve consciously recognizing that these preferences are emotionally rewarding. If children do not comply with expectations for individual deportment, then much of their experience will remain at the level of structural relationships. Interactions will be infrequent and of minimal duration, rewarding allyships will be transient, and friendships will not develop.

Rewarding allyships are not necessarily based upon affective preferences (Goffman, 1959:77–105). Two or more children may interact frequently as a team simply because they are the best match possible within the group of classmates from whom to choose. Their interests and skills coincide to a greater extent than with any of their other classmates, but given a larger pool of more homogeneous eligibles they probably would not choose each other. Their teaming remains a situationally-based convenience grouping. One of the most vivid examples occurred the only time the center provided before and after school care. For the most part Bill, an eight-year-old third-grader, held himself aloof or acted as a disruptive force, shouting out answers far ahead of anyone else during learning exercises and picking on the younger children. Frank was the only child to regularly play with Bill, mostly roughhousing. Frank was one of the oldest and largest four-year-olds at the center. During the bulk of the day when Bill was at school, Frank was predominantly in a friendship grouping which included himself, Matthew and Rita. Both Matthew and Rita were also loud and outgoing four-year-olds. Matthew was the leader, labelled "the trouble maker" by staff. Rita was initially misidentified by all the research participant observers as a boy. She exhibited frequent mood swings between disruptive behavior (especially when Matthew was present) and cooperative behavior (with Frank and others when she was not with Matthew). The teaming between Bill and Frank then seemed to be based upon the fact that Frank was one of the largest of the day care children and also a child who was characteristically a follower of a more aggressive leader. It is unlikely that Bill would have teamed up with Frank if there had been another child with similar interests and skills present who was closer to Bill's own age.

FRIENDSHIPS

Friendships emerge when children identify emotionally with others as equals. This was the case with Kimberly and Brian. Initially Brian was Kimberly's side-kick. He was neither as aggressive nor as confident as she. She initiated, he participated. When she stopped, he lost interest. As they spent increasing amounts of time together, they began to be reported as acting in concert rather than as initiator and follower. They painted pictures together, ate together, danced together and even shared the same emotions. For example, Brian would say to another, "Kimberly and I are mad at you." As allyships develop into friendships, children replace the singular pronoun "I" with the plural pronoun "We" (Roedell, et al., 1977:58).

Appropriate allyships are rewarded within the social structure of the day care environment. Friendships are individually rewarding as well. Provided that children's social exchanges meet teachers' behavioral expectations for relationships and interactions, exclusive preferences will be respected by the teachers. Not only are preferences respected, but they are subtly reinforced by teachers trained to place a high value on interactions between children. Two or three children acting together are much more likely to have the ability to acquire valued resources, such as eliciting responses from teachers, than is a child acting individually. The phrase, "Please give us . . ." communicates to the teacher that children are sharing, and thereby contributing to a harmonious group environment (Maccoby, 1971).

From the child's perspective, sharing a teacher's time with preferred others can be a rewarding trade-off if quality of time does not have to be sacrificed for quantity of time. For example, if a teacher has primary responsibility for six children and equitably tries to spend the same amount of time with each child, then any one child could receive ten minutes of attention per hour. If three of the children interact sufficiently to enjoy the same activities at the same time, then they can collectively share thirty minutes of time. Moreover, a teacher is less likely to be concerned about showing favoritism to certain children when time is spent with a group than when time is spent with an individual. Teachers are likely to spend longer periods of uninterrupted time with groups than with individuals. A small cohesive group can also be more effective in drawing the teacher away from an activity involving an individual child. Friendships are very powerful tools for controlling scarce resources and ensuring a constant supply of rewards (Maier, 1969:276, 281–282). Moreover, resources acquired in a spirit of friendship facilitate further learning and development (Roedell, *et al.*, 1977:58). In contrast, resources acquired through disruptive behaviors (such as tantrums) focus energies on controlling behavior.

When children are placed into situational relationship with each other through enrollment at a day care center, some already have a competitive advantage (Werner, 1957). They have the kinds of behavioral attributes that lead the research participant observers to label these children as having basically friendly personalities (Campbell, 1964:304–307; Isaacs, 1933:272–279; Roedell, *et al.*, 1977:58–59; Rubin, 1980:51). That is how researchers described Michael during the first year of our observations. He was the youngest child at age two years, three months. He was a favorite with the other children. They seemed to take pleasure in hugging him, cuddling him, even occasionally kissing him, and in many ways playing "parent" to him. They called him their "baby." Michael either looked bewildered or seemed to enjoy the attention. Michael was self-directed and unselfish, equally willing to engage in an activity on his own or share in it with others. Michael also delivered rewards by making the other children feel good about themselves. For example, another two-year-old, Sarah, came over and got on the rocker with him and the two of them rocked together for nearly fifteen minutes. Generally, he did not show any evidence of possessiveness towards materials. When he was playing in the sandbox with a little shovel, another-two-year old, Barry ran over and asked to use the shovel. Michael gave it to him and then continued digging in the sand with his hands. In other situations, Michael showed this same adaptability and flexibility of being able to substitute alternative methods for engaging in the same activity. Michael was never observed to cry, whereas other young or inexperienced children would tantrum or leave an activity when another child encroached upon their territory.

When a young or inexperienced child is basically self-directed and also is consistently positively responsive to interactions initiated by others, allyships develop quickly and frequently. The child's basic personality structure seems to elicit the norm of reciprocity, the desire to nurture and instruct, in more experienced children (Berscheid and Walster, 1969). For example, Brian, a four-year-old, was at the bottom of the jungle gym trying to help Michael get down. Brian said, "Come on little Michael, it's easy."

For older or more experienced children there is a complementary personality structure which seems conducive to friendship formation. Older or more experienced children can take advantage of their seniority to initiate interactions as well as being responsive to interactions initiated by others. Children who are behaviorally altruistic and able to empathize emotionally have a competitive advantage. They are more likely to initiate or maintain interactions in such a way that others will respond positively. For example, when Kimberly hit Sarah hard enough to make her cry, Kimberly then knelt beside her, touched her face, and generally tried to make Sarah feel better. Kimberly showed the desire to make amends and comfort children she had hurt. With up to twenty-five children in a relatively restricted area, such minor injuries are not uncommon. Kimberly also behaved altruistically, to cherish and protect others, even when she had not perpetrated the incidents. On one occasion, Anne was pushing at Bobbi's face. Kimberly came over and hugged Bobbi. Anne looked very sad and said, "I'm sorry," to Bobbi. Kimberly gave Anne a pat on the back. The incident was handled in such a way that all three girls ended up interacting happily.

Altruism and empathy can be expressed in many different ways. Sometimes the behavior is very obvious as when one child hugs another. At other times it is more subtle, as was the case when a group of children were playing musical chairs. Michael was unable to grasp the rules of the game and kept deviating from them. The other children would bump into him making it difficult for them all to play the game. Kimberly said as she took his hand, "Come on Michael, you can stand by me." The game continued smoothly with Kimberly providing Michael the necessary guidance. Altruism and empathy can also be expressed by modifying the rules. This happened on another occasion when Brian's solution was to say to Michael, "That's O.K., we'll go slow at first."

Occasionally altruism and empathy will be expressed through a gift. For example, when Bobbi left a game in tears, Anne went over to her and gave her a penny. The penny was a prized possession which Anne had brought from home and had been displaying to the other children off and on all morning. For children, giving the extrinsic possession is not the same as an adult providing a material object as a substitute for affection. For a child the prized possession and the affect coincide (Isaacs, 1933:272–274).

Children also provide services for each other. For example, when a new staff member was having difficulty putting on Sarah's snowsuit, Anne came over and put it on quickly. Kimberly, Bobbi and others had also gathered around telling the teacher what to do.

It is through numerous repetitions of interactions such as these that friendships develop. The children need not be the same age or even at the same developmental stage (Rowen, 1973:153). Sarah, Kimberly, Anne and Bobbi (2, 4, 3 and 3 years old respectively) interacted with each other frequently and for relatively long periods of time. Over one of the six-month observational periods, they grew more possessive of each other's time as well as more protective of each other. They rarely argued.

When children are confident and secure about their existing friendships they can be open to making new friendships with many others. Sarah, Kimberly, Bobbi and Anne welcomed others who joined them in their activities. They had friendships with other classmates as well as with each other. In such a situation, the children are rewarded personally by their friendships and the whole group profits from the harmonious environment engendered by the friendships. Both interpersonal and structural rewards are maximized. Teachers and other children augment the interpersonal rewards provided by the friendship.

Friendships can also be exclusive and confining as was the case for Dorothy, Paula and Kiki, a group observed at a different time. Altruism and empathy alternated with self-centered behavior and ridicule. Dorothy constantly sought approval from the researchers, "Don't I eat well?" "See that picture on the wall? I drew it. Isn't it good?" "Don't I look nice today? I have new shoes." Paula would hold herself aloof from many teacher-initiated activities, for example, refusing to participate in races on the playground. Paula also overreacted when another child bumped into her during the course of a day, screaming as if mortally wounded. Kiki would make fun of other children's attempts at an activity. She would laugh at someone's attempt to do a puzzle although she herself had trouble putting puzzles together. The three girls played with each other frequently, sometimes for relatively long periods of time. But frequently, their play was disrupted by arguments. They used withdrawal of friendship to threaten each other. Paula would say to Kiki, "You won't be Dorothy's friend any more, will you? You don't like her." If Paula was successful, she and Kiki would go off to play together leaving Dorothy temporarily alone. Each of the girls sometimes enlisted other classmates to verbalize the power of friendships as an exclusionary tactic. Dorothy would react to Paula, or initiate an argument with Paula without apparent provocation, by saying to another classmate, "You won't be Paula's friend, will you? You're only my friend. Don't play with her." The friendship between Dorothy, Paula and Kiki provided both interpersonal rewards and frustrations. It did not maximize further learning and development. Teachers were most often enlisted to manage behavior and classmates to act as allies in arguments. Dorothy, Paula and Kiki were successful in obtaining the attention of others. But in this situation, neither teachers nor classmates could enhance or augment over a sustained period of time the interpersonal competencies developed through the friendship.

Friendships which are exclusive and confining do provide opportunities to expand social, emotional and cognitive skills, whether the friendships are conflict-ridden or tranquil. They have developmental value for the children involved. But they do not have the added advantage of serving as a secure base of confidence and trust from which the individuals operate to acquire additional skills and resources. Friendships which are diffused and open to others provide opportunities both to practice current skills and to extend these skills forward to new stages of mastery.

DISCUSSION

Most importantly, the present research demonstrates the viability of studying the structuring of friendship formation among very young children. By explicating the stages in the process from situational relationships to interactions to allyships to friendships, a conceptual framework is provided from within which: (1) variables are identified for further research; (2) categories for assessing social and emotional development are suggested; and (3) strategic intervention points for increasing classroom teaching effectiveness are highlighted.

Particularly important towards this end is the evidence demonstrating the importance of friendships for furthering cognitive development. The data are consistent with other research on adults that suggests: The higher one's level of social and emotional development, the greater is one's cognitive complexity (Hale and Delia, 1976). The day care center is the preparatory arena for compulsory education. The data suggests that readiness for specific academic learnimg will develop unevenly, partially dependent upon children's abilities to form allyships and friendships. The quality or effectiveness of a day care environment could be rated according to the proportion of children who are involved in behaviorally appropriate allyships and friendships.

Young children's play is their work. For older children and adults, friendships may overlap with, but are distinct from, time spent with others at school or work. For young children who require constant supervision, friendships and time spent with others in day care coincide to a significantly greater extent. Day care children's friends are their classmates, although not all of their classmates are their friends. In the future, as much attention must be directed towards understanding children's social and emotional relationships as has been the case for measuring their cognitive, linguistic and physical development.

ACKNOWLEDGMENT

I am grateful to Richard White, Nick Curtis, Joyce Gab, Laura Heil, Susan Seligman, James Borgelt, Jan Dropik, Michael Hampton, and Patricia Kanter who collected the observational data and to Penelope P. Croghan, Kathie Gregory, Vincent Keenan, Mary Ellen O'Neil and Marylin Weber for assistance with the initial data analysis.

NOTE

1. Name is a pseudonym for this child as is the case for all other names used subsequently.

REFERENCES

Aronson, Elliott
   1960   The Social Animal. San Francisco, Calif.: W. H. Freeman.
Berger, Charles R., Marylin D. Weber, Mary Ellen Munley, and James T. Dixon
   1977   "Interpersonal relationship levels and interpersonal attraction." Pp. 245–261 in Brent D. Ruben (ed.), Communication Yearbook I. New Brunswick, N.J.: Transaction.
Berscheid, Ellen, and Elaine Hatfield Walster
   1969   Interpersonal Attraction. Reading, Mass.: Addison-Wesley.
Bossard, James H., and Eleanor Stoker Boll
   1966   The Sociology of Child Development. Fourth Edition. New York: Harper and Row.
Byrne, D., and W. Griffitt
   1969   "Similarity and awareness of similarity of personality characteristics." Journal of Experimental Research in Personality 3:179–186.
Campbell, John D.
   1964   "Peer relations in childhood." Pp. 289–322 in Martin L. Hoffman and Lois Wladis Hoffman (eds.), Review of Child Development Research. Volume 1. New York: Russell Sage Foundation.

Chein, I.
   1954   "The environment as a determinant of behavior." Journal of Social Psychology
          39:115–127.
Clausen, John A.
   1968   "Perspectives on childhood socialization." Pp. 130–181 in John A. Clausen (ed.),
          Socialization and Society. Boston, Mass.: Little, Brown.
Denzin, Norman K.
   1977   Childhood Socialization: Studies in the Development of Language, Social Be-
          havior, and Identity. San Francisco, Calif.: Jossey-Bass.
Douvan, Elizabeth, and Martin Gold
   1966   "Modal patterns in American adolescence." Pp. 469–528 in Lois Wladis Hoffman
          and Martin L. Hoffman (eds.), Review of Child Development Research. Volume
          2. New York: Russell Sage Foundation.
Duck, Steven W.
   1973   Personal Relationships and Personal Constructs: A Study of Friendship Formation.
          New York: John Wiley.
Duck, Steven W., and Christopher Spencer
   1972   "Personal constructs and friendship formation." Journal of Personality and Social
          Psychology 23:40–45.
Erikson, Erik H.
   1972   "Play and actuality." Pp. 127–167 in Maria W. Piers (ed.), Play and Development.
          New York: W. W. Norton.
Evans, Ellis D.
   1975   Contemporary Influences in Early Childhood Education. Second Edition. New
          York: Holt, Rinehart and Winston.
Fein, Greta G., and Alison Clarke-Stewart
   1973   Day Care in Context. New York: John Wiley.
Goffman, Erving
   1959   The Presentation of Self in Everyday Life. Garden City, New York: Doubleday
          Anchor.
Hale, Claudia L., and Jesse G. Delia
   1976   "Cognitive complexity and social perspective-taking." Communication Mono-
          graphs 43:195–203.
Herron, R. E., and Brian Sutton-Smith
   1971   Child's Play. New York: John Wiley.
Ilg, Frances L., and Louise Bates Ames
   1955   Child Behavior: From Birth to Ten. New York: Harper and Row Perennial.
Isaacs, Susan
   [1929] The Nursery Years: The Mind of the Child from Birth to Six Years. New York:
   1968   Schocken.
Isaacs, Susan
   [1933] Social Development in Young Children. New York: Schocken.
   1972
Levitan, Sar A., and Karen Cleary Alderman
   1975   Child Care and ABC's Too. Baltimore, Md.: Johns Hopkins University Press.
Maccoby, Eleanor E.
   1971   "Role-taking in childhood and its consequences for social learning." Pp. 343–356
          in George G. Thompson (ed.), Social Development and Personality. New York:
          John Wiley.
Maier, Henry W.
   1969   Three Theories of Child Development: The Contributions of Erik H. Erikson,

Jean Piaget, and Robert R. Sears, and Their Application. New York: Harper and Row.

Mead, George H.
1934 Mind, Self and Society. Chicago, Ill.: University of Chicago Press.

Newcomb, T. M.
1961 The Acquaintance Process. New York: Holt, Rinehart and Winston.

Rodnick, R., and B. Wood
1973 "The communication strategies of children." The Speech Teacher 22:114–124.

Roedell, Wendy C., Ronald G. Slaby, and Halbert B. Robinson
1977 Social Development in Young Children. Monterey, Calif.: Brooks/Cole.

Rowen, Betty
1973 The Children We See: An Observational Approach to Child Study. New York: Holt, Rinehart, and Winston.

Rubin, Zick
1980 Children's Friendships. Cambridge, Mass.: Harvard University Press.

Shipman, M. D.
1972 Exploring Education: Childhood, A Sociological Perspective. Lancs, Great Britain: NFER.

Smart, Mollie S., and Russell C. Smart
1967 Children: Development and Relationships. New York: Macmillan.

Snapper, Kurt J., and JoAnne S. Ohms
1978 The Status of Children 1977. Washington, D.C.: Department of Health, Education and Welfare.

Stone, L. Joseph, and Joseph Church
1973 Childhood and Adolescence: A Psychology of the Growing Person. Third Edition. New York: Random House.

Weber, Marylin Daly
1977 Social Situation, Uncertainty, Communication and Interpersonal Attraction. Ph.D. dissertation, Northwestern University.

Werner, H.
1957 Comparative Psychology of Mental Development. New York: International University Press.

FEMINISM, FEMALE FRIENDS, AND THE RECONSTRUCTION OF INTIMACY

Joan Acker, Kate Barry and Joke Esseveld

INTRODUCTION

a change in the facts of life (vital statistics) does not necessarily and automatically
lead to a change in the facts of life (social interaction) . . . The nature of social
interaction changes when individuals or groups decide to change it, and set about
doing so, overcoming the opposition of other individuals and groups (Frankenberg,
1976).

This quote captures the overall perspective of this report of our study of
change in the lives of a group of middle aged American women.

The demographic transformation in American women's lives is old
news. Increasing proportions of adult women work for pay, the percent
of a woman's lifetime devoted to mothering has dramatically fallen, more
women are single heads of households, most women can expect to spend

some of their adult lives without the companionship of a man. These changes have made the contradictions between our society's ideology of equality and the reality of female disadvantage more visible than ever before. Working women can see their disadvantages of pay and promotion; sex discrimination cases become news reported in the media; a new image of the successful woman emerges. But, what impact has this had on the daily lives of the average woman?

The Women's Movement can be interpreted as a response to, and an influence on, these changes in the demographic facts of life. One of its goals is to alter social interaction or personal relations to make them more congruent both with the structural reality of women's increasing participation in the society outside the family and with beliefs about equality and freedom. This requires a redefinition and a restructuring of many social relations, particularily the more intimate ones which have traditionally been based on different values and interactions. The question is: Have the changing life patterns and the ideas of the women's movement influenced women's interpretation of, and feelings about, personal relations and led them to reconstruct those relations? This is the question that we will discuss, but not unequivocally answer, in later portions of this paper.

THE STATUS OF PERSONAL RELATIONS IN SOCIOLOGICAL THEORY

Our discussion is limited to certain personal relations in the private sphere, women's ties with female friends and kin and their intimate connections with men, whether husbands or lovers. This choice is based on theoretical considerations as well as upon our intention to contribute to the subject matter of this volume. Questions relating to these close personal bonds are being seen as important for understanding the larger social structure. This has not always been so, even though the family, usually defined as the focus of intimate social relations, has been viewed at the most general theoretical level as an important element in social structure (Parsons, 1954). Intimate social relations and their significance for society have been neglected, at least partly, because of concerns of the dominant structural theories, whether Marxist or structural-functionalist. In both traditions, the family has been seen as a relatively conservative, status quo preserving institution, with varying consequences for the theoretical status of intimacy.

In structural functionalism, the significance of family relations is defined in terms of the important functions they perform for the larger social structure, i.e., socialization and tension management. The family is seen as a stabilizing institution which is essential for assuring continuity, social cohesion, and a sense of meaning for individuals. A consequence of this view of the family's functions has been a sociological concentration on certain questions to the neglect of others. For example, there has been much more interest in socialization—the learning of acceptable behavior—than on how children feel about parents. There has been much more attention paid to the effects of wives' gainful employment on husbands' attitudes, marital happiness, and children's adjustment than on wives' feelings about themselves and about the emotional relationships they have with other family members (Hochschild, 1975). Only recently, with the rise of the Women's Movement have sociological studies on such questions been done. (See, e.g., Birnbaum, 1975; Macke, *et al.*, 1979; and Richardson, 1979).

Another consequence of the way in which the family has been conceptualized in much of sociology is the failure to give much theoretical or empirical attention to intimate relations within the family and with outsiders and their potential for understanding society. The family is seen as a bounded social structure. In an image of society as a system with subsystems (of which the family is one), all of the subsystems have more or less permeable boundaries. Implicitly, the boundaries of the family have been seen as well defined and not too permeable; the family is isolated in modern society, separate from the public structures of economy and polity. As a consequence, internal structures have been given the most attention in family sociology and when the external world is considered, it is in its impact on the internal structure rather than on the reciprocal interpenetration of structures. (For a different view, see Kanter, 1977). Moreover, the theoretical isolation of the family has been paralleled by the isolation of family sociology. What started as an ideology of the family as a haven in the 19th Century has been reified in the theory and structure of an academic discipline. Since significant intimate relations are seen as occurring within this isolated institution, the study of wife-husband, parent-child and other kin relations is placed in an isolated position, on the periphery of the sociological enterprise. Another result of this mode of conceptualization is that intimate relations that fall outside family boundaries, such as friendships and non-marital sexual ties, are hardly theorized about at all. As Bart (1975) has pointed out, female-female relationships (one of our concerns in this paper) have been little studied partly because they have been viewed as irrelevant to social structure.

In the Marxist tradition, the family has also been seen as a conservative institution. But the interpretation of the theoretical significance of the support of the status quo differs from that of the mainstream theories discussed above. Rather than a source of stability and continuity, the family is seen as an impediment to desirable social change; no longer the location of production, it also has become peripheral to the main determinants of class and revolutionary change. Consequently, the family, including the social relations of intimacy, has been of little interest to Marxist theorists. Although some strands of Marxist thought such as Critical Theory (Horkheimer, 1972 and Reich, 1972) gave some primacy to internal family relations in their attempt to understand the success of authoritarian movements and the defeat of socialist aims, their focus was still on the family as a source of resistance to positive social change. Their attempts to bring the family into Marxist analysis did not have a broad effect on other sectors in this theoretical tradition. In sum, we can say that the family and, most particularly, intimate social relations have been placed outside the domain of central concern by the dominant theories of Western sociology.

Recent history has undermined this theoretical placement of the family and personal relations. Family and marriage, with all the discontent, boredom and conflict that often characterize life in these institutions, are no longer taken as natural and inevitable. People want happiness and, in an affluent society, seek it through divorce, "new life styles," encounter groups and new religious sects. Traditional sociologists and other commentators interpret this as a failure of personal relations and the family (e.g., Slater, 1971; Lasch, 1979). The supposed decay of the family has even become a political issue; for example, conservative candidates promise to save the family, and the President of the U.S. calls a White House Conference on the Family. Some theorists, such as Eli Zaretsky (1978), argue that the growing demand for a personally satisfying private life has the potential for generating a new revolutionary movement. Others, such as Christopher Lasch (1979), contend that the search for "new life styles" is part of the malaise of advanced capitalism in which all private relations become absorbed into the cash nexus. Far from finding any revolutionary hope in the turmoil that disturbs our personal worlds, Lasch finds only the basis of despair. Thus, personal relationships force their way into the consciousness of sociologists as theoretically and empirically relevant to questions about the process of change in the larger structure.

THE STATUS OF PERSONAL RELATIONS
IN FEMINIST THEORY

Feminist thought has provided one of the most powerful sources for the emergence of a general theoretical position that puts personal social relations and emotions on the level of macro-structures in regard to their importance for understanding contemporary societies. Confronting the cross-cultural and trans-historical perpetuation of the subordination of women, these theorists were forced to admit that approaches focussing on economy, class, politics and other large institutional structures were not adequate in explaining societal life (e.g., Mitchell, 1971). They neglected other social relations such as patterns of domination and inequality built into sexuality, human reproduction, the socialization of children and the division of labor in the family as well as into the many structures outside the private sphere. And these patterns seemed very resistant to change. Attention of feminist theorists became, therefore, focussed in the direction of the personal and the intimate. The search for solutions has led some into a neo-Freudian analysis of unconscious process (Mitchell, 1974; Chodorow, 1978). Other analyses are more concerned with the social construction of meaning and consciousness within changing structural constraints (Rowbotham, 1972; Smith, 1977).

Whatever the theoretical perspective, feminist thinking points to the centrality of female-female relations and female-male relations of the sexual kind in understanding social structures and the position of women within them (Seiden and Bart, 1975). "Sisterhood is Powerful" and "The Personal is Political" are the Women's Movement metaphors for these theoretical positions. "Sisterhood is Powerful" is a slogan that seeks to countermand and deny the traditional stereotypes of women as passive, weak and unable to work together to alleviate their oppression. Behind the idea of sisterhood lies the understanding that all women have been subjected to the same values of femininity, the same sex roles, that prescribed a willing submission to an inferior state. Sisterhood implies a common fate, but a shared experience that has been mystified and obscured in a society in which each woman is a lonely competitor in the race to get and hold a man. Women will be able to forge new bonds with each other, this view suggests, as they begin to break down the barriers that separate them and come to understand that the way to solving their problems is in sympathetic and supportive cooperation with each other, not in hostile or suspicious competition.

Consciousness raising groups, although not the only avenue to an altered and feminist perspective, have been the primary organizational form for developing a sense of shared experience and a new interpretation of that experience. Getting together regularly in small groups, women talk about their lives and their feelings about those lives, often revealing for the first time emotions that they had tried to keep secret because there had seemed to be no legitimation for such reactions. For example, one of the secrets revealed over and over again was that many women pretend to have orgasms when actually nothing of the kind is happening to them. Feelings of inadequacy, guilt toward the mate, ambivalence toward sex often contributed to depression and a general joylessness. These feelings went unarticulated, except perhaps with a psychotherapist, because women saw them as trivial, shameful and extremely private and personal. The feminist interpretation pointed out that the personal—even the most private sexual feeling—is political, allowing women to understand and validate their experience within a social-structural framework. Sexual dysfunctions, along with anger, hostility, feelings of isolation and inadequacy, could all be understood as reactions to an oppressive social system in which men have a systematic advantage over women, an advantage they perpetuate in the personnel office, on the psychiatrist's couch, and in the marital bed.

"The Personal is Political" amounted to a devastating critique of social relations. Relegated to a powerless and dependent position by the social structure, the very relationship that was to provide economic security and emotional support, the relationship with a man of one's own, was the instrument of oppression. This relationship was also the source of structural barriers and emotional distrust between women. Thus, there is a theoretical link between the nature of the female-male—most often the wife-husband—relationship and close friendships between women (Caplan and Bujra, 1978). Such a linkage between these two types of intimate relationships is also suggested by a functional analysis that contends that the structural isolation of the couple makes that bond more and more central in private life, reducing the opportunities as well as the desirability of other close emotional ties that might compete with the exclusiveness of the marital dyad. The feminist analysis adds that this is all very dysfunctional for the woman.

This feminist analysis constitutes both an emerging social theory and a counter-ideology. While, at this point, we are discussing the theoretical background to this research, it should also be understood that many of the women we interviewed were to varying degrees also being exposed to and coming to adopt a feminist world view.

FEMALE FRIENDS AND HETEROSEXUAL TIES—THE LITERATURE

Before proceeding to see how these ideas affected the intimate ties of women who were trying to alter their lives in the late 1970s, we will briefly survey what is known about female friendships and heterosexual intimacy prior to the emergence of our present Women's Movement. Have women been isolated from other women in American society? Has intimacy in the marital pair been more myth than reality, a smokescreen to hide relations of domination? What does the available research show?

In the 19th Century, Carroll Smith-Rosenberg (1979) argues, women of the upper and middle classes had close relationships of reciprocal communication, sharing and emotional support. A network of women, mothers, daughters, sisters and friends, provided the love and nurturance that all of them needed for coping with the crises and traumas of life. Within this female world, men played a separate and peripheral part. Did these close and sustaining ties disappear with the further development of a mobile, competitive capitalist society? Both Seiden and Bart (1975) and Long Laws (1979) suggest that women continued to have emotionally significant relationships with each other, but that these were interpreted as unimportant and hidden by an ideology that supported male dominance. "The ideology (belief system) that women can not trust other women, can not work for other women, in short, can not be sisterly, serves" a function for the society. "The purpose it serves for the patriarchal society in which we live is to reinforce women's dependence on men. For if women can not trust or work for or be friends with women, then they must, of course, turn to men" (Seiden and Bart, 1975 p. 194).

Thus, accepting such an ideology, women may fail to notice the importance of their female friends. Researchers may also have failed to notice; they have not paid much attention to the nature of female-female relationships, especially to the question of the degree of intimacy, sharing of confidences and emotional closeness in these relationships. There are some exceptions, although studies tell us more about the frequency of woman to woman interaction than about the salience and closeness of the relation. Lopata (1971) provides a great deal of data on neighboring relationships, showing variations in the frequency and content of these interactions. She found the highest levels of neighboring among suburban housewives, with both socializing and service exchanges as important elements. Factors such as age, education, type of housing and community, and presence of young children account for some of the variation. Sometimes intensive neighboring produces close friendships, but it is not clear from Lopata's account how frequent this is nor how intimate the friendships become. In a subsample of 571 respondents in Lopata's study, 44 percent of the women reported that they talk daily on the telephone with women friends. These women also reported frequent contacts with their mothers and mothers-in-law. However, Lopata provides little information on the content of these calls and we can only infer some degree of closeness from the high frequency.

Rubin (1976) emphasizes the absence of female friends among the working class wives she interviewed, although she does mention that neighboring during the day time is important in the lives of full-time housewives. Friendships, in Rubin's study, are limited by the demands of relationships with the extended family, but it is not clear whether female relatives provide some of the intimacy and support that are part of friendships for other women. It does seem clear that the sex-segregated social relations reported in earlier studies of working class life (Bott, 1957; Young and Wilmott, 1957) were not prevalent in the California communities that Rubin studied.

A few other studies are relevant to the question of the prevalence and nature of female-female friendships. In a pilot study of 12 female feminists, Seiden and Bart (1975) found that nine had always had close women friends. In a small sample of college-educated couples, Babchuk and Bates (1963) found that wives tended to identify the husband's male friends among their own three closest friends and tended to more frequently identify men rather than women as their closest friends. Married women had fewer close friends than women who were divorced, widowed or single, in a study reported by Booth and Hess (1974). There is a problem, in addition to the social invisibility of female friendships alluded to above, in interpreting these findings. That is the problem of the meaning, to the survey respondent, of the term "friendship." Neighbors and friends are different concepts, as is evident in the studies of both Lopata (1971) and Rubin (1976). Friends may be people who are invited into the home for couple-companionate socializing. Women who visit during the day for gossip and chit-chat may not be consciously identified as friends. Allan (1977) notes this problem in studying friendship in Britain, suggesting that there may be class differences in the meaning of the concept, that it is important to discover how the individual defines and experiences relationships if findings are to be interpreted with any accuracy.

No clear conclusions can be drawn from the sparse literature on friendships among women in the contemporary U.S. There are indications that the ideal of the marital relationship as the primary locus of intimacy has spread to the working class (Rubin, 1976) as well as the middle class (Lopata, 1971). The corollary to this ideal is that other bonds, such as female-female ties, are secondary and not so intimate. At the same time, there are data showing that many women, especially when they are housewives with children, have frequent social contacts with other women, share confidences, and talk about feelings (Lopata, 1975). We do not know much about the concrete content of these feelings and confidences, nor about the felt significance of these relationships.

What can we say about marital intimacy? As with friendship, marital intimacy is a concept that may have different meanings to different people. As an ideal it is central to the idea of the companionate marriage. Intimacy includes, according to Glazer (1975), dependency, confidence sharing, emotional involvement, and the relationship as primary. A low level of conflict between the partners is also included in Glazer's concept of intimacy. Salamon (1977) makes a useful distinction in her discussion of family and kin bonds. In defining a close personal relationship, she says, "the affiliation should: (1) be of some duration; (2) involve a sharing of personal knowledge; (3) contain mutual understandings for behavior; (4) possess a commitment, to the extent that the tie would be counted on for aid and support" (Salamon, 1977, p. 809). Such relations are significant for the creation of the self and meaning, but they are not necessarily "close," that is, confidences, fears and joys may not be shared. Intimacy develops, along with the context for self-revelation, when a positive affect is added to the other elements of what Salamon calls "a personalized" bond. Intimacy also implies reciprocity, as Glazer suggests. We add that it probably also assumes equality and shared life experience.

We return to the basic question, to what extent has marital intimacy been a reality, to what extent only an ideology? Glazer (1975), in a review of community studies that contain some evidence on this question, notes the sex segregation and lack of communication between blue-collar couples. Rainwater, as early as 1959, records the wistful wishes of blue-collar wives for greater closeness with their husbands. Rubin's study of working class wives in the 1970s much more clearly shows that women in this class desire, but do not experience, intimacy with their husbands. Seeley and associates (1956) in the 50's and Cuber and Harroff (1966) in the 60's both found indications that middle class marriages of long standing often lacked the close personal and positive bonds of intimacy.[1] On the other hand, Lopata's (1971) study suggests that at least some proportion of better educated middle class women are able to achieve the ideal of the companionate marriage, including intimacy with the spouse.

Much research suggests that the conditions for intimacy between men and women do not yet exist in our society. The evidence on the lack of equality in the economic and occupational realm as well as in the division of labor within the home is massive (see, e.g., Stromberg and Harkess, 1979). Both feminist writers and sociologists such as Goffman (1979) have detailed the processes of interpersonal interaction that maintain patterns of dominance and deference in the private sphere. In addition, there is evidence of lack of reciprocity and divergent rather than shared experience. Studies of perceptions and evaluations of married life have for years shown that there are low levels of agreement between members of married pairs about dimensions of the marriage (Long Laws, 1971; Bernard, 1972).

Glazer (1975) shows similar findings in a recent study of marital intimacy. She found a particularly low correlation between mates on how primary the emotional bond between them was. Thus, Jessie Bernard's (1972) observation that there is "her marriage" and "his marriage" is repeatedly confirmed. While people with divergent experience may be able to communicate about their differences, this may be a more strained and difficult process than communication between those who share a perceptual stance. Berger and Kellner (1970) have argued that marriage involves the process of developing a shared and exclusive set of meanings and interpretations. What they do not recognize is that these meanings are often constructed around the perceptions of the man, misting over with veils of mutuality the underlying patterns of sexual inequality described by Goffman (1979). Thus, we hypothesize that many women who may identify their marriage as an intimate one will alter that definition as they begin to see relations of power and domination within the marriage and reinterpret feelings of frustration and diminished self-worth.

The consciousness raising group experience is indirect evidence on the state of intimacy between the sexes. Although there is no way to determine how many women have participated in these groups, the lists of those who have go far beyond any formal list of members of feminist organizations (Evans, 1980). Women who have been in such groups attest to the uniqueness of the emotional relationships experienced there and the contrasting poverty of content of other relationships, including the heterosexual bond. While some might argue that consciousness raising appealed only to a minority of women who had not been able to achieve a positive relationship with men, we believe that such groups appealed to those women who, for a variety of reasons, could not or would not continue to cast themselves in the role of the subordinant, the follower, the powerless.

We conclude, as we concluded with our discussion of the evidence on the nature of female-female bonds in our society, that the social science evidence is inadequate, spotty and often circumstantial. Given these severe restrictions, there seems to be more evidence for intimacy as a cultural ideal than intimacy as part of everyday experience. We intend in this paper to make a small addition to the data on this subject, acknowledging that we leave unanswered most of the questions that we have raised.

THE SAMPLE AND THE METHOD

This paper is part of a larger study of changes in the lives of women in their middle years. It is based on the experiences of 28 women who were in the process of consciously trying to change their lives after long periods during which their primary identities were as housewives and mothers. Their median age was 45 at the time of the first interview. About a third would be categorized as working class and about two-thirds as middle class on the basis of their husbands' occupations. Almost all of them would be identified as working class on the basis of their own occupations or potential occupations. No clear class differences emerged in responses to the feminist movement or in female-female friendships or heterosexual bonds. Therefore, we do not include class in the analysis.

Our method of thinking sociologically and carrying out research owes much to the work of Dorothy Smith (1974, 1975, 1977). We agree with Smith that women's lives and experiences have been outside or peripheral to the framework of sociological thinking, to the "world sociology knows" (Smith, 1977, p. 18). We also agree that we want to contribute to a sociological analysis that "would be capable of providing for women analyses, descriptions, and understandings of their situation, of their everyday world and its determinations in the larger socio-economic organization" (Smith, 1977, p. 22). This requires, as Smith argues, starting with the everyday experience of those who live it, rather than starting with an organization of the topic, including frameworks and concepts, that predetermine what is problematic. A sociology *for* women must take as problematic the actual experiences of women. As Smith puts it, "if we are to offer those who live in our society (including ourselves) a means to understand how our social world comes about, then we must have a method of arriving at adequate description and analysis of *how it actually works*. Our methods cannot rest in problems of validating theories, which to a large extent have become procedures for deciding among different formalized "opinions" about the world. When we approach the problem of experience, we are, and must be, looking for answers in terms of actual socially organized practices. Situations, types, forms of social organization are then seen to recur because there is an underlying organization of social relations which generates them as "the same" (Smith, 1977, p. 26).

While we were convinced that we should start our study of change in the lives of middle aged women from the accounts of the women themselves, we also recognized that we were approaching the work with our own theoretical organizations of the social world. Nor did we wish to eliminate or blank out our own conceptual systems, since obviously one can see nothing without some notion that there is something there to see and we believed that our feminist theoretical views would help us to see things that other theories might obscure. In a process of ongoing discussion among those who were doing the interviewing, we tried to make as clear and conscious as possible our own conceptions of reality and to continually check those out against the accounts of the women participating in the study. In this way, we hoped not only to reveal to ourselves our own implicit assumptions about what life is like and how it works, but also to understand the views of others.

Data were gathered by the three authors of this paper through unstructured, in-depth interviews focussed on change in the lives of the interviewees. We started by asking them to tell us about current changes in their lives and what seemed most important to them. In the context of the discussion about the present, we asked about past history, beginning with adolescence unless the interviewee herself wanted to talk about earlier experiences. We obtained accounts of significant childhood experiences, as the women perceive them in the present, from most of those we interviewed. We also gathered information on education and work experience, on relationships with parents, husbands, children and friends, and on their aspirations and hopes for the future. The women whose lives are the basis for this paper were all interviewed at least twice over a period of three years, 1976 to 1979. We also participated with many of them in informal settings such as women's centers and in formal meetings of women's organizations.

Our data are intended to reveal processes of social relationships rather than statistical patterns or correlations between variables. Therefore, we selected interviewees who we believed could be expert informants on the processes of change in social relations that are part of conscious efforts to effect change. These would be women who were actually trying to change their lives. Since, so far as possible, we wanted to talk with women who started the change process from comparable positions and who might, therefore, be facing similar problems and experiencing similar processes, we tried to locate women whose children were in high school or beyond (although some still had one or two younger children) and who had been primarily mothers or wives, even though they might also have had paying jobs. Contacts were made through friends and acquaintances, counselors (both vocational and educational), therapists, Parents Without Partners, workshops at the local community college, Women's Studies classes, and by referral from women who had already been interviewed.

Our sample is a purposive one and, thus, we cannot make generalizing statements of the type, "fifty percent of white, middle aged American women have no close female friends," or of the type, "high intimacy with female friends is positively correlated with high participation in the Women's Movement." We suspect that the first statement is false and that the second statement is true, but we do not have evidence to support either contention.

THE RECONSTRUCTION OF RELATIONSHIPS WITH WOMEN

The women we talked to were actively attempting to remake the conditions of their lives. For most of them, this process took the form of going to school though some were working or looking for a job. Only one of them had a previous college degree and some had not finished high school. All of the women we interviewed live in the Northwest United States, some in rural areas, some in small towns, others in larger cities, though many of the interviews were done in a small city dominated by a large university. This is an agricultural state without the kinds of manufacturing and corporate offices that employ large numbers of women. It is an area which is predominantly white having little public visibility of class differences. In this community, returning to school is a publicized and available option. Educational opportunities abound, but the number of well educated women exceeds the number of traditional female jobs. Our focus here is not on going back to school or work as events which mirror general demographic trends for women, but on the ways in which the women we interviewed restructured their intimate relationships with other women as they made these changes. For though the particular opportunities available to these women may be specific to the context of this community, the social meaning of their experiences is not.

The Formation of New Female Friendships

Contact with an organized group, class, or program for women—that is, the movement into structures outside the family—was an important early event in the formation of new and different kinds of female friendships for almost all the women in the study. These programs and locations were themselves structured through feminism; though not necessarily labeled as feminist, they are tangible results of the Women's Movement, responses to a heightened awareness of women's problems. As such, these contexts are informed implicitly or explicitly by feminist ideas, and they provide contact with other women who have already developed feminist understandings. Their search for new interpretations of what it means to be a woman in this society or for a different mode of existence led to participation in new contexts and forming new friendships. At the same time, new contacts with other women helped to produce altered perspectives on their own lives and possibilities, including a new value and support from these contacts. Each constituted the other. In this way, involvement in feminist contexts did not mean that positive feelings about other women were simply embraced as a necessary part of feminist ideology. Rather, they emerged from the attempts to cope with daily life which were possible in this particular setting at this particular time.

These experiences could be startling and exhilarating. Their settings were readily available, as in Women's Centers in colleges and universities, Women's Studies classes, and community college workshops for mature women. The latter seem to have been particularly important for several women, because what began as a gathering of strangers responding to a newspaper advertisement evolved into a group of friends continuing to meet regularly after the workshop had ended. As one woman commented:

> I began to get restless about being just at home and taking care of the kids and yet I didn't know quite what direction I was going to go. I took a class called Life Planning for Adult Women through the community college. It was for women who are trying to make life changes and seeking new directions. There were divorced women and widows and married people like me and everybody seeking.

This woman decided to remain a full-time homemaker, but not long after the class ended, the instructor called to ask her if she wanted to join a consciousness raising group along with some others who had been in the class. She agreed and the women in the group became her best friends.

> These seven women are all doing exciting things in the community, but having some real pain involved in what they are doing. We have just been through an incredible two and a half years together and I am extremely close to them. We would just get together at one of the people's houses, one night a week from 7:30 until one or two in the morning and drink wine. Nobody put on airs or anything, and it was always open ended. We talked about whether we should have topics, should one person lead it? That never happened because somebody would come every week with something they would want to talk about, or more than one thing. And we would just go from there.

For another woman, the wife of a heavy equipment operator, the formation of new friendships and a transformation of her life began through the efforts of a community college counselor who was a feminist and through involvement in the college Women's Center. Feeling estranged from the wives of her husband's friends and her own life as a housewife, the trip to the local community college to find out about courses was a daring venture into an unknown world. What began as a tentative inquiry ended in her registering for classes and obtaining a job in the Women's Center. The interviewer asked:

> "How did you get to the Women's Center?"

> I don't know, I just decided I wanted to work at the Women's Center . . . I thought that at least I could do something there . . . from hearing and a little reading I was getting, picking up things about the Women's Center, wanting to know more about it. And a woman that I admired very much suggested that I would do very well if I would work there, that I would probably enjoy it so that boosted my ego and I thought that's where I'll go. I wrote this long letter telling them that they just had to have me work for them. It was great." The center introduced her to a new world of friends. "It's amazing. I've never had this many warm friends at one time. I feel a real sisterhood. I'm very aware of women and not as something to compete with, which is something really nice. It's like we need to be together if we're going to make it, if it's ever going to be any different. I just feel really good about it.

Another avenue to new female friends was the formation of self-help groups. One such group was started by four middle-aged women who found themselves in a number of college classes together and decided to form an organization of older women students. Meetings had organizational goals—developing information for returning women students, fund raising, organizing events and get-togethers so that women could share experiences and offer each other support. As the group expanded and the work went on, close ties of mutual aid developed.

The presence of an ideology of sisterhood is important in these contexts. The idea that it is essential for women to share with and support one another, the implications of the commonalities embodied in women's experience, structures the kinds of communication possible, the affection and intimacy which is offered. Comprehension of the mutual features of experience which attributes value and commitment to other women contains the potential for a new sense of self. Female friendships become relationships of empathy and support, easy intimacies where words and actions do not have to be explained or justified, they are immediately understood. As such, these new female friendships have a political dimension, they become sources of resistance to the conditions of daily life.

Female Friends, Old and New

As we suggested earlier in this paper, discussions of sisterhood carry assumptions of reassessing how one thinks, acts and feels in relation to other women. New female friends are not simply more recent acquaintanceships, they are different kinds of relationships. However, as we also suggested above, it can be argued that women have always maintained close personal relationships with other women, relations which have remained unrecognized, certainly in sociological discourse and often in private life. How did this work out for the women we talked to—did a context of feminism transform their relationships with other women or had female friends always been a part of their intimate lives? There is no possibility of generalization here, since their experiences differed.

Some of the women we talked to had always had close relationships with other women, often maintained over many years. These friendships were important and provided affection and support. In one woman's case, when she and her family moved to another city, her close friend persuaded her husband to accept a job in the same town. A feminist conception of female solidarity is not new to these women, but perhaps consolidates the value of such friendships and gives them a public legitimacy. Certainly for some, the isolation of the nuclear family had not always prevented female ties.

For others, new relationships with women were different from old friendships, involving a more candid sharing of life experiences and feelings than had previously been possible. In particular, men, husbands and lovers, became topics to be discussed in a different way. Feminism transformed a taken for granted connection between intimacy and relationships with men by both analyzing the politics of intimate relationships and giving a voice to women's unmet needs within them. The private world of the couple became the subject of public discourse. Consider the following response.

I think that most of the women that I know have always pretended to be perfectly content with their lot and they're happy. And their husbands are marvellous and their children never get into any trouble. And I say, 'Well, gee, my husband is drunk some of the time and my kids get into trouble. And I hate washing diapers and cleaning the same floor over and over and not going out for five years at a time.' Women of my generation weren't honest about what was going on . . . and that made me feel like something was wrong with me . . . It (feminism) frees me up so much; it just feels so good to me to see it on a piece of paper—to see a whole book written about things that I've been thinking for the last twenty years and thinking 'wow, there's something wrong with you if you're thinking this and no one else feels like this.' And here's book after book of people feeling just that way.

Others had had friends with whom husbands and children were not taboo subjects, but with whom the complaining was always kept on a superficial level.

"We never really faced talking about the real issues. We'd talk about the physical complaints (she and her friends were pregnant) and how the husbands could never understand what you're feeling. Mostly we giggled and gossiped and got drunk." Or, "we used to have Tupperware parties, you know. That's about it. I've always had one friend, but there were always so many areas that were just never talked about.

Nobody would dare run their husbands or boyfriends down. That was bad, bad image for you. But everybody did. That's all we talked about, how lousy our men were, but we never zeroed in on it. It's not like I have now, not the kind of really warm way down deep, 'I care that you are there, you hurt and I know and I want to help'. Not like that, not like I've gotten here."

Of course, this talk about 'how lousy men are' is the kind of communication that takes place between women when men are not around, and as such contains elements of subversion, as women's 'gossip' sessions have done for generations, but since it respects the insularity of the couple it is a subversion which ultimately protects the position of the male. Previous relationships with women had held to this tacit agreement, that the first allegiance was to the husband. Thus, one could complain about him, but never reveal the deep hurt and anger or the indifference that underlay these complaints. Forming new friendships in a feminist context dissolved this protective stance, and it became possible to speak of and validate previously hidden experiences. Finding new meaning and content in relationships with women—discovering sisterhood in this sense—has been part of the Women's Movement from the beginning. Yet, feminism is often thought of as the domain of specific, and by implication, atypical groups of women rather than as an ideology and social theory with the most general and radical implications. What is significant here is that these implications were still being recognized and acted upon in the late seventies in the lives of women who were not highly educated, were not professionals, had practically no contact with popular self-actualization therapies and no background of political activism or radical allegiances.

The adoption of a feminist perspective can make old friendships difficult. There is less and less to talk about, more hesitations and more silences. Yet, old allegiances are maintained by many women who become feminists. They are maintained because of loyalty or because they are part of networks of family friends. This results in a double life.

> I have two lives. I belong to a woman's support group, mostly women younger than I am. I feel a nurturance and a support there that I've never had in my life. Then, I have my peers, most of whom are totally involved in doing things for their husbands and children. In the families, the couples we get together with, if they all knew how I really felt, they would think I'm a radical Women's Libber. As it is, I just get teased about it. I don't say anything. They just don't know who I am.

Couple relationships, usually established through the husband's work, continued for most of the women who were still married. If change involved a separation or divorce, these friendships were no longer available; couple friends tended to rally around the man or to just fade away. This produced considerable bitterness, even though as time went on, such regret dissipated.

Transformation of relationships with other women includes those with mothers and daughters. For many women, coming to a feminist perspective means a reassessment of the mother. A mother who was demanding, restrictive, and critical comes to be seen as a woman who was struggling against great odds to give her children a better life. A mother who had been perceived as weak and passive is understood in new terms, as a survivor and finally as a woman with guts and perseverance. Although some of this reassessment can be attributed to maturity—a coming to terms with oneself as less than perfect—feminist insights did seem to have contributed to closer and more appreciative relationships with mothers.

Daughters present different problems. These feminist mothers felt very close to their daughters, and were anxious that their daughters not make the same mistakes that they themselves had made. For example,

> My advice to my daughter over two years ago, she was at college and struggling with man-woman relationships, was to let him see what you are and do not pretend to be something that he likes because it will cost you your relationship. Later, some day, he will despise you when he discovers that you were living a lie, did not tell him the truth. He sees you for what you are and everything will be lost.

Another woman outlined the lessons she was trying to teach her daughters, lessons that she paid a high price to learn. First, "It's your body, you decide what you want to happen to it. You don't trade sex for anything, ever." Second, "marriage is not forever and you need to have your own money. Always save a little whenever you have any extra money, but keep it a secret, in your hiding place." Thus, the main concern in regard to daughters is that they should be independent people and women who will not allow themselves to sacrifice honesty and integrity for the sake of an ephemeral intimacy with a man, an intimacy that is inevitably undermined by the efforts to maintain it. Most of the daughters were a source of pride and pleasure to these mothers although some had adopted very traditional relationships with men and notions about their own femininity. When this happened, it was a source of distress and discomfort. These were exceptions; many of the women in transition who had any feminist perceptions were in the middle of a three-generation female network that provided them support and comfort and embedded them in systems of obligation.

Feminism - Popular Distortions and Reality

The actuality of these women's lives contradicts the stereotypes of feminists as self-oriented people trying to break away from family ties into a new, but sterile, freedom. Within capitalist social relations such stereotypes are easily generated. Articulated demands for autonomy are seen as being satisfied through individual success and achievement and mythologized as such in magazines for the "new woman." The search for a satisfying and independent personal life is translated into a conception of self in which one's own needs are primary and detached from those of others, and it is popularized as a technique for managing everyday life—assertiveness training—which is aimed at women and labeled as feminist. Feminist critiques of the family are seen as proposals for lives free of warmth, nurturance and obligation. This is true for conservative political movements and radical theorists for whom the family is a (male) haven in a heartless world. For the women we talked to, coming to feminism meant none of this. Feminism did not undermine

the family in the minds and lives of the women in our study. It strength-
ened family ties with mothers and daughters, while new relationships
extended the bonds of family to a wider circle of women. For many, the
obligation and necessity of providing help and support to other women
was not confined to close relationships, but was a central part of their
lives in general.

The experience of the women who formed the group for older women
students is instructive here.

> I called a woman on our council one night because I forgot . . . her daughter has
> epilepsy and she said she felt so alone. So, I called her up and said, 'If you need
> to go to the hospital with her . . . I'm up most of the night every night anyhow—
> just call me'. As she said later that, that coming when it did—although it was a
> small thing for me—was probably one of the biggest things that ever happened to
> her because she suddenly didn't feel frightened anymore. Because, one night her
> car wouldn't start and she didn't have anyone to call. And I said, 'other people
> help me out when I need help and I have no qualms about calling them.' I think
> that kind of support and everything we'll find out as we are organizing this—that
> these are the important things.

The mutual aid these women offered to each other, especially for the
early organizers of the group, was often emotionally draining and time
consuming as well as gratifying.

> As soon as the group got going, I got calls. I would have to map out a big space
> because I knew that the woman on the other end of the line had a very real need
> to tell her story. I knew the call was going to take half an hour at least. I think it's
> a good thing, a positive thing for women to do, but part of the time you really don't
> have time to do it.

Or a desperate call for help would come at 2:00 a.m. from a woman who
was drunk, alone and tearful. Driving to the other end of town to listen
with sympathy sometimes meant missing a class the next day. The kinds
of help offered and received in this group was informed by a feminist
spirit. For these women, feminism did not mean a celebration of self at
the expense of others, but the recognition that control of one's own life
was to be found in overcoming the relations of domination which structure all women's lives. Their dedication was to helping their sisters cope
with their oppression, while at the same time using this means to confront
their own anger at male domination and advantage. For other women
this dedication shaped future job choices and possibilities, which could
be as general as "wanting to work with and for women" or as specific
as seeking out student placements in agencies where a future career and
feminist politics could be in some sense combined. Still others were
engaged in volunteer work in feminist organizations—women's centers,
rape crisis networks, a shelter home for battered women.

These women were attempting to incorporate the feminist insight that the "personal is political" into the practice of their daily lives. This radical kernel of feminist theory has always implied more than the private realization of the ways in which personal life is socially structured, it also means the movement from that realization to social action. This movement sharply differentiates feminism from other popular modes of self-discovery in which private discontent is turned back on itself into personal and individualized solutions. Of course, not all of the women we talked to were engaged in this kind of action. For some, their feminism was contained in the restructuring of their personal lives. In part this can be attributed to the difficulties of overcoming the ideology of a privatized culture, in which politics can become equated with life-styles. But for many, the problems in transforming insights into action were based in the real conditions of their lives. In a world in which it takes all your energy to survive, there is little time for anything else.

The women who were politically active were not exempt from these conditions. When the boundaries of limited, legitimate demands that characterized many of the old female relationships were broken, an emphasis on caring for an extended group produced its own dilemmas. For those who were not in crisis and thus found themselves often in the position of nurturer, support could seem to be only going in one direction:

> I haven't found a lot of support from the women I am working with. And I understand that. They're coming from a shitty place and so, the place you have to be in order to give some support that counts—you have to be up a little ways yourself. And it's really hard. It's like beating a dead dog with a stick to try and make it stand up. A lot of these women—just dealing with their everyday living is hard enough and expecting you to support each other . . . I'm not so sure that that's not unrealistic. It's another trip we're laying on ourselves, saying, let's do it all ourselves.

Yet, the most active women still believed that giving care and attention to others is one of the very positive things about women that often makes them different from men, and is a characteristic that should be protected and developed: "People shouldn't turn their backs on each other. This is the way it ought to be. I wouldn't like myself if I turned my back. But I do get tired." For them, feminism echoes the values they put on nurturance—values which are essential to their conception of a 'good person.'

CHANGING RELATIONS BETWEEN THE SEXES

The discussion at the beginning of this paper of the feminist critique of relations between the sexes and the review of the literature on marital intimacy suggested several questions. Is the idea of intimacy between the sexes in the companionate marriage more mirage than actuality? How does a woman's feminist understanding affect her intimate relations with men? What alternatives are available to mature women who, from desire or necessity, attempt to reorder their relationships with men? The accounts women gave us of their lives provide the basis for partial answers to these questions for these particular women. Their experiences give some insight into the processes of changing expectations of marriage and the structural limitations to the changes that can actually be achieved. Altering relationships with men was a matter of immediate concern to all the women we interviewed, regardless of their marital status at the time of the first interview. At that time, 12 of our respondents were married, 11 were divorced, and 5 were separated from their husbands. They had been married for between 15 and 35 years.

Intimacy—Myth or Reality?

Jessie Bernard's (1972) argument that there is "her" marriage and "his" marriage, discussed above, suggests that the structural conditions for intimacy, equality and shared experience, rarely exist in marriage. This can be interpreted as a basic contradiction within the marriage institution, in its modern or companionate version, between the ideology that sustains it and the social relations that constitute its real existence in daily life. The belief in equal partners sharing a common fate in life is belied, particularly in the case of the woman who is for long periods a full-time homemaker, by the reality of her economic and social dependence. The experiences of the women we interviewed reveal some of the many ways that this contradiction is reflected in the betrayal of intimacy between wife and husband.

The betrayal of intimacy can come slowly in the process of trying to accommodate to a condition of inequality, but one that is not seen as such. One woman, for example, spent the first 15 years of her marriage trying to be the perfect woman according to the standards of her husband and the next ten years of the marriage trying to figure out why she was so nervous and generally distressed. She gradually came to see that there was no openness, honesty, or reciprocity in their relationship. Transgressions of intimacy had started early in the marriage. She told about one incident.

> I hadn't planned a child for maybe another couple of years. I wasn't feeling well on the job and my husband suggested I go to a doctor for a pregnancy test. I said no, I couldn't possibly be pregnant . . . we aren't going to do that for a couple of years yet. I went to the doctor and sure enough the rabbit died and it came out that he had been keeping a little black book of my menstrual periods and that he wanted a child. He had it all timed. So, there in the doctor's office, in absolute turmoil, confusion and disappointment, I made him promise that we wouldn't tell anyone

until I had decided how I felt about it and knew what to say. This was in 1950 and women had the babies they were pregnant with. I went back to work and when I came home I found that he had told sixteen people on the way home.

This marriage illustrates other common ways that intimacy is violated or even prevented from developing. For example, closeness is prevented by the inability of the man to express his feelings and by his withdrawal from emotional contact (Balswick and Peek, 1971). "We had many stormy fights and he would pout. He would punish me during our quarrels by not talking to me for five days. He could stand that; I was destroyed." Another example is the discrepancy that often exists between the woman's view and the man's view of the relationship between intimacy and sex.

In looking back on it, my husband and I really placed opposing values on almost everything. An illustration is the man-woman relationship. I said that before I could go to bed with a man, he would have to be my friend. My husband laughed and said, 'You can't be friends with a woman.' This was in direct opposition to his life, because he had many women friends made through his work. But, underneath lay his real conviction that the woman you sleep with is not your friend. So I was not his friend.

In spite of the rebuffs, she tried to live according to the gospel of togetherness of the period and to help her husband become a success.

I became the world's greatest volunteer. At home I worked 24 hours, around the clock. I would do anything to help that man. But I was never really able to let him see who I was, had he been interested. He used to say that I was a diamond in the rough and that if he worked at it long enough he'd have his perfect product. In the last few years I was finally able to let him see who I was and he grieved. He is still grieving because I am not what he wanted.

But, she was not angry, rather she blamed herself for the betrayal of intimacy through the slow accretion of lies, until the person she presented to her husband and the person she felt to be herself had different identities.

This story, with different details, was repeated in the experiences of a number of other women in our study. The desperate attempts to live up to the expectations of a dominant husband which generated feelings of inadequacy and failure were common. It was also common that these were feelings that could not be talked about, again undercutting intimacy. Even some of the women who had been most successfully married by their own criteria had experienced an estrangement from an idealized image of self as exemplary wife and mother. This, too, was an estrangement that could not be expressed, except at the risk of disturbing the shared interpretations of the couple. One woman said, "I felt like a queen on a pedastel. Nobody would let me come down and that's the way it was. I was too good to go to a tavern. I felt like I had to play this role and that's the way he (her husband) wanted me to be."

The creation of a shared world of meaning and interpretation in the process of interaction between wife and husband, so well described by Berger and Kellner (1970) as functional for the wider society, may create barriers to intimacy that ultimately undermine the relationship itself. Definitions of reality mutually constructed by the pair at one' time may be later eroded by experience, particularly if the definitions favor the dominance of one partner, usually the man. Yet, there may be great reluctance to talk about feelings of rejection of this socially constructed microcosm, because such discussions may threaten the very existence of this private world. This could happen in couples with supposedly egalitarian marriages or in couples who had a traditional male-dominant pattern, as in the following example. A woman in her early fifties, still married and close to her successful husband, described their agreement about what a marriage and family should be, an agreement they had faithfully carried out. They were religious and followed their church's teaching that the man should be the head of the family, but that everything should be discussed within the couple,

> the couple should work as a unit and the wife should do her work and the husband should do his work. There were things that I decided on and things that he decided on, depending on what they were. The father was actually the final authority after the mother's viewpoint was, of course, taken into consideration.

Her agreement that this was a desirable pattern for her life was slowly eroded as, influenced by the writings of the Women's Movement, she began to see that her self confidence and independence had also been eroded. She was able to talk with her husband about sexual inequality and women's rights, but not about her own feelings. As she put it, "My husband is trying to understand, and well, frankly, I would be afraid to have a confrontation, because that usually means just about one thing and that is a divorce, which I am not ready for and don't at this point, want."

The undermining of intimacy in cases of this kind may have been exacerbated by growing inequalities within the couple. Not only were these women economically dependent upon their husbands, in every case the men had rapidly increased the discrepancies between themselves and their wives in education, status and power. As the men earned graduate degrees and advanced in their professions or moved into more highly paid work, the women stayed at home caring for children or worked at routine jobs to help the men on their way. As the age of the marriage increased, the gap in life circumstances between the spouses increased, heightening the impossibility of maintaining reciprocal sharing of feelings and experience.

The transgression of intimacy seemed to come suddenly and violently for some women in our study in the form of the unexpected decision by the husband to leave. Yet, as the women began to unravel and reinterpret the past, they began to see that what they had assumed to be a shared reality had not actually existed. Some of them found that there had been a difference in the meaning and content of the intimate relationship itself. Female expectations of reciprocal openness and empathy may not be shared by men who look to their wives for support and comfort but do not see themselves providing such care. One woman, evaluating the reasons for the break up of her marriage, located a change point in the relationship with her husband when she withdrew this onesided support: "I think I started rejecting him sexually. I quit nurturing. I stopped wanting to rub his feet and stopped wanting to fix him his coffee." She feels that she stopped being a model wife and that for this reason her husband withdrew. Yet, her rejection meant that she stopped being the person who provided the warmth and comfort in daily life; she violated an intimacy that was on his terms.

Is intimacy between the sexes in the companionate marriage a mirage or a reality? The accounts of the women we interviewed add to the evidence that such intimacy is rare and difficult to achieve. The women we are discussing in this paper were all in the process of trying to effect changes in their lives, which in practical terms included changes in relationships with men, so we should probably expect that heterosexual intimacy would be problematic to them. A few of these women had empathetic and supportive husbands who were trying to go through a process of change with their wives. These couples were trying to reconstruct their shared world into a more egalitarian one. This change process produced new problems and ambiguities for them, much as it did for others in the study. These new dilemmas will be discussed below.

The Effects of Feminism on Women's Relations with Men

The development of feminist understandings by the women in our study gave them new ways to interpret the failure of intimacy and new and more positive ways to resist the deterioration of sense of self that had been a product of marriage for many of them. As we noted above, negative feelings about marriage and men, feelings long held in secret, became validated in a public forum, altering the way these women viewed themselves in the marital pair.

Feminism also contributed to the growing realization of many of these women that they must establish greater independence from men. Previously content with a traditional division of labor in the family, women now felt a necessity to become economically independent. "Now I think that the true way to independence is to have your own job and support yourself. Otherwise, you are not a member, you have no voice in this society. You don't pay taxes, you don't have your own tax return, nothing." They also realized that their lives had become restricted by a social dependence, often manifested by a fear of going into strange places or of traveling alone. Going on a trip by themselves, staying overnight in a motel, or even going alone into a local restaurant were positive and difficult acts of resistance undertaken by many of these women in their attempts to establish a separate and self-sufficient self.

Feminism supported other acts of resistance, such as refusals to perform as expected according to the norms of their marriages. Thus, women who had previously engaged in a world of couple friendships, refused to have anything to do with that world. One woman, for twenty years an exemplary company wife, refused to perform anymore. As she described it,

> My husband's very uneasy with me because he doesn't know what I'm going to say to people, because I don't play that role anymore of being afraid to say something to someone, or don't antagonize someone because we need the business. I really don't care what happens to that. So, if they say something to me that I don't like, or do something that I think is really disgusting, I just tell them what I feel. I'm tired of having to just stand there.

Other women rejected the non-verbal sexual signals which are endemic to casual encounters between women and men. One woman's rejection was through gaining weight:

> I think I thought if I put on twenty or thirty pounds that I wouldn't have to deal with all that, you know, the games, the come-ons, the looks, all the things that men do with women. I don't want to flirt with men anymore. I thought that was a way to stop them flirting with me.

A changing consciousness resulted in the heightened visibility of other implicit rules of female-male interaction. For example, techniques of dominance and control in ordinary conversation became obvious.

> If you start talking about some sort of a controversial subject with a man, you sense after you're standing up for your side of the controversy that you'd better not stand up for your side anymore. It's much better if you let the conversation kind of fade away and leave them with a feeling that they've won.

This is one way of dealing with sexist behavior. Those who felt the necessity of confronting sexism more directly faced some conflict between that imperative and a reluctance to deal with men who fail to understand women's position.

> We're really hurt when a sister doesn't help us. But, Jesus, they're in the same boat, most of them. Yet we aren't expecting anything from men, any help. No expectations are laid on them. I just want to say (to men) 'Be quiet.' And women will say, 'Well, we have to raise their consciousness.' I don't want to. Shit. Let them go and raise their own goddam consciousness.

These efforts to reassess and reconstruct relationships with men raised problems, dilemmas, and often painful contradictions. Almost all of the women in this study were heterosexual and most wanted a close sexual relationship with a man. But these women were developing new criteria for intimacy. They no longer would accept relationships in which a new found and hard won sense of personal autonomy is eroded into forms of subservience, deference and dependence. They did not want to be the nurturers to men who see intimacy as receiving nurturance rather than giving it. They wanted both intimacy and autonomy, needs which as Easton (1978) points out, turn out to be contradictory, given the way that many men define their desires. As one woman put it:

> No man will ever be everything to me again. I will not live to take care of a home and to take care of a husband and to take care of kids. I won't do that anymore and that's not very attractive to a man that wants to be taken care of. . . . I've met a man. . . . he said, 'I would not want you to become an attorney. I would would want you to iron my shirts and I would want to see you every day. I would not want to stay home while you were out tooting your horn'. So I would not be what he would want me to be. It seems that the men I meet put me in touch with the way I'm changing because men want certain things from women. They want sex and they want softness, and they want to be smarter, they want to have all the answers.

New feminist awareness revealed to some women that they were still attracted to men who were likely to recreate relations of dependence and they were struggling to redefine what is sexually attractive about a man.

> I married a man who always projected having it all together. I find I'm still attracted to men who project that image. The man I have been most sexually attracted to since my divorce is a macho male. This other man who is my good platonic friend whose wife just left him, is crying with me, tells me he wants to scream. He's wishy-washy, he's a bucket of mush and I understand all those emotions because I felt them myself and it's a total turn-off when they're coming from a male. I hate them. He's not attractive to me at all because of expressing those emotions. It's so dumb, because he's so human and he's letting me see his humanness much more than Mr. Macho. I'd be a lot better off if I could relate to the bucket of mush because he's more human, but it's a turnoff . . .

She was struggling not only with gaps between understandings and feelings, but with the content of those feelings. The man who was attractive was the man who exploits and dominates. She could not give herself up to intimacy with a man who wanted her to conform to his ideas of what a woman should be, and yet he was who she wanted.

The adoption of a feminist ideology did not make man-haters of the women in this study, but it did validate and provide explanations for their ambivalent feelings about the men in their lives. Their new understandings of the failures of intimacy in their marriages and of the tension between their drive toward autonomy and their need for sexual and emotional closeness with a man produced new problems. For some, it posed the question of whether female-male intimacy is even possible or desirable with present social arrangements.

Toward Resolutions of the Heterosexual Dilemma

The possibilities for resolving the heterosexual dilemma by finding a new man who can enter into a relationship of mutual trust, caring, and openness are limited by demographic facts and cultural conventions, as well as male difficulties in meeting the expectations of changing women. The male death rate exceeds the female death rate, as women age the supply of available men dwindles. And, surviving males who might be looking for a new mate often choose a considerably younger woman, while the older woman in a similar situation is rarely chosen by a younger man. While two women in our study entered new and happy relationships with men and another became a lesbian, over the three years that we were in touch with the others, they had only two realistic possibilities: to continue the relationships with their husbands or to build a single life.

In spite of estrangements and discontents within their marriages, and the effects of the new ideas of feminism, all of the married women we are discussing stayed married and three of the five separated women had returned to their husbands by the time this study ended. A number of the married women had tried living alone and had come to the conclusion that on many counts a somewhat unsatisfactory husband was better than no husband at all. The structures of age and sex discrimination often underlying this preference were clear in one woman's discussion about why she was going back to a husband who had been psychologically abusive to her for 30 years. She was 54 at the time of the interview and had recently graduated from college with honors. "It's not realistic to think I'll be able to make it. They'll hire someone around 30 if they want to hire an older woman. Who'd want to hire me?" This assessment was based on experience. The problems were not only economic; she also wanted an intimate relationship with a man, and, as she said, "there just

aren't any marvelous men out there.'' She felt that her age was a factor
here, too. "Older women are a surplus on the market and you know
what happens to value when there's a surplus. Supply and demand.''
There were also positives in her relationship with her husband. They
shared many values and he was still concerned and involved in the lives
of their five children. Moreover, they had had a good sexual relationship.
Her experience with feminist ideas had put her own problems into a
different framework for her. She could now, in contrast to the past, see
her troubles as largely originating in the wider society. No longer blaming
herself for everything that went wrong, she felt that she could handle
the situation with her husband better, and that, everything considered,
going back to him was worth a try.

Seeking solutions to the contradictions between intimacy and autonomy, these women tried a variety of ways to reconstruct their marital
relations. One resolution to this dilemma is to reduce the centrality of
a relationship with a man, making it specific and circumscribed, while
looking to women for the more diffuse and intimate relations of caring,
empathy and support. The separation of sexuality from emotional closeness is an attempt to shift the centrality of heterosexual ties. As one
woman put it:

I'm not so sure what the circumstances would be that I would want to get involved
with another man. I don't know. I really like the excitement of it. It might only be
for that. And I like it as far as exploring my sexuality. I had a relationship with a
younger man. And I was not not sensitive to him. I liked him very much. But I
really wanted to find out if I was capable of multiple orgasms. I have never felt
guilty about my sexual feelings and I've particularly not felt that most men satisfied
my sexual feelings . . . and so in this way, in this relationship, this man was a very
able lover and was delightful. So that part was good. But, you know, after a while,
I really got bored with him.

Such attempts to isolate sexual bonds from other ties with men do not
mean that relationships with men become instrumental and embody, in
Lasch's (1979) terms, a "flight from feeling." Rather, these attempts
embody a practical recognition of what can and what cannot be expected
of men, a knowledge of the potential for male control and female vulnerability. She "was not not sensitive to him." But this also means she
could not successfully resolve the paradox of autonomy and intimacy
by making this separation between sexuality and emotional closeness.

Another sort of attempt to shift the centrality of male relationships
involved a renegotiation of the relationship with the husband to establish
a sphere of independence. That sphere might be as small as 'a room of
one's own,' a bedroom vacated by a grown child, made over into a
study. Or, the sphere of independence could expand into most of daily

life, leaving the relationship with the husband in the background, still providing a degree of security, legitimacy, economic support and some companionship. Such women, there were several in the study, live with their husbands, yet lead completely separate existences, no longer functioning as part of a couple.

> I have a lot of friends and they're all women, absolutely no men friends and no couple friends. We don't go any place as a couple. We don't do anything. We haven't had a couple friendship since I worked. I'm not a wife in the traditional sense. I go places with my friends, go to the coast, mutual friends and I go there together for weekends, and I just tell him, well I am going for this weekend and I am doing this and I am going there, goodbye.

For other women, the solution was an effort to compartmentalize their lives, to maintain two distinct existences, one life with their husbands and one life of their own. This effort to carve out a sphere of independence without reducing commitments to the family could not always be managed or maintained. Obligations that came from being a wife and mother tended to disrupt the new sphere of independence. In the words of one woman,

> So here I am, I'm struggling along. It's taken me nine years to go to school already. I really wanted to graduate last term and I couldn't. I couldn't graduate last term because I had to go on a trip with my husband. It was a business oriented trip. . . . it's just another time that I have to postpone my goals. It's another time. I had to postpone graduation and I had to drop out for a term.

This arrangement, which on the surface might seem the best of both worlds, had its own contradictions and pitfalls; these did not only arise from the demands of being a "company wife."

> We have a workable arrangement, and we have periods of calm where I like him and he likes me. Everything is OK as long as he lets me do my thing and doesn't try and sabotage me. And even then, all I'd have to do is smile and fake it. He can believe he's happy so long as I put my tensions elsewhere. But I've stopped manipulating that way. I'd really like a contract, he leaves me alone and I'll leave him alone.

There is little intimacy here and tremendous energy goes into keeping two worlds going, but there is a degree of comradeship when things are calm, and it is workable, as she says.

A few women in this study were trying to reconstruct intimacy with their husbands while at the same time they were trying to more clearly demarcate their own identity in the couple. In these cases, they were building on relationships that had always been empathetic. One husband was willing to admit that it was now his wife's turn to do the things important to her and he was even willing to move and look for a new job if that were needed. In other couples, the division of household labor was in the process of change. The husbands in these couples were also going through periods of questioning their lives and looking for change. The wives were understanding and sympathetic about the frustrations and limitations in their husbands' lives. "I can see that my husband is just as trapped as I was. And I do care about that." But, the process of working toward an intimacy satisfying to both of them at the same time that the wife was trying to establish a new autonomous identity, was difficult. This woman continued,

> I can't fight his battles as well as fight my own . . . I don't have enough energy. Sometimes it totally drains me. He sees so much of what I do as a personal rejection and I've said to him what I need from you now is not to take the things I am doing as a personal rejection. I know there are times when I hold you at arms length. It's so that I can keep my own head above water—it's not a personal rejection. But I haven't gotten through to him . . . and he doesn't have any outside supports, none at all. He has said to me, 'I don't have anyone but you,' and it's just like, 'Oh, don't say that.' He's trying and it's because he's trying that we're still together. I think he's much more scared than I am.

A year later, she was still contending with her contradictory desires for independence and emotional closeness while her husband was working out his reactions to the alterations in their lives by seeing a counselor. Three years later they were still together, feeling much closer to each other and to the building of a life that satisfied them both. This is a success story and there are economic as well as individual explanations. The woman in this case was able to find a well paying job after a brief period of retraining. Her choice of field was propitious, a male dominated occupation with relatively high incomes and high demand for workers. During the period that she was getting established, her husband was briefly unemployed and then made a career change. In a sense, they were starting over together, providing an egalitarian base on which to renegotiate their personal lives.

Many of the women we talked to were no longer with their husbands, but were attempting to construct new lives alone. The single life was not the resolution of choice for any of them. There seemed to be several reasons for this. The ideology of the heterosexual tie is strong; this is the relationship that defines a woman's life. As one woman said, "Your life-time relationship is with a man. If you don't have one, something is missing." Women alone are excluded from the round of couple socializing. Such women have women friends with whom they go to restaurants, movies, the theatre, yet they speak of having "no social life." In the absence of a normative structure that values relationships between women, it is sometimes difficult to recognize their importance. In addition, living alone, for most of the women in this study, meant giving up sexual relationships entirely. This was painful; the sexual and emotional loneliness they experienced was sometimes extreme. Although the lack of sexual companionship was partly a consequence of the unavailability of men, as noted above, this statement must be qualified. These women felt that they had to forego sexual activity because of the lack of suitable men. Even the oldest women we talked with had had their encounters with men who saw themselves as potential lovers. It was the woman who had made the negative choice; the man was not one with whom she could have an egalitarian relationship, or perhaps he was simply boring. Life experience and a feminist awareness of the difficulties of the heterosexual tie had made these women wary and considerably changed their perceptions of men. One woman put it this way. "They're all pretty pitiful, you know." Yet, she still would have liked a sustaining sexual relationship.

The women who were living alone were building satisfying lives, even though they were coming to the conclusion that sexual relationships were not going to be possible for them in the future. They might desire relationships with men, but this desire was not rooted in desperation, rather in a practical acceptance of a sorry state of affairs, the poor selection of potential husbands and lovers. They were finding satisfactions in their daily activities and a pride in themselves through their work or their success in school. They liked the women they had become better than the women they used to be, and were not prepared to compromise what they saw as "a second chance to belong to myself," for an intimacy that would be much less than the intimacy they desired.

CONCLUSION

We began this paper with several questions about the sphere of personal relations, both as important for locating the meaning of women's experiences and for understanding the structure of social relations at a time when the demographic facts of women's lives are changing. We wanted to look at those changes as women live them in daily life, how such changes affect close friendships between women and heterosexual intimacy, and the problems and possibilities the changes raise.

For these women, relationships with other women were central in structuring their lives. They were sources of support, affection and resistance, as well as sources of the commitment and obligation which for several women cohered in various forms of feminist action. Yet, there were structural limitations to these friendships. Feminist insights alone could not remove the social conditions in which they were grounded and there were real barriers to making feminist ideology reality. Sisterhood for many of these women meant an extensive network of demands and obligations, demands which are difficult to meet when you are also struggling to win a degree of autonomy in your own life. Personal survival may take all the time and energy available, and there are few structural supports for relationships between women, as there are for heterosexual relationships, which could make this survival easier.

Sisterhood with women, at least in part, comes with and from a critique of relationships with men. Heterosexual intimacy comes to be seen as structured through relations of domination. Coming to this realization does not mean one can step outside those relations; these women were still tied to men in different and overlapping ways—economically, socially, emotionally and sexually. Thus, feminism did not remove the contradictions endemic in relations between the sexes, it raised them in new forms. Coping with these new dilemmas of autonomy and intimacy proved hard. Often the choices were structured between remaining within, or returning to a less than satisfactory relationship which, despite compromises, could provide sources or areas of independence; or life as a single woman, a life without what most women still define as the central relationship.

Despite these painful gaps between ideology and reality, what feminist consciousness and relationships with other women did produce was a sense of self worth and integrity. These women no longer blamed themselves for the conditions of their lives. They could face the issues involved without personal devastation:

> I think that having a feminist consciousness and learning about what you do—I really validated a lot of the things that I believed to be true about me that I would not have done otherwise. I feel better about me. And those same things can happen to you without a feminist consciousness and you will feel that it is because you are a more shitty person. . . . I think I can sort it out more objectively.

NOTE

1. The literature on marital happiness over the life cycle may be relevant here, but the controversies over methodology and meaning make it very difficult to unravel the implications for intimacy and since that probably would take another paper, we do not deal with it here. See, e.g., Long Laws 1971.

REFERENCES

Allan, George
　　1977   "Class variations in friendship patterns." British Journal of Sociology 28 Spring:
　　　　389–93.
Babchuk, Nicholas, and Alan P. Bates
　　1963   "The primary relations of middle-class couples: A Study in male dominance."
　　　　American Sociological Review 28, 3, 377–84.
Balswick, Jack, and Charles Peek
　　1971   "The inexpressive male: a tragedy of American society." Family Coordinator 20,
　　　　363–68.

Berger, Peter L., and Hansfried Kellner
1970   "Marriage and the construction of reality." In Hans Peter Dreitzel (ed.), Recent Sociology 2. London: Macmillan.
Bernard, Jessie
1972   The Future of Marriage. New York: World Publishing Co.
Birnbaum, Judith Abelew
1975   "Life patterns and self-esteem in gifted family oriented and career committed women." In Martha Mednick, Sandra Tangri and Lois Hoffman (eds.), Women and Achievement, New York: Wiley.
Booth, Alan, and Elaine Hess
1974   "Cross-sex Friendships," Marriage and Family 36:38–47. Fall.
Bott, Elizabeth
1957   Family and Social Network, London: Tavistock.
Caplan, Patricia, and Janet M. Burjra
1978   Women United, Women Divided. London: Tavistock.
Chodorow, Nancy
1978   The Reproduction of Mothering. Berkeley: University of California Press.
Cuber, John F., and Peggy B. Harroff
1966   Sex and the Significant Americans, Baltimore, Md: Penguin.
Easton, Barbara
1977   "The decline of patriarchy and the rise of feminism: a critique of feminist theory." Catalyst 10–11, Summer: 104–124.
Evans, Sara
1980   Personal Politics. New York: Vintage.
Frankenberg, Ronald
1976   "In the production of their lives, men(?) . . . sex and gender in British Community Studies." In Diana Leonard Barker and Sheila Allan (eds.), Sexual Divisions and Society: Process and Change. London: Tavistock.
Glazer, Nona
1975   "Man and woman: interpersonal relationships in the marital pair." In Nona Glazer Malbin (ed.), Old Family/New Family. New York: Van Nostrand.
Goffman, Irving
1977   "The Arrangement Between the Sexes." Theory and Society, Fall: 301–331.
Hochschild, Arlie Russell
1975   "The sociology of feeling and emotion: selected possibilities." In Marcia Millman and Rosabeth Moss Kanter (eds.), Another Voice. Garden City, New York: Anchor.
Horkheimer, Max, and Theodor W. Adorno
1972   Aspects of Sociology. Boston, Mass.: Beacon.
Kanter, Rosabeth Moss
1977   Work and Family in the United States: A Critical Review and Agenda for Research and Policy. New York: Russell Sage.
Lasch, Christopher
1979   Culture of Narcissism. New York: W.W. Norton.
Laws, Judith Long
1971   "A feminist review of the marital adjustment literature: the rape of the locke." Journal of Marriage and Family 33 (3) August: 483–516.
Laws, Judith Long
1979   The Second X., New York: Elsevier.
Lopata, Helena Z.
1971   Occupation: Housewife. New York: Oxford.

Lopata, Helena Z.
1975 "Couple-companionate relationships in marriage and widowhood." In Nona
       Glazer (ed.), Old Family/New Family. New York: Van Nostrand.
Macke, Statham Anne, George W. Bohrnstedt, and Ilene N. Bernstein
1979 "Housewives' self-esteem and their husbands' success: the myth of vicarious
       involvement," Journal of Marriage and Family 41, 1: 51–58.
Mitchell, Juliet
1971 Woman's Estate. Harmondsworth, Middlesex, England: Penguin.
Mitchell, Juliet
1975 Psychoanalysis and Feminism. New York: Vintage.
Parsons, Talcott
1954 "A revised analytical approach to the theory of social stratification." In Talcott
       Parsons, Essay in Sociological Theory. Glencoe, Ill.: Free Press.
Rainwater, Lee, Richard P. Coleman, and Gerald Handel
1959 Workingman's Wife. New York: Oceana Publications.
Reich, Wilhelm
1972 Sex-Pol. New York: Vintage.
Richardson, John G.
1979 "Wife occupational superiority and marital troubles: an examination of the hy-
       pothesis." Journal of Marriage and Family 41, 1: 63–74.
Rowbotham, Sheila
1973 Woman's Consciousness, Man's World. Harmondsworth, England: Penguin.
Rubin, Lillian B.
1976 World of Pain, New York: Basic Books.
Salamon, Sonya
1977 "Family bounds and friendship bonds: Japan and West Germany." Journal of
       Marriage and Family 39: 807–20
Seeley, John R., R. Alexander Sim, and Elizabeth W. Loosley
1956 Crestwood Heights, New York: Basic Books.
Seiden, Anne M., and Pauline B. Bart
1975 "Woman to woman: is sisterhood powerful?" In Nona Glazer (ed.) Old Family/
       New Family. New York: Van Nostrand.
Slater, Philip E.
1970 The Pursuit of Loneliness. Boston, Mass.: Beacon Press.
Smith, Dorothy E.
1974 "Women's Perspective as a Radical Critique of Sociology." Sociological Inquiry
       4, 1: 7–13.
Smith, Dorothy E.
1975 "An analysis of ideological structures and how women are excluded." Canadian
       Review of Sociology and Anthropology 12, 4: 353–369.
Smith, Dorothy E.
1977 "Some implications of a sociology for women." In Nona Glazer and Helen Waeh-
       rer (eds.), Woman in a Man-Made World. Chicago: Rand McNally.
Smith-Rosenberg, Carol
1979 "The female world of love and ritual." In Nancy R. Cott and Elizabeth H. Pleck
       (eds.), A Heritage of Her Own. New York: Simon and Schuster.
Stromberg, Ann H., and Shirley Harkess
1978 Women Working. Palo Alto: Mayfield.
Young, Michael, and Peter Willmott
1957 Family and Kinship in East London, New York: The Free Press.
Zaretsky, Eli
1976 Capitalism, the Family and Personal Life. New York: Harper Colophon.

EFFECTS OF FRIENDSHIP SUPPORT ON THE PSYCHOLOGICAL WELL-BEING OF WIDOWS

Elizabeth A. Bankoff

The question of why some people have exceptional difficulty adjusting to major life crises is a crucial problem in mental health research. While a life crisis, such as death of one's spouse, is traumatic for most everyone experiencing it, it remains unclear why some widowed people experience a more difficult adjustment process than do others. As the classical studies of Durkheim (1951) made clear, even such a relatively unambiguous trauma as conjugal bereavement can produce varied reactions depending upon such factors as family constellations, lifestage, sex and culture.

This chapter addresses the issue of differential adjustment to the death of a husband. The study to be reported began with the assumptions that such a loss is a stressful experience associated with low morale; that adjustment to widowhood is a lengthy process; and that personal relationships with significant others are important in determining the widow's psychological well-being throughout her adjustment process. The study was concerned with the ways in which various friendship relationships can enhance or lessen widows' psychological well-being both shortly after the death of their husbands and over time. Three basic issues were addressed by the research:

First, how do the various *types* of support provided by the widow's friendship network (e.g., companionship, guidance, emotional support) affect her psychological well-being? Does the relative importance of particular types of support vary in an orderly fashion during the adjustment process? That is, are some types of support more helpful than others depending upon the phase of widowhood?

Second, how are the widow's *sources* of support within her friendship network (i.e., married friends, widowed or single friends, or neighborhood friends) related to her psychological well-being? Does the relative importance of these various support sources change during the adjustment process?

Finally, how do *specific types* of support provided by *specific* friendship *sources* affect the widow's well-being both shortly after the death of her husband and over time?

WIDOWHOOD AND ADAPTATION

The death of her husband is likely to severely disorganize a woman's life. Her living environment is radically altered, her social life is fundamentally disrupted, her emotional security is removed and, frequently, her financial security is undercut. This loss introduces into her life new difficulties which she must deal with on her own, apart from the help she may receive, for a time, from friends and kin (Glick, *et al.,* 1974; Lopata, 1973, 1979; Parkes, 1972).

The widowed have long been considered a high-risk population in terms of psychopathology. As early as 1897, Emile Durkheim called attention to the relatively high suicide rates of the widowed and noted:

> The suicides occurring at the crisis of widowhood . . . are really due to domestic anomie resulting from the death of a husband or wife. A family catastrophe occurs which affects the survivor. He is not adapted to the new situation in which he finds himself and accordingly offers less resistance to suicide.
>
> (Durkheim, 1951:259)

In fact, the millions[1] of women in our society who are widowed are more likely than their married or ever-single peers to be poverty stricken, socially isolated, psychologically or emotionally troubled, and left without a meaningful life pattern or social function (Bradburn, 1969; Gorer, 1969; Gurin, *et al.*, 1960; Harvey and Bahr, 1974; Hiltz, 1977; Lopata, 1973, 1979; Maddison and Walker, 1967; Parkes, 1964a, 1964b, 1972). Moreover, persons suffering a conjugal bereavement also suffer an elevated risk of physical deterioration and death (Jacobs and Ostfeld, 1977; Kraus and Lutkins, 1967; Rees and Lutkins, 1967; Young, *et al.*, 1963).

However, despite the fact that widowhood is accompanied by an elevated risk of psychopathology, most widows do not suffer psychopathological outcomes. As Lopata notes: "In spite of some tendencies in that direction most women do not become fatally ill, commit suicide, or become institutionalized in mental hospitals after the death of the husband . . . life continues in passive acceptance or in assertion of a new life style" (1973:75). In fact, about half of Lopata's sample indicated that they enjoyed some compensations attributed to the death of the husband, including less work, living alone, independence and peace of mind.

Nevertheless, within the conjugal bereavement literature much emphasis has been placed on the psychological pathologies resulting from the event itself. Perhaps the primary reason why the consequent pathologies have been so heavily stressed is that little attention has been given to the adaptation of the widowed over time. Instead, the focus has been on early reactions to the loss. With few exceptions, clinical observations as well as empirical investigations have focused on what may be called the *crisis loss phase* of bereavement. It is by now well documented that during this phase, which begins at the onset of bereavement, the widowed person typically experiences shock, often accompanied by denial of the loss, followed by a period of intense grief, which is succeeded by depression and apathy as the bereaved person becomes resigned to the loss (Hiltz, 1977; Lindemann, 1944; Parkes, 1972; Vachon, 1976). It is this phase to which Raphael (1971) refers when she speaks of bereavement as a specific event which tests the intrapsychic adaptive mechanisms beyond their normal homeostatic range; one which can be seen as a crisis of high probability of occurrence and low frequency of predictability; one with high likelihood that the individual will be adversely affected.

Although Lindemann (1944), in his pioneering work with the bereaved, believed that individuals may rapidly recover from grief, his emphasis, too, was on describing the normal and pathological reactions during the crisis loss phase. However, it is becoming increasingly clear that while this early phase is time-limited, it is followed by what may be conceptualized as a *transition phase* when the widowed person's intense grief has lessened and new plans and assumptions about the world and the self are built up. During this phase the widowed person faces the task of attempting to build a normal, but new, life with a new set of role relationships and a new identity (Hiltz, 1977; Parkes, 1971, 1972; Vachon, 1976). Glick, *et al.*'s (1974) longitudinal study of widows indicates that this transition phase may last at least four years after the death of the spouse. As Parkes reports, "We do not know how long these reactions to bereavement continue. Other studies suggest that they may last for many years, but as our own study did not continue beyond the fourth year, we can set no limit to the duration" (1975:135).

Most stress models emphasize short-term pathological effects of stressful life events (Dohrenwend and Dohrenwend, 1974), and therefore are not appropriate for studying a long-term process of psychosocial adaptation to a stressful life event such as widowhood. Our conceptual model of the process of conjugal bereavement assumes that adjustment to widowhood is a lengthy process which is characterized by two general phases of bereavement—the crisis loss phase and the transition phase (Figure 1). In addition, as psychopathology is not a universal, or even a typical outcome of widowhood, our model does not assume a pathological outcome. Rather, the model suggests that adaptation to this critical event can range from psychological growth and well-being to psychopathology, depending on mediating situational and psychological factors.

Figure 1. Model of the Process of Conjugal Bereavement

Situational and Psychological Mediators

DEATH OF SPOUSE → CRISIS LOSS PHASE → TRANSITION PHASE

(−) Well-being (+)   (−) Well-being (+)

Time ────────────────────────────────────→

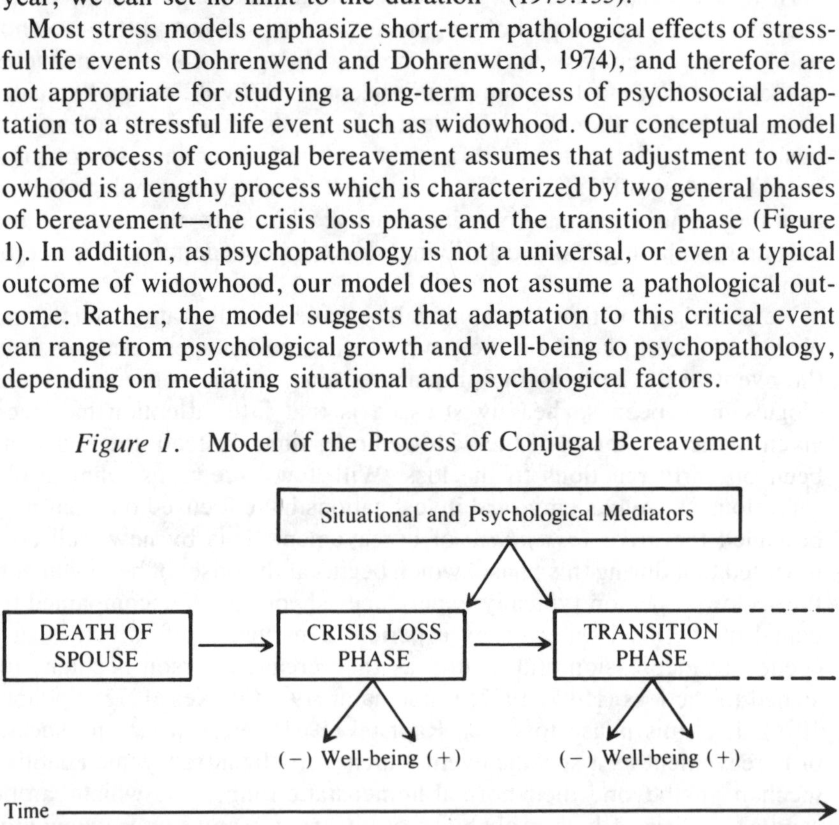

While most of the "outcome" research on the bereaved has focused on the crisis loss phase, with attempts to understand the effects of psychological mediators on early outcome, this study focuses on situational factors that may influence the overall psychological well-being of the widow in both adjustment phases.

THE ROLE OF THE SOCIAL NETWORK IN ADAPTATION TO WIDOWHOOD

Explanations for differential reactions to such an experience as conjugal bereavement might focus on such factors as ego strength of the individual, the subjective meaning of the event to the individual, as well as on the more specific objective nature of the crisis event. In addition, explanation may be sought in the individual's social surroundings. Certainly there are many different aspects of the environment which may contribute to an individual's psychological well-being. However, there is a growing consensus that a person's social network plays a crucial role by serving as a buffer between life events and adaptation (Cobb, 1976; Gourash, 1978; Henderson, 1977; Pearlin, 1975). Theories of community mental health postulate that an individual's mental health is crucially effected by his interactions with others in his community (Blackman and Goldstein, 1968). The theory of preventive intervention holds that "among the significant factors which will determine the mental health of an individual are those relating to his emotional milieu, with special reference to the quality of interpersonal relationships with significant people in his immediate environment" (Caplan, 1974:52).

And, indeed, there is a growing body of literature which attests to the importance of the social network as a support system which mitigates the effects of stressful life events (Gourash, 1978). It has been shown that the emotional support provided by an active social network reduces psychological distress among college students (Liem and Liem, 1976); that psychiatric symptoms arising from job-related stress can be minimized by social network support (Burke and Weir, 1977); that social support can retard further health decline among heart attack victims (Finlayson, 1976). Moreover, there is evidence that intimacy and frequency of contact with members of the social network influences the morale of the widowed person (Bornstein, *et al.*, 1973; Clayton, *et al.*, 1972; Lowenthal and Haven, 1968; Parkes, 1972; Pomeroy, 1975). In short, there is ample reason to believe that network support can play a major role in combatting poor mental health in general, and in particular, can aid widows in their process of adjustment.

The notion of social network is usually taken to mean ". . . a specified set of linkages among a defined set of persons, with the additional property that the characteristics of these linkages as a whole may be used to interpret the social behavior of the persons involved" (Mitchell, 1969:2). This network can include relatives, friends, neighbors, fellow employees or professionals paid for their services. However, in this paper we focus primarily on relationships based upon free choice, and mutual positive orientations and attractions; that is, upon *friendship* relations (Laumann, 1973; Litwak and Szelenyi, 1969). We chose to closely examine the effects of this subset of the widowed person's social network because we were guided by the notions that friendship groups can best help with issues involving change and fluctuation (Litwak and Szelenyi, 1969); that support from friendship groups may be particularly critical at times in the life cycle when friends are experiencing similar role changes and, therefore, can facilitate both the learning of new roles and the relinquishment of old ones (Hess, 1972); that friendship, in contrast to kinship, provides individuals with a wider choice of role models of the same age and sex (Rosow, 1967, 1974).

In fact, there is pertinent evidence which underscores our decision.[2] Pihlblad and Adams (1972) have shown that contact with friends is associated with higher life satisfaction among the widowed than contact with family. Widowed persons with no friends had lower life satisfaction than widowed persons without children or siblings, while those with high friend contact had higher satisfaction than those with high family contact. They conclude from their study: "There is little doubt that friend association 'explains' more of the satisfaction variance in widowhood than did family association, and that the level of friend contact is more linearly related to satisfaction increase than was the case with level of family contact" (1972:327). Similarly, Arling (1976) found a positive association between friendship and morale of the widowed and no association between family involvement and morale. Lopata (1973, 1979), too, has emphasized the importance of friendship for the widow's happiness. From her extensive sociological investigation of urban widows she has maintained that friendship is important to the urban woman and can be expected to become more important. Moreover, she asserts that many women could be happier if they had friendships to expand their social life space, and concludes that ". . . the society could contribute to the welfare of its older widows by increasing the opportunity for them to become involved in primary relations" (1973:217).

Unfortunately, as Maddison and Raphael (1975) have recently lamented, much of the research on bereavement and its consequences fails to take social network factors into account. Even those who argue for the importance of a supportive social network have tended to take a monolithic view of support, conceptually equating support solely with emotional supportiveness while measuring support by assessing frequency of contact with network members. Thus, there has been little consideration given to the relative importance of other types of support a widows' network can provide. Moreover, there has been an implicit assumption that the social support needs of the widow are relatively fixed and, therefore, *what* is good, as well as *who* is good for a widow during one phase of widowhood are equally good for her at a different phase.

TYPES OF SUPPORT AND ADAPTATION

Although there is little hard evidence on what constitutes the essential components of care or support (Henderson, 1977), a variety of support functions have been suggested. Robert Weiss' (1969) theory of the functional specificity of relationships, developed through his work with once-married individuals who were single by virtue of divorce or death, identifies five types of support essential for well being: intimacy, social integration, reassurance of worth, nurturance and assurance of assistance. In addition, he posits a sixth, guidance, which for some people may also be necessary. Lopata (1973) has suggested that the functions friends perform for a widow may include "attention which acknowledges that she is going through social and personal difficulties, active engagement in social interaction, and easement of her transition from one lifestyle to another" (1973:197). The work by Glick, *et al.* (1974), Lowenthal and Haven (1968), and Maddison and Walker (1967) all indicate that the network's providing opportunities to express personal, intimate concerns and problems being experienced is critical for the well-being of the widow.

The adjustment tasks and problems of the widow differ, depending on which phase she is experiencing (Hiltz, 1977; Parkes, 1972; Walker, *et al.*, 1977). As Hiltz (1977) describes it, the problems of widowhood can be analytically separated into two kinds. First (during the critical loss phase), there are the emotional and psychological traumas of grief and mourning, of finally letting go of one's old emotional ties and roles which centered on the husband. She next faces, during the transition phase, issues of building a new life, new role relationships and a new identity. Thus, as the widowed person's problems and adjustment tasks vary by phase of widowhood, it is reasonable to assume that her support needs, and thus the salient friendship support functions, would accordingly vary. As Parkes maintains:

> If the early stage of bereavement is a time when family, friends and others should rally round and relieve the newly bereaved person of some of his roles and obligations, the later stage is one when the bereaved person should be helped to establish his own autonomy. It may be important for a bereaved person to grieve. It is also important for him to stop grieving, to give up his withdrawal from life and to start building a new identity.
>
> (1972:175)

SOURCES OF SUPPORT AND ADAPTATION

Previous work suggests that some kinds of friends will have different effects from others on positive adaptation to widowhood; they should also provide different services. Interactions with still-married friends may become less frequent and less rewarding because of a new asymmetry in life styles and concerns (Blau, 1961; Lopata, 1979; Silverman, 1970,

1972). Other widows may assume a new importance by becoming important sources of knowledge for problems unique to widowhood (Silverman, 1970). Moreover, Silverman (1972) has argued that homogeneity in marital status among friends is a key factor in a widow's positive adjustment, because the most effective emotional support for the widowed is given by people who have also been widowed. Although the marital status of neighborhood friends may vary, Litwak and Szelenyi (1969) suggest that the unique structural features of this friendship subset, namely, face-to-face contact and residential proximity, make it best for providing one particular type of support: emergency assistance.

Therefore, in the present study these three subsets of widows' friendship networks—their married friends, their widowed or single friends, and their neighborhood friends—were examined in terms of the relative importance of the support they provide for widows' well-being, in both phases of widowhood. And, as the relevant literature suggests several types of support which may be important for a widow adjusting to the death of her spouse, these types of support—attention, intimacy, companionship for social activities, approval of a new life style, emotional support, assurance of emergency assistance and guidance—were evaluated in the present study in terms of their relative importance as mediators between the impact of widowhood and the widow's psychological well-being during both of her adjustment phases.

METHODS

Study Sample

The findings presented here are derived from a comprehensive national study—Self-help and Urban Problems: Alternative Help Systems, conducted at the University of Chicago. The data for this paper are based on a sample of widows that is part of a larger sample comprising widows and widowers, new mothers, mothers of twins, and bereaved parents. Approximately half of this larger sample had been or were then members of self-help groups. To obtain the widowed sample, lists of names of widowed people were obtained from two organizations of widowed people, one centralized in Chicago and the other nation-wide. These lists included names of widowed people who were members of these organizations as well as names of widowed people who had been invited to join the organization, but did not join. Thus, the sample comprises widowed people who had access to a friendship network. A total of 2,798 questionnaires were mailed. Thirteen hundred eighty questionnaires were returned (50.3 percent of those delivered).

From these returns two groups were identified for the present study.

The Crisis Loss Phase group (n = 126) consisted of women who had been widowed less than 18 months *and* reported that they were still in the midst of intense grief. Women who had been widowed more than two years, but less than five years, *and* reported that they were still grieving but to a limited extent, constituted the Transition Phase group (n = 321). Since the purpose of this study was to explore network factors which facilitate well-being during the process of adjustment to widowhood, widows who reported that they were no longer grieving were excluded from further analyses, as were all of the widowers.

To suggest that differences between these two groups of widows in the effects of their friendship networks is due to the differences in their phases of adjustment to widowhood, it is necessary to establish first that these two groups are alike on relevant background characteristics. It has been argued that the following factors may influence friendship patterns and friendship needs: socioeconomic status, religious affiliation, age/lifestage, level of economic distress, race, working status, size of community, length of residency in hometown community, living arrangements, level of prior dependency on spouse and need for affiliation (cf. Blau, 1961; Cantor, 1979; Hiltz, 1977; Kasarda and Janowitz, 1976; Laumann, 1973; Lopata, 1973, 1979; Park and Burgess, 1921, 1925; Parkes, 1975; Toennies, 1887; Wirth, 1938). Thus, the widows in the crisis loss phase sample were compared on the above characteristics with the widows in the transition phase sample. These two groups of women did not differ significantly on any of the above characteristics (Table 1). Therefore, it appears that these two groups are basically the same "type" of women. Any friendship-related differences cannot be attributed to any confounding differences in "types" of people. Sixty percent of our sample were employed at least part time, 49 percent lived alone, although 95 percent were mothers. Fifty percent were Catholics, 50 percent were Protestants; 100 percent were Caucasians; 19 percent had earned at least a bachelor's degree, while 14 percent had not completed high school. The mean age was 53.6 years, the average number of living children was 2.9, the average number of children still at home was 1.1, and the average number of years lived in their present community was 2.5.

Although placement into one of the phase of widowhood groups was based on subjective (i.e., self-reported level of grief) as well as objective (i.e., time since the loss) criteria, it was, nevertheless, important to explore the validity of the claim that these two groups are composed of women in different phases of their bereavement. Since one would expect widows in the crisis loss phase to be experiencing more acute psychological pain and distress than widows in the transition phase, a comparison of numerous indicators of psychological distress was undertaken. As expected, compared with their counterparts in the transition phase,

Table 1. Comparison Between Crisis Loss Phase Sample and
Transition Phase Sample on Personal and Background
Characteristics and Indicators of Psychological Distress

| Dimensions of Comparison | Phase of Widowhood | | Significance[a] |
	Crisis Loss Phase (n = 126)	Transition Phase (n = 321)	
I. Personal and Background Characteristics			
Age (Years)	52.1	54.1	NS
Employed	57.0%	61.0%	NS[b]
SES	47.1	45.2	NS
Education	12.9	12.8	NS
Economic distress	1.6	1.7	NS
Length of residency (Years)	27.3	31.6	NS
Size of community	4.7	4.4	NS
Number of living children	2.9 (n = 114)	3.0 (n = 313)	NS
Number of children living at home	1.2	1.1	NS
Catholic	55.0%	47.0%	NS[b]
Protestant	44.0%	53.0%	NS[b]
Caucasion	100.0%	100.0%	NS[b]
Need for affiliation	2.4	2.4	NS
Prior dependency on spouse	2.7	2.8	NS
II. Indicators of Psychological Distress			
Overall Psychological Well-Being	0.3	0.9[c]	.02
Overall Psychological Distress	2.0	1.8[c]	.005
Depression	2.4	2.1[c]	.0001
Anxiety	1.8	1.6[c]	.02

[a] Unless otherwise indicated, all statistical analyses are calculated by ANOVA between crisis loss phase and transition phase means.
[b] Fisher's Exact Test.
[c] This group is less distressed.

the widows in the crisis loss phase showed significantly less overall psychological well-being and significantly greater depression, anxiety and psychological distress (Table 1).

Thus, in summary, it appears reasonable to assume that, in the aggregate, these two samples comprise the same types of women. The only major difference is that they are in different phases in their adjustment to the loss of their spouse.

Measures

The Affect Balance Scale (Bradburn, 1969) was our indicator of psychosocial adaptation. Although a variety of mental health measures were considered, this measure of psychological well-being was felt to be most appropriate for several reasons. First, low morale (i.e., lack of "felt happiness") is a common denominator throughout the adjustment process, whereas more pathological reactions tend to be localized in the crisis loss phase. Second, the Affect Balance Scale enables us to make fine discriminations among individuals, distinguishing, when necessary, as many as nine points along the scale. Third, this scale comprises independent negative and positive affect dimensions. Therefore, in addition to being a measure of psychological well-being, the Affect Balance Scale gives us a richer conceptual framework for investigating the social support correlates of psychological well-being (Bradburn, 1969). For example, it is conceivable that the presence or absence of a particular type of friendship support may relate only to one type of affective experience and may influence the sense of well-being only through one side of the Affect Balance Scale. In these cases, we shall be concerned with the measure of that one type of affect, that is, either positive or negative. Where the presence or absence of a particular support function is related to both positive and negative affect, we shall use the Affect Balance Scale as the best measure of the relationship between these types of support and psychological well-being.

The measures of attention, intimacy, and assurance of emergency assistance were developed for a study of life events and adaptation in adulthood by Pearlin and Lieberman (cf. Brown, 1979, 1978; Lieberman and Glidewell, 1978). The attention scale indicates the amount of contact the widows have had with their married, widowed or single, and neighborhood friends. The intimacy support scale determines the frequency with which the widows have discussed their important personal problems with members of each of these friendship subgroups. The assurance of emergency assistance support scale measures the extent to which the widows have felt they could depend on members of each of the three subgroups in an emergency. Similar scales were developed to measure the amount of emotional support received from each subgroup (e.g., "How much can you depend on your married friends for support and comfort when you are feeling down?"); the amount of guidance received from each of the friendship subgroups (e.g., "How much can you depend on your neighbors for information and advice about what to do or who to see about problems you are experiencing as a widowed person?"); and the amount of approval received from members of each of the friendship subgroups for starting to lead an active social life (e.g., "How much do your widowed or single friends approve of you, as a widowed person, having [or wanting to have] an active social life?"). A measure of social companionship support was derived from a combination of two questions: the first indicated the frequency with which the widows went out for recreation, entertainment, or social activities, the second determined with which network members, if any, they were likely to go.

FINDINGS

Types of Friendship Support and Psychological Well-Being

The first task in our analyses was to determine how the various types of support from the entire friendship network related to the psychological well-being of the widows in each phase of widowhood. Therefore, the mean levels of each type of support from all three categories of friends (i.e., married friends, widowed or single friends, and neighborhood friends) were multiply regressed on each of our indicators of well-being: overall, positive affect, and negative affect. Separate analyses were performed for each of the two groups in order to determine whether the same or different kinds of support affect well-being in the different phases of adjustment to widowhood.

The analyses of the relationship between the psychological well-being of widows in each phase of widowhood and the types of support provided by the friendship network are reported in Table 2. For widows in the crisis loss phase of widowhood the best predictors for overall well-being are their friends' social companionship and the lack of their friends' approval of a new life style. Social companionship and intimacy are important contributors to the positive dimension of well-being for these early widows. However, approval for a new life style and the lack of dependability supports from friends were significantly associated with the negative dimension of their well-being.

Together these findings suggest that it is important for newly bereaved widows who are still in the midst of their grief to have the social companionship of their friends, to be able to talk to their friends about their personal problems, and to know that they can depend on their friends for emergency help. In addition it would appear that, perhaps counter to what we might at first think, having their friends' approval for developing a new active social life style has a negative impact on these intensely grieving widows.

For widows in the transition phase of their adjustment to widowhood, the best predictors for their overall well-being are having their friends' social companionship and guidance, but also *not* having the assurance that they can turn to their friends for help in an emergency. Guidance from their friends, social companionship and intimacy with their friends, and the lack of assurance of their friends' dependability, all contributed to the positive dimension of the well-being of the transition phase widows. However, we find that the presence of intimacy from their friends also has a negative impact on the well-being of these widows, as does the absence of their friends' social companionship.

Thus, it would appear that the friends of widows who are no longer newly bereaved but are still grieving to a limited extent while making the transition to a new life can best contribute to their overall well-being by providing them with social companionship as well as guidance and information on handling the problems that they are experiencing due to being widowed. Although being able to confide in their friends has a positive effect on the widows' well-being, it apparently can also be dysfunctional. Finally, for widows in the transition phase of their adjustment, knowing that they can always turn to their friends for help has a curiously negative effect on their well-being.

In order to interpret the results of these two sets of findings, it is important to keep in mind the psychological states, adjustment tasks and particular problems of widows in these different phases of widowhood. As was noted earlier, widows in the crisis loss phase of their adjustment are experiencing intense grief, often accompanied by denial of the loss and refusal to let go of their old emotional ties and roles which centered on the husband. It, therefore, makes sense that these early widows would benefit most from having the companionship of their friends and from being able to depend on their friends for help. Moreover, our finding that it is important for these widows to be able to talk to their friends about their serious personal problems is corroborated by previous research with the bereaved. The research has consistently found that talking about their grief (i.e., "grief work") is critical for the mental health of a newly bereaved (Glick, *et al.*, 1974; Lindemann, 1944; Maddison, 1968; Maddison and Raphael, 1975). The finding that having their friends' approval for adopting a new life style has a negative impact on the well-being of these newly bereaved widows was initially puzzling. Why would such approval make a negative difference? If newly bereaved widows are, in fact, reluctant to let go of their husbands and, thus, their roles and routines which centered on them, then it is possible that friends' approval for adopting new roles and routines that are devoid of husbands may be perceived by new widows as pushing them to do something they are not yet prepared to do.

Widows in the transition phase of their adjustment to widowhood are no longer in the midst of intense grief. Although they are still grieving, they are no longer traumatized by their grief. However, they are now facing a whole new set of adjustment tasks and problems of building a new independent life, new role relationships, and a new identity. Thus,

Table 2. Stepwise Multiple Regression Analyses: Significant Friendship Support Predictors for Psychological Well-Being[2]

Phase of Widowhood	Dependent Variable	Type of Support	Standardized Beta	R^2	F	Significance	Overall R^2	Overall F	Overall Significance
Crisis Loss Phase (n = 103)	Overall Psychological Well-Being								
		Social Companionship	.28	.08	5.61	<.025			
		Approval of new life style	−.21	.05	3.37	<.10	.13	4.72	<.025
	Positive Affect								
		Social Companionship	.31	.10	7.05	<.01			
		Intimacy	−.23	.06	4.09	<.05	.16	5.91	<.005
	Negative Affect								
		Approval of new life style	.31	.07	6.81	<.025			
		Dependability	−.26	.05	4.50	<.05	.13	4.63	<.025

122

Transition Phase (n = 229)	Overall Psychological Well-Being	β		F	p	R²	F	p
	Social Companionship	.22	.04	11.71	<.001	.07	4.39	<.005
	Guidance	.21	.01	6.87	<.025			
	Dependability	−.16	.02	4.03	<.05			
Positive Affect	Guidance	.25	.06	10.21	<.005	.12	6.82	<.001
	Social Companionship	.19	.04	8.90	<.005			
	Intimacy	.16	.01	3.87	<.05			
	Dependability	−.13	.01	2.80	<.10			
Negative Affect	Intimacy	.16	.03	6.14	<.025	.06	5.51	<.005
	Social Companionship	−.15	.03	5.03	<.025			

[a] Support functions were entered into the predictive equation only if they had a significant effect on the dependent variable.

123

it is understandable that these transition widows not only benefit from social companionship with their friends, but are worse off if they do not have it. In addition, it is understandable that widows who are attempting to forge a new life for themselves benefit from guidance and information from their friends about what to do or whom to see about widowhood-related problems they are experiencing. Perhaps, as Brown (1980) has suggested elsewhere in this book, widowhood does rekindle peer socialization as one of the functions of friendship.

The effects of talking to their friends about personal problems are more perplexing. Confiding in their friends appears to have at once a positive and a negative effect on the well-being of these transition phase widows. Perhaps the explanation for these findings as well as for the negative impact of knowing that they can always rely on their friends for help stems from the fact that these widows are striving to become more self-sufficient in their new lives. Therefore, although they derive some benefit by talking to their friends about their problems, they also may feel that in doing so they are being too dependent on their friends. Similarly, perhaps knowing that they can always turn to their friends for help strikes at the core of their attempts to become self-sufficient. This explanation is consistent with Parkes' (1972) assertion that while the newly bereaved need a great deal of rallying support and assistance from family, friends, and neighbors, later on they need to be helped to establish their own autonomy. Of course, there is another possible explanation for intimacy being both positively and negatively associated with the well-being of these transition phase widows. Perhaps within their total friendship network there are some friends with whom sharing personal problems and depending upon for emergency assistance has a positive effect, while there are other friends with whom doing so has a negative effect.

Sources of Friendship Support and Psychological Well-Being

How are the various *sources* of support from within the friendship network related to the well-being of the widow throughout her adjustment process? An overall support score was first determined for each of the three friendship subgroups (i.e., married friends, widowed or single friends, and neighborhood friends). These three summary scores were derived by taking the mean score across all of the seven types of support provided by each of the friendship subgroups. For example, the summary support score for the married friends represents the average combined amounts of guidance, emotional support, social companionship, attention or contact, dependability, approval for a new life style and intimacy supports provided the widow by her married friends. The summary support scores for each of the three friendship groups were then individually regressed on each of our indicators of well-being. Again separate analyses were performed for each of the two samples in order to determine whether the same or different sources of friendship support affect well-being in the different phases of widowhood.

The analyses of the relationship between the psychological well-being of the widows in each phase of widowhood and the overall support provided by each friendship support group are reported in Table 3. For widows in the crisis loss phase of adjustment the results appear to be simple and straight forward. Overall support from married friends appears to have a positive effect on their well-being, while the overall support from their widowed or single friends as well as that from their neighborhood friends appears to have no significant effect on their well-being.

The results of the analyses for the transition phase widows are more complicated. Although the overall support from the married friends of these widows has a significant negative effect on their well-being, there is still some indication that support from these still married friends also has a positive effect on their well-being. Similarly, although the overall support from the neighborhood friends of these transition phase widows has a strong positive impact in terms of their well-being, there is also a negative component to the effect. And finally, while apparently overall support from these widows' widowed or single friends has no important positive effect on their well-being, the absence of overall support from this friendship source has a significantly negative effect on the widows' sense of well-being. In other words, having overall support from their widowed or single friends does not appear to make the transition phase widows any "happier." However, not having the overall support from this friendship source does seem to make them "unhappier."

These results suggest some interesting considerations. First, it would appear that regardless of phase of widowhood, source of support is an important factor in determining whether or not the support has a positive, negative or neutral effect on the widows. Second, although it has been suggested that the most effective support for widows comes from other widows who have experienced the same loss themselves (Silverman, 1972), our findings suggest a more complicated pattern of effective support. Although 83 percent of our widows in the crisis loss phase indicate that the widowed or single friendship category was a relevant category for them (i.e., they have at least one widowed or single friend), the overall support provided them by these friends does not effect their well-being. On the contrary, it is these widows' still married friends who were the critical support providers. It is possible that these widows' married friends are their long-standing friends, while their widowed or single friends are new friends. If this is true, then the greater importance attached to the married friends may be a function of the fact that the

Table 3. Regression Analyses: The Effects of Support From Friendship Sources on Psychological Well-Being

Phase of Widowhood	(N)	Support Source	Dependent Variable	Standardized Beta	R^2	F	Significance
Crisis Loss Phase	(116)	Married friends	Overall Well-Being	.16	.03	2.98	<.10
			Positive Affect	.25	.06	7.80	<.01
			Negative Affect				NS
	(105)	Widowed/single friends	Overall Well-Being				NS
			Positive Affect				NS
			Negative Affect				NS
	(116)	Neighborhood friends	Overall Well-Being				NS
			Positive Affect				NS
			Negative Affect				NS
Transition Phase	(306)	Married friends	Overall Well-Being				NS
			Positive Affect	.12	.01	4.41	<.10
			Negative Affect	.16	.03	7.91	<.01
	(307)	Widowed/single friends	Overall Well-Being				NS
			Positive Affect				NS
			Negative Affect	-.16	.03	7.87	<.005
	(311)	Neighborhood friends	Overall Well-Being				NS
			Positive Affect	.16	.03	8.51	<.005
			Negative Affect	.15	.02	7.56	<.01

widows feel closer to their old friends than they do to their new friends, regardless of the commonality (or lack of) of their marital statuses. However, if this old versus new friends assumption is true, then our findings also suggest that, at least during their first eighteen months of widowhood, the widows' old married friends do not, in general, remove themselves as a source of support. This would be contrary to the popular notion that widows suddenly find themselves in a social vacuum, abandoned by their married friends. It appears that during the crisis loss phase such a vacuum, indeed, is not created.

The third consideration suggested by these findings is that the relative importance of sources of friendship support for the well-being of widows changes during their adjustment process. Whereas support received from the new widows' married friends makes only a positive contribution to their well-being, in the transition phase it has a predominantly negative effect (while still retaining some positive aspects). Concomitantly, although overall support received from the new widows' widowed or single friends has no important effect on their well-being, in the later phase of widowhood overall support from this source becomes very important. In other words, although well-being in the crisis loss phase apparently is not adversely affected if widows do not receive overall support from widowed or single friends, it suffers when they are in the transition phase. Thus, we find that the salience of overall support from widowed or single friends increases from one phase of adjustment to the next, while the salience of overall support from married friends decreases, even making some negative impact in the second phase.

When we compare the amount of contact widows in the first phase of adjustment have with each of their friendship support sources with the amount of contact widows in the second phase have with theirs, a difference emerges. As we might expect, the widows in the first phase have more contact with married friends and less contact with widowed or single friends than do widows in the second phase (Table 4). This may, in part, explain both why the overall support from married friends is more important for widows in the first phase than in the second phase, and why the overall support from their widowed or single friends is more important for the widows in the second phase than in the first. However, it does not help to explain why the overall support received in the transition phase from married friends is predominantly negative. If it is true that even with less contact with married friends, the support they do receive is largely dysfunctional for transition phase widows, then perhaps, contrary to popular notions, married friends do not drift or pull away from their friends who become widowed. Rather, it may be the widows themselves who, finding the "support" they receive from their married friends to be adversive, initiate the separation.

Table 4. T-Tests: Amount of Contact with Friendship Sources

Friendship Support Source[a]	Phase of Widowhood		Significance
	Crisis Loss	Transition	
Married friends	2.4[b] (n = 120)	2.2 (n = 309)	.05
Widowed and single friends	2.2 (n = 116)	2.9[b] (n = 325)	.00
Neighborhood friends	2.4 (n = 125)	2.4 (n = 326)	NS

[a] Entries are mean scores.
[b] This group had more contact with the friendship support source.

The relationship between overall support from neighborhood friends and well-being in each phase of widowhood suggests that the overall support received from neighbors has no impact on the new widows' well-being, but has both positive and negative effects on longer-standing widows. The reason for the change in salience of this support source is not immediately apparent. T-test comparisons suggest that the reason is not related to difference in amount of contact with their neighborhood friends: there is no significant difference between the two groups of widows on this dimension (see Table 4). Moreover, if we consider age, level of economic distress and work status to be indicators of degree of mobility or confinement, then, we can rule out difference in mobility, since they did not differ in these respects. Similarly, these widows do not differ in length of time in their community or its size. Thus, it is not that they have less or more established neighborhood ties nor live in less or more urban environments. Perhaps the explanation lies in the specific types of support the neighborhood friends provide for their widowed friends, as we shall explore below.

Specific Types of Support from Specific Friendship Support Sources and Psychological Well-Being

We can now ask is there a significant interaction between source of support and type of support? In other words, does it seem to be important for widows to receive specific *types* of support from specific *sources*?

Stepwise multiple regression analyses were used to address this question. Each widow had indicated in her questionnaire how much of each type of support she had received from each of the three friendship subgroups. These data yielded support-by-source scores which were multiply regressed on our indicators of well-being, for both phases of widowhood.

From these findings (see Table 5) we now see that, depending upon who gives it, the same type of support can have very different effects on the same group of widows. We also see that the effects of a particular

Table 5. Stepwise Multiple Regression Analyses: Significant Type of Support by Friendship Source Predictors for Psychological Well-Being[a]

Phase of Widowhood	Dependent Variable	Type of Support	Source of Support	Standardized Beta	R²	F	Significance	Overall R²	Overall F	Overall Significance
Crisis Loss Phase (n = 98)	Overall Well-Being	Intimacy	from married friends	.28	.10	5.47	<.025	.16	5.84	<.005
		Guidance	from widowed friends	.25	.06	4.32	<.05			
	Positive Affect	Intimacy	from married friends	.32	.14	8.02	<.01	.21	8.24	<.001
		Emotional	from widowed friends	.28	.07	5.86	<.025			
	Negative Affect[b]									
Transition Phase (n = 250)	Overall Well-Being	Guidance	from neighbors	.24	.08	9.37	<.005	.13	7.53	<.001
		Intimacy	from widowed friends	.15	.02	5.07	<.025			
		Dependability	from neighbors	.20	.02	6.43	<.025			
	Positive Affect	Guidance	from widowed friends	.25	.08	13.22	<.001	.12	12.87	<.001
		Emotional	from neighbors	.20	.04	8.20	<.005			
	Negative Affect	Guidance	from neighbors	-.26	.04	10.44	<.005	.10	3.94	<.001
		Dependability	from neighbors	-.20	.02	5.10	<.025			
		Intimacy	from married friends	.18	.01	4.04	<.05			
		Contact	from married friends	-.21	.02	5.04	<.025			
		Dependability	from married friends	.16	.01	3.01	<.10			

[a] Type of support by friendship source predictors were entered into the equation only if they had a significant affect on the dependent variable.
[b] None of the predictors were significant.

friendship support group can vary radically, depending on the type of support given as well as on phase of widowhood.

While we know that social companionship and assurance of emergency assistance from their total friendship network is important in the crisis loss phase, we can now confirm that no particular friendship subgroup is a critical source for these particular types of support. Similarly, we found that having the approval of members of their total friendship network for leading a new, socially active life style had a negative impact on the well-being of these new widows; we also can now say that no one subgroup's approval makes a significant impact.

However, these further findings do indicate that particular subgroups of the friendship network do make unique and important contributions to the well-being of widows in both phases of adjustment. Turning first to the crisis loss phase, we see that although our earlier findings indicated that intimacy was an important type of friendship support for the well-being of these early widows, it is now apparent that it is not intimacy support from the total friendship network that is important, but rather, intimacy support specifically from married friends. It is apparently very important for the well-being of widows in the crisis loss phase to be able to talk to their married friends about their personal problems. However, confiding in their widowed or neighborhood friends seems to make little difference. We had also found that the overall support provided by married friends was important for their well-being. It is now apparent that it is not all types of support from this set of new widows' friends which are important for their sense of well-being. It is only intimacy support. Similarly, although our findings have suggested that receiving overall support from widowed or single friends was irrelevant, we now see that to receive particular types of support from this set of friends does seem to increase sense of well-being. The more emotional support they receive from widowed or single friends the happier they are. The more this set of friends provides guidance about how to handle their widowhood related problems the more their overall well-being is enhanced.

As Lindemann (1944) has suggested, working through grief by expressing it with significant others should be important for the mental health of the newly bereaved. It, therefore, is understandable that our widows in the crisis loss phase seem to benefit from being able to talk to their friends about important personal problems. But why would such intimacy support be effective only when it comes from married friends? In addition, although it is understandable that newly bereaved widows also need emotional support and guidance, why do these types of support only make a difference when they come from widowed or single friends?

If these married friends for the most part are long-standing ones, perhaps these widows only feel comfortable unburdening their sorrow and pain to friends who have known them through the years and with whom they have had a history of reciprocal problem sharing. On the other hand, despite such comfort and closeness, there seem to be limits to the type of support such friends can provide. Widowed or single friends seem to be best able to provide emotional support—to comfort and soothe when these new widows are in pain. This is likely to be so because as the new widows face their loss and the particular pain of widowhood, these friends are best equipped to understand and empathize. They can also provide advice and information about how to deal with widowhood related problems.

It is interesting to note that for our sample of new widows struggling with acute grief, their support needs are intense but localized. That is, relatively few types of support make a big difference in terms of the well-being of widows in the crisis loss phase. Those that do, however, make a big difference. The findings for transition phase widows, on the other hand, suggest that as widows' grief lessens and they begin struggling to forge new lives for themselves, the intensity of their support needs also lessens. However, the variety of their support needs increases, as does the variety of relevant support sources.

Where guidance from their widowed friends was helpful to the crisis loss phase widows, this type of support appears to be even more important for the well-being of the transition phase widows (Table 5). Perhaps this is because of increasing needs for socialization as they reorganize their lives. This type of support from widowed friends has a slightly greater effect on widows in the transition phase than on new widows. Additionally, the overall well-being of the transition phase widows is also enhanced by receiving such support from neighborhood friends, as well. Moreover, our findings indicate that the less guidance support the transition phase widows receive from their neighborhood friends, the more unhappy they are.

There also is some indication that the respective roles of widows' married and widowed friends change during the adjustment process. Although it was extremely important for the crisis loss phase widows to be able to share their important personal problems with their married friends, for the transition phase widows it is their widowed or single friends who emerge as the important suppliers of this intimate type of support. In fact, our findings suggest that the more the transition phase widows confide in their married friends, the worse off they are. Concomitantly, the more these widows depend on their married friends the more their sense of well-being is decreased. Thus, it appears that the married friends of the transition phase widows hurt them more than they help. One can speculate that transition phase widows might be better off cutting back on ties with their married friends. However, our findings also tentatively suggest that the less contact these widows have with this same group of friends, the more unhappy they are. What can be made of this seeming paradox?

Perhaps where there once was a close bond between these widows and their married friends, drastic differences in life situations may now be eroding that bond. But while transition phase widows might feel hurt and abandoned if and when their married friends stop calling, they also find that when they try to confide in these once close friends, they are no longer understood. It is now those friends in similar life circumstances who seem to understand. Furthermore, if an important adjustment task for these transition phase widows is to build a new, more independent life for themselves, then perhaps to continue to depend on this cohort of friends from their prewidowhood days has a dampening effect on this building process. It may also be true that, over time, these married friends, in fact, have become less reliable. Offers of help may not be followed up (Parkes, 1972), and therefore, to depend on them for help even in an emergency may lead to disappointments.

Litwak and Szelenyi (1969) provide a model which may explain why depending on neighborhood friends, as opposed to married friends, for emergency assistance is positively related to the transition phase widows' sense of well-being. They argue that different primary groups have different and unique structures. Each of these unique structures is linked to the particular task it can best perform. According to this task-specific model, neighbors are the most effective network source for emergency assistance; clearly, they are best equipped because they live in close proximity. However, neighborhood friends seem to perform other important support functions for the transition phase widows. Neighbors also seem to be an important source of guidance and emotional support for these widows. The more advice and information their neighborhood friends provide about how to handle widowhood related problems and the more emotional support their neighborhood friends provide for them, the greater is these widows' well-being. It is not immediately clear why neighborhood friends are such an important source for these supports for these widows. Nor is it clear why this set of friends is a more salient support source for these widows than for those in the crisis loss phase.

As earlier noted, there are no differences between our samples of widows in terms of their age, work status, length of residency in their communities and size of their communities. Thus, differences in mobility or confinement, length of time lived in their neighborhoods, and size of their communities do not explain the apparent difference in saliency of neighborhood friends for our two samples. We also know that this difference in salience is not because of any differences in amount of contact with their respective neighborhood friends. Furthermore, t-test comparisons (see Table 6) also indicate that the transition phase widows do not receive more guidance, dependability, or emotional support from their neighborhood friends than the crisis loss phase widows receive from theirs. Therefore, it is not availability nor quantity differences which create the difference in saliency.

Perhaps the difference in the salience of neighborhood friends is related to differences in amount of concerned attention they are getting from their total social network, and differences in their focal problems and adjustment tasks. For example, previous work suggests that friends, family and neighbors rally around to support newly bereaved widows. Consequently, many of their day-to-day problems and responsibilities are attended to by a host of significant others (Parkes, 1972). Thus, although early widows apparently need assurance of emergency assistance, perhaps because of the implosion of dependable support from their entire social network, no single source of this support is most critical. The greater efficiency of neighborhood friends to perform this function on an ongoing basis (cf. Litwak and Szelenyi, 1969) has not (yet) become pertinent. However, by the time widows move into the transition phase their overall social network has, in large part, ceased to rally around them (Parkes, 1972). It may even be that their old friends become less dependable as their problems and concerns begin to diverge from those of the widows. Consequently, the efficiency of the neighborhood friends for performing the function of dependability in emergencies becomes more relevant.

We can also speculate that widows in the transition phase, now less preoccupied with their grief, have begun to be more concerned with how they are going to handle the multitude of day-to-day problems for the first time faced alone. Now that their grief has lessened they are psychologically more free to worry about more mundane, widowhood-related problems, such as how they are going to get the storm windows up before winter sets in; when they should have the oil changed in their car; who is going to cut the grass or unclog the drains, etc. Perhaps it

Table 6. T-Tests: Amount of Support from Neighborhood Friends

Support Provided by Neighborhood Friends	Phase of Widowhood		Significance
	Crisis Loss	Transition	
Guidance	1.95[b] (n = 114)	1.80 (n = 299)	NS
Dependability	2.22[b] (n = 116)	2.20 (n = 303)	NS
Emotional Support	2.17[b] (n = 122)	2.09 (n = 312)	NS

[a] Entries are mean scores.
[b] This group received more support.

is their neighbors' advice and information on how to handle this class of problems that is beneficial to the transition phase widow, while still irrelevant to the concerns of the widow in the crisis loss phase. It is also probable that at least some neighborhood friends are also widowed and thus, the similarity of their circumstances (i.e., being without their spouses in the same neighborhood) has made these neighborhood friends particularly salient over the years since the transition phase widows lost their spouses. This could explain why neighborhood friends are not only important sources of guidance and assurance of emergency assistance, but also more important sources of emotional support for the transition phase widows than for the crisis loss phase widows.

At present such explanations are speculative and need to be empirically tested. It is possible that these findings merely reflect an idiosyncratic relationship between our sample of transition phase widows and their neighbors, since our sample is not, in fact, drawn from a true random sample of widows. However, these findings do suggest that a closer examination of the contributions neighborhood friends can and do make to widows in the transition phase of their adjustment to widowhood may be a fruitful line of future inquiry.

CONCLUSIONS

Our data suggest that whether or not friendship support helps, hurts, or is inconsequential for the well-being of widows during their long process of adjustment depends on at least three factors: the problems and adjustment tasks currently faced by the widow, the specific type of support provided, and the source of that support. That is, different adjustment tasks and focal problems apparently create different support needs. Therefore, types of support which are helpful for widows with one set of problems and adjustment tasks may be irrelevant or even unhelpful for widows with a different set. Moreover, the effect of even the same type of support may vary radically depending on its source. It seems that certain characteristics of widows' friends—whether they are married or not, live close by or not, are long-standing friends or not—influence their effectiveness.

Our specific findings, of course, require replication on a true random sample of widows. Nevertheless, several important implications emerge for future research. One of the major implications of our research is that researchers who study widows and their informal support systems should differentiate widows in terms of their primary concerns and adjustment tasks. The support needs of widows do not remain fixed throughout the adjustment process. A second implication is that researchers should investigate the relative importance of a range of specific types of support provided by the network. Support should not be viewed as a monolithic entity. There are many and varied types of support the network can provide, each having its own effect. A third implication is that investigators be sensitive to the fact that different types of support may require primary groups with different characteristics. That is, due to their unique characteristics one subgroup of the social network may be best suited and therefore more effective, suppliers of particular types of support.

Finally, our data illustrate the importance of *simultaneously* considering *specific types of support, specific support sources* and *specific adjustment phases*. Such detailed analyses can help us to more precisely specify the ways in which friends or other primary groups can enhance or lessen widows' psychological well-being throughout the adjustment process. Moreover, such specificity may begin to give us some leverage on what it might take to improve the quality of life for widows and, thereby, facilitate positive psychosocial adaptation to widowhood.

ACKNOWLEDGMENTS

The research reported here was supported with a grant from the National Institute of Mental Health (Self-Help and Urban Problems: Alternative Help Systems, PHS #5, ROl-MH30742). Morton A. Lieberman and Leonard D. Borman were the co-principal investigators. Initial findings from this larger study which investigated the formation, functioning, and impact of self-help groups as they respond to a wide range of life events and crises, including widowhood, have been reported elsewhere (cf. Lieberman and Borman, 1979).

NOTES

1. In 1974 there were 9,814,000 widows in the United States. This is about 13% of all women over the age of 18 (Bureau of the Census, 1974).

2. There is also considerable evidence for a significant association between friendship and positive well-being of the elderly (cf. Carp, 1966; Hochschild, 1973; Lemon, *et al.*, 1972; Pihblad and McNamara, 1965; Phillips, 1973; and Rosow, 1967).

REFERENCES

Arling, Greg
    1976 "The elderly widow and her family, neighbors and friends." Journal of Marriage
          and the Family 38(4): 757–768.
Blackman, S., and K. M. Goldstein
    1968 "Some aspects of a theory of community mental health." Community Mental
          Health Journal 4(1): 85–90.
Blau, Z. S.
    1961 "Structural constraints on friendships in old age." American Sociological Review
          26: 429–439.
Bornstein, P. E., P. J. Clayton, J. A. Halidas, W. L. Maurice, and E. Robins
    1973 "The depression of widowhood after thirteen months." British Journal of Psy-
          chiatry 122: 561–566.

Bradburn, N.
1969 Structure of Psychological Well-Being. Chicago: Aldine.
Brenner, M. H., and W. Mandell
1965 Economic Conditions and Functional Psychosis. Paper presented at the meeting of the Eastern Sociological Association, New York.
Brown, B. B.
1980 "A life-span approach to friendship: Age-related dimensions of an ageless relationship." In H. Lopata and D. Maines (eds.), Research on the Interweave of Social Roles; Friendship, Vol. 2, Greenwich, Conn.: J.A.I. Press.
Brown, B. B.
1979 Predicting Patterns of Help-Seeking in Coping with Stress in Adulthood. Unpublished doctoral dissertation, University of Chicago.
Brown, B. B.
1978 "Social and psychological correlates of help-seeking behavior among urban adults." American Journal of Community Psychology 6(5), 425–439.
Bureau of the Census, Marital status and living arrangements
1974 Current Population Reports, Series P–20 March: No. 271.
Burke, R. J., and T. Weir
1977 "Marital helping relationships: The moderators between stress and well-being." Journal of Psychology 95, 121–130.
Campbell, A., P. E. Converse, and W. L. Rodgers
1976 The Quality of American Life. New York: Russell Sage Foundation.
Cantor, M.
1979 "Neighbors and friends: An overlooked resource in the informal support system." Research on Aging 1(4): 434–463.
Caplan, G.
1974 Support Systems and Community Mental Health: Lectures on Concept Development. New York: Behavioural Publications.
Carp, Frances M.
1966 The Future of the Aged: Victoria Plaza and Its Residents. Austin, University of Texas Press.
Clayton, P. J., J. A. Halikas, and W. L. Maurice
1972 "The depression of widowhood." British Journal of Psychiatry 120: 71–77.
Cobb, S.
1976 "Social support as a moderator of life stress." Psychosomatic Medicine 38(5).
Dohrenwend, B. S.
1978 "Social stress and community psychology." American Journal of Community Psychology 6, 1–14.
Dohrenwend, B. S., and B. P. Dohrenwend
1974 "A brief historical introduction to research on stressful life events." In B. S. Dohrenwend and B. B. Dohrenwend (eds.), Stressful Life Events: Their Nature and Effects. New York: John Wiley, 1–6.
Durkheim, E.
1951 Suicide: A Study in Sociology. Glencoe, Ill.: The Free Press.
Finlayson, A.
1976 "Social networks as coping resources: Lay help and consultation patterns used by women in husbands' post-infarction career." Social Science and Medicine 10: 97–108.
Glick, I. O., R. S. Weiss, and C. M. Parkes
1974 The First Year of Bereavement. New York: John Wiley and Sons.
Gorer, G.
1965 Death, Grief and Mourning. New York: Doubleday and Co.

Gourash, N.
1978 "Help-seeking: A review of the literature." American Journal of Community Psychology 6(5): 413–423.
Gurin, G., J. Veroff, and S. Feld
1960 Americans View Their Mental Health. New York: Basic Books.
Harvey, C. D., and H. M. Bahr
1974 "Widowhood, morale and affiliation." Journal of Marriage and the Family 36, 97–106.
Henderson, S.
1977 "The social network, support and neurosis: The function of attachment in adult life." British Journal of Psychiatry 131: 185–191.
Hess, B.
1972 Friendship. In M. W. Riley, et al. (eds.), Aging and Society. New York: Russell Sage.
Hiltz, S. R.
1977 Creating Community Services for Widows: A Pilot Project. Port Washington, N.Y.: National University Publications.
Hochschild, Arlie R.
1973 The Unexpected Community. Englewood Cliffs, N.J.: Prentice-Hall.
Jacobs, S., and A. Ostfeld
1977 "An epidemiological review of the mortality of bereavement." Psychosomatic Medicine 39(5): 344–357.
Kasarda, J. D., and M. Janowitz
1974 "Community attachment in mass society." American Sociological Review 39: 328–339.
Kraus, A. S., and S. G. Lutkins
1967 "Mortality of bereavement." British Medical Journal 4: 13–16.
Laumann, E. O.
1973 Bonds of Pluralism: The Form and Substance of Urban Social Networks. New York: John Wiley and Sons.
Lemon, B. W., V. Bengtson, and J. Peterson
1972 "An exploration of the activity theory of aging." Journal of Gerontology 27: 511–523.
Lieberman, M. A., and L. D. Borman and Associates
1979 Self-Help Groups for Coping with Crisis: Origins, Members, Processes and Impact. San Francisco: Jossey-Bass.
Lieberman, M. A., and J. C. Glidewell
1978 Overview: Special issue on the helping process. American Journal of Community Psychology 6(5): 405–411.
Liem, J. H., and R. Liem
1976 Life Events, Social Supports and Physical and Psychological Well-Being. Paper presented at the meeting of the American Psychological Association, September.
Lindemann, E.
1944 "Symptomatology and management of acute grief." American Journal of Psychiatry 101: 141–148.
Litwak, E., and I. Szelenyi
1969 "Primary group structures and their functions: Kin, neighbors, and friends." American Sociological Review 34: 465–481.
Lopata, H. Z.
1973 Widowhood in an American City. Cambridge, Mass.: Schenkman Publishing Co.
Lopata, H. Z.
1979 Women or Widows: Support Systems. New York: Elsevier.

Lowenthal, M. F., and C. Haven
    1968   "Interaction and adaptation: Intimacy as a critical variable." American Socio-
            logical Review 33: 20–30.
Maddison, D.
    1968   "The relevance of conjugal bereavement for preventive psychiatry." British Jour-
            nal of Medical Psychology 41: 223–233.
Maddison, D., and B. Raphael
    1975   "Conjugal bereavement and the social network." In B. Schoenberg, I. Gerber,
            A. Wiener, A. Kutscher, D. Peretz and A. C. Carr (eds.), Bereavement: Its
            Psychosocial Aspects. New York: Columbia University Press, 26–40.
Maddison, D., and W. Waler
    1967   "Factors affecting the outcome of conjugal bereavement." British Journal of
            Psychiatry, 133: 1057–1067.
Mitchell, J. D.
    1969   "The concept and use of social networks." In J. C. Mitchell (ed.), Social Networks
            in Urban Situations. Manchester: Manchester University Press, 1–50.
Park, R. E., and E. W. Burgess
    1925   The City. Chicago: University of Chicago Press.
Park, R. E., and E. W. Burgess
    1921   Introduction to the Science of Sociology. Chicago: University of Chicago Press.
Parkes, C. M.
    1975   "Unexpected and untimely bereavement: A statistical study of young Boston
            widows and widowers." In B. S. Schoenberg, I. Gerber, A. Wiener, A. H.
            Kutscher, D. Peretz, A. C. Carr (eds.), Bereavement: Its Psychosocial Aspects.
            New York: Columbia University Press, 119–138.
Parkes, C. M.
    1972   Bereavement: Studies of Grief in Adult Life. New York: International Universities
            Press.
Parkes, C. M.
    1971   "The first year of bereavement: A longitudinal study of the reaction of London
            widows to the death of their husbands." Psychiatry 33: 444–467.
Parkes, C. M.
    1964a   "Recent bereavement as a cause of mental illness." British Journal of Psychiatry
            110, 198–204.
Parkes, C. M.
    1964b   "Effects of bereavement on physical and mental health—A study of the medical
            records of widows." British Medical Journal 2: 274–279.
Pearlin, L.
    1975   "Sex roles and depression." In N. Datan and L. Ginsberg (eds.), Life Span
            Developmental Psychology: Normative Life Crises. New York: Academic Press,
            183–198.
Pihlblad, C. T., and D. Adams
    1972   "Widowhood, social participation and life satisfaction." Aging and Human De-
            velopment 3, 323–330.
Pihlblad, C. T., and R. McNamara
    1965   "Social adjustment of elderly people in three small towns." In A. Rose and W.
            Peterson (eds.), Older People and Their Social World. Philadelphia: F. A. Davis.
Phillips, Derek, L.
    1973   "Social participation and happiness." In J. N. Edwards and A. Booth (eds.),
            Social Participation in Urban Society. Cambridge, Mass.: Schenkman.

Pinneau, R.
 1975 Effects of Social Support on Psychological and Physiological Status. Dissertation, University of Michigan.
Pomeroy, E. L.
 1975 Relationship Between Mourner Characteristics and Factors Affecting Grief Work. Dissertation, University of Southern California.
Raphael, B.
 1971 "Crisis intervention: Theoretical and methodological considerations." Aust. N. Z., J. Psychiatry 5: 183–191.
Rees, W. D., and S. G. Lutkins
 1967 Mortality of bereavement. British Medical Journal 4: 13–21.
Rosow, I.
 1974 Socialization for Old Age. Berkeley: University of California Press.
Rosow, Irving
 1967 Social Integration of the Aged. New York: Free Press.
Silverman, P. R.
 1972 "Widowhood and preventative intervention." Family Life Coordinator 21: 95–104.
Silverman, Phyllis R.
 1970 "The widow as caregiver in a program of preventive intervention with other widows." Mental Hygiene 54(4): 540–547.
Toennies, F.
 1887 Gemeinschaft and Gesellschaft. Leipzig: Fues's Verlag.
Vachon, M. L. S.
 1976 "Grief and bereavement following the death of a spouse." Canadian Psychiatric Association Journal 21: 35–44.
Walker, K. N., A. MacBride, and M. L. S. Vachon
 1977 "Social support networks and the crises of bereavement." Social Science and Medicine 2: 35–41.
Weiss, R.
 1969 "The fund of sociability." Trans-action 6: 36–43.
Wirth, L.
 1938 "Urbanism as a way of life." American Journal of Sociology 44: 3–24.
Young, M., B. Benjamin, and C. Wallis
 1963 "Mortality of widowers." Lancet 2: 454–463.

PART II
SITUATED FRIENDSHIP: FACILITATORS AND CONSTRAINTS

FRIENDSHIP DILEMMAS AND THE INTERSECTION OF SOCIAL WORLDS:
RE-ENTRY WOMEN ON THE COLLEGE CAMPUS

Judith A. Levy

As Simmel (1955) observed, people in modern society typically belong to many social circles and relational networks, each having a unique structure, set of demands, and cohesive force. Yet despite a large body of research concerning friendship within particular settings and contexts, little attention has been paid to the problems of managing friendship across multiple and often competing worlds. This paper examines the experience of older women who return to school as an example of how entry into a new social universe can create friendship dilemmas for individuals across two networks of social relationships. The analysis focuses on the difficulties re-entry women encounter in making friends on campus, the role of student duties and common identity in serving as a basis for friendship, and the effect of the re-entry woman's university relationships on friendships drawn from family and neighborhood ties. Many of the findings are generalizable to women entering the labor force as well as any who make role changes when entering new social realms. A social world perspective, following the tradition of Shibutani (1955), Bucher and Strauss (1961), Becker (1974) and more recently Unruh (1979) and Wiener (1980), has been used in conceptualizing and analyzing the data. This perspective is useful because it draws attention to how group boundaries and segments within society create both opportunities for change and a climate for conflict (Strauss, 1978).

DATA AND METHODS

Data for the analysis are based on 60 in-depth interviews with women who returned to school after at least a four-year break in their education or who were over thirty when they enrolled. The re-entry women are students in the College of Arts and Sciences at a small private mid-western university. The university started keeping records on older students for a year and a half preceding the study. A computer search through the university's records as well as a snowball technique resulted in a sample of thirty graduate and thirty undergraduate women.

The objectifying interview (Lofland, 1971), encouraging participants to discuss their experience in a natural manner, provided the framework for discussion of the re-entry woman's experience at the university. The average length of each interview was two and a half hours.

The ages of the women ranged from 25 to 63 with a median age of 35. Forty-three of the women were married, thirteen were separated, widowed or divorced, and four had never married. Of the sixty women who were in the sample, nine dropped out or temporarily had withdrawn from the university, ten had graduated, and forty-one were in school when interviewed.

ENCOUNTERS AND INTERACTIVE STRATEGIES

Although universities are accommodating an increasing number of older students who have come back to school to complete their education, the re-entry woman is still a distinct minority on most college campuses (Van Dusen and Sheldon, 1976; Brandenburg, 1978). Like most outsiders who move into new social territories (Schutz, 1944), the returning woman faces the problem of finding a place for herself within an established order where there are no clear roles for her to play.

Because of a strong normative system surrounding age appropriate behavior, most individuals have a general sense of the proper order and timing of significant life events and their own particular place within this ordering (Neugarten, *et al.*, 1965). One function of age-grading is that it provides a cohort of individuals who can guide and support each other through the transition from one stage to another (Benedict, 1938). Individuals, however, who are off-time in their scheduling have to make the transition without this support. Re-entry women know they are off-time and out of sequence for a traditional educational career, and this knowledge becomes a source of embarrassment and discomfort when they find themselves in a classroom with much younger students. One informant remarked:

> I have a real thing about being old in classes with young students. Very often I feel out of place, I feel old and uncomfortable. I think, my God, what an ass, sitting here among all these kids.

Faculty and student behavior toward the women suggest that others on campus also feel something unusual is occurring. Upon first encountering a re-entry woman in the classroom, students are inclined to insulate themselves against the intrusion by creating a protective distance between themselves and the returnee. One informant reported on the phenomenon:

> I found pretty much until this year that in a new class when I go in there are usually two empty seats on either side of me for about the first week.

Faculty typically elect to maintain the "polite fiction" (Burns, 1953) that re-entrants are no different from other students. Rather than interacting with them as equals based upon shared adulthood, faculty maintain the traditional fiduciary distance appropriate between teacher and pupil. For re-entry students, then, age becomes a master status that influences their interaction with students, while studenthood overrides all other characteristics in social transactions with faculty.

Because it is not always clear what is expected of someone their age who is also a student, re-entry women occasionally overstep normative boundaries or do things that prove embarrassing. "When you have a student who doesn't fit in," one re-entrant remarked, "it's like having a puppy that's not housebroken." She went on to explain:

> My sense of appropriateness wasn't always situationally appropriate. That first quarter, I must have bothered some of the students. One young man blurted out, 'Do we have to listen to this?' The teacher and the [other] students were supportive. It indicated I was different.

To ease the awkwardness of the situation for themselves and others, re-entry women develop various tactics to manage their deviant status. Some women use these strategies occasionally while others develop a repertoire of tactics they regularly use in managing their on-campus lives. One common maneuver is to try to *blend in* with the younger students. The process of blending includes not asking unnecessary questions or noticeably outperforming other students in class. Within this context, "grade grabbing" is seen as a way to alienate oneself from the others.[1] Presenting the correct appearance also is critical in establishing an acceptable identity (Stone, 1962). When language and dress styles are too different, they are altered to conform to campus standards. As one re-entry woman explained:

> I looked like little Miss Junior League. They wouldn't think I was anything but a suburban housewife. So in the beginning I tried to alter my dress and make-up and hair so that I would look like the rest.

Flaunting, the opposite of blending in, is seen as potentially leading to outcast status. The attitude, "I'm back in school, see how wonderful I am" is offered as an example of what not to do in managing the situation. Similarly, calling attention to being different or what Levitin (1975) calls *deviance avowal* is perceived as evoking negative reactions from faculty and students:

> I spent about the first few weeks explaining to other students who I was and why I was there. Finally a male student took me aside and said, 'Look, nobody cares.' I found out that the one most concerned about age was me.

Some individuals actively court a marginal status because of the advantages such a position may offer (Riesman, 1954). Within this context, *capitalizing* on being older by asking for special favors or "kissing up to professors" also is viewed by re-entry women as inappropriate behavior.

Women with a youthful self-image credit their appearance with making it easier for them to fit-in by disguising differences between themselves and younger students. Women who look young often choose to disclose their nonschool selves in bits and pieces as they feel others are willing to accept them. One respondent who routinely uses a tactic of *gradual disclosure* explains it in this way:

> The ones I know well, I have no secrets from. Other people, when I first meet them, ask how many children do you have? I say I have an eleven year old and let it go at that and never mention the older ones. Let them find out in gradual stages.

But prevarication can result in unpleasantness when people base their behavior on inaccurate or incorrect definitions. Another respondent recalls that a friendly relationship with a young man ended when he found out about her secret self:

> He used to sit behind me in my Spanish class and he used to flirt with me. Then he found out I was married and had three kids. It was a blow; he stopped flirting.

Women can avoid this predicament by being *up front* about their marital and family circumstances before misunderstandings occur. In being up front, the woman works her personal biography into conversation when talking with someone for the first time. Yet there can be a fine line between up front and deviance avowal as some women discover when students chide them for being overly conscious of their age or differing status.

Being taken as young provides women with the temptation to *pass* in situations where disclosing their age may prove embarrassing or put them at a disadvantage.[2] One explains:

> I didn't want to be categorized. I've been the victim of ageism before. If people were going to accept me for younger than I was, I was going to play it for that. If it was going to get me a better social life than I would have otherwise . . . sometimes when people knew right away how old I was I could just see the barriers go up before we even got acquainted.

Some women repeatedly use this strategy. These women are often the ones who reject the notion of special programs for returning women because they do not want to call attention to their differing status. Nevertheless, problems can occur when others fail to respond to the woman according to her own self-definition. One woman remarks: "It startles me when someone says something that implies an age difference. I think, oh yes, I really have gray hair, don't I?" Women who choose to pass live under the constant threat that others will blow their cover and give away their secret. One informant, for example, told how her family and marital status became publicly known when another student excitedly announced in class, "Did you know she has a son in college?" Another threat to an undisclosed self comes from professors and teaching assistants who single out the women for special recognition and in doing so create and call attention to their differing status. Husbands and children may also become a threat if their presence poses a contradiction to the image women have created for themselves. At parties and student affairs, a husband may prove particularly embarrassing to the woman's image if he says something inappropriate or behaves in a manner inconsistent with general student norms.

While the re-entry woman's tactics prove useful in fitting into the general milieu of campus, the more successful strategies are based upon either minimizing or hiding personal characteristics typically accepted within the normal context of friendship. Yet, as Suttles (1970:100) points out, unless people are willing to disclose their identities and have reason to believe they are interacting with one another's "real self," friendship is impossible for each individual believes he or she "cannot detect the person behind the actor." In general, people expect friends to accept who they are and to overlook personal quirks and idiosyncrasies. When fitting-in strategies are used, they can interfere with the process of self-disclosure even though they may ameliorate other problems. For the re-entry woman, then, friendship acquisition requires some degree of risk-taking in terms of personal disclosure. As we shall see, it also involves overcoming friendship problematics rooted in the university system as well as the life-cycle biographies of the women.

FRIENDSHIP DILEMMAS FOR THE RE-ENTRY WOMAN

Social relationships are not formed at random but are lodged in systems of meaning and circumstance (Simmel, 1955). Many social settings provide institutionalized means for new participants to enter into on-going activities and become friendly with other co-participants. University networks, for example, provide a similarity of circumstance that brings students together who otherwise might not know one another. These formal and informal groupings include fraternities and sororities, extra-mural sports organizations, and student cafeteria crowds. All these contexts serve a purpose in structuring the process of friendship formation (Becker, et al., 1968). Many of these networks are not practically available to re-entry students; for these friendship and affiliation opportunities depend upon activities typically organized around interests specific to a young cohort. The 40-year-old woman with two teenage children seems out of place at a college mixer or hanging around with the crowd at the pinball machines in the student union. Even in less obviously youthful activities, the re-entry student discovers that age norms and life cycle assumptions make it difficult for them to enter. Friendship dilemmas for re-entry women stem from two sources: the structure of the university which is organized around processing young cohorts of students, and the discontinuity in life-cycle that comes from entering a status position usually completed at an earlier age. First, what are the organizational properties of the university which impede or complicate friendship formation for the older student?

University Limitation on Friendship

The social stratification system of a university is organized around a ranking system that places faculty, graduate students, and undergraduates at successively diminishing points on a hierarchical scale. Typically, students determine their positions within the pecking order according to established criteria based upon age and educational standing. But re-entry women comprise a highly diverse group, new to campus; there is no predetermined position for them to assume. They are scattered through the undergraduate years, according to their prior experience and education. As students they are marginal, caught between the role requirements of a younger student and the adult responsibilities and accomplishments that make them closer in status to the faculty (see Hughes, 1945). These contradictions provide a dilemma for the woman who is uncertain as to which group she belongs:

> I remember thinking I had to decide whether I was with the professors or with the students. It was kind of a dual role. I know professors from other situations and I was on an equal basis with them in the outside world. Yet, I was a student when I was within the university and the other students thought that I was on the professor's side. So I really didn't fit into either group.

The ambiguities surrounding re-entry women can be equally confusing for those faculty members who find it difficult to imagine an older woman as a student. One informant told the following story:

> A group of us went to a bar one evening. It's a place where professors like to go and they had invited us to come. When we showed up, everyone was amazed that I was there. Several professors said to me, 'Don't you need to be at home? What are your kids doing?' It was as if I was out of character. They couldn't believe I came to school, went home, took care of the kids and that wasn't my total experience. They couldn't see me doing what all other grad students do.

Younger students have similar problems in knowing how to relate to the women. Another woman recalled the intense surprise of a young man who found himself seated next to her—his former Sunday School teacher. Still another informant mentioned the difficulties others encounter in placing re-entry women within a specific social role:

> They (the students) have me at 25–26 which is really nice but . . . as soon as they hear I have children, they immediately group me with their mothers as if I were 55.

Women who feel the least ambiguity are those for whom the lines of status demarcation are clearly drawn. ''I never expected to be friends

with the faculty," is typical of their attitude, "so I never felt disap-
pointed." Or in regard to the younger students, "I didn't come back to
school looking for a social life, I'm glad that's behind me."

Like most individuals who occupy an uncertain or stigmatized status
(Berk, 1977), re-entry women face a dilemma between seeking out intimate and potentially satisfying relationships and protecting themselves
from possible rejection. To avoid embarrassing themselves or others, re-
entry women search for cues as to where they belong or where friendly
overtures can be anticipated. One informant, for example, remarked that
she often hinted to younger students that she would like to be included
in their activities. She would then wait to see if they invited her. Another
returning woman explained that she learned to avoid rejection by "feeling
out" faculty members before inviting them to her home.

While the hierarchical structure of the university creates one set of
problems, the sex and age composition of certain departments results
in others.[3] Those departments organized around substantive areas traditionally dominated by men offer little encouragement or opportunity
for friendship. As one re-entrant explained:

> The department has never been very open toward women. There are no women
> professors and there are often few women graduate students. The general feeling
> is that women don't have the intellectual equipment that is needed. The graduate
> school culture tends to be nil because the women are so few.

In contrast, departments with women professors, a number of women
students, or sometimes other returnees, are seen by women as providing
a homogeneous group of like individuals with whom friendship can be
established.

University policy of processing students according to undergraduate
and graduate cohorts also results in differing friendship opportunities for
re-entrants at each level. Graduate students typically meet regularly with
one another in small seminars and at departmental gatherings. Repeated
contact under conditions of mutual interest provide a beginning basis for
friendship. In addition, teaching and research obligations bring graduate
students into close contact with faculty. As students get closer to graduation, status differences tend to become less salient and friendship with
faculty becomes easier. Undergraduates do not have the same structural
support. They are generally in large classes where students have little
contact with one another. Personal interaction with faculty is generally
minimal. Social relationships typically are forged in after school activities
and between classes. Because they are not part of most youthful campus
activities, most re-entry undergraduate women find it very difficult to
break into traditional undergraduate circles. For the most part, their roles

as undergraduates also keep them at a distance from faculty. The problems involved in being an atypical student within a large impersonal bureaucracy makes it much more difficult for returning undergraduates than graduate women to develop regular contact with others on campus that lead to friendship.

Life Cycle Discontinuities

While university structure strongly influences friendship opportunities, life-cycle differences between students and the returnees create additional and often related barriers. One example is differences in living arrangements. Students at private universities generally are required to live on campus where the sequestering effect of dormitory living creates friendship networks and promotes in-group feelings (Schein, 1967). Dormitory residents often study together and room and board fees typically include group meal arrangements. The returning woman is not part of this campus world. Rather, her ties tend to be with the neighborhood and off-campus networks. One young mother summarizes the difference by saying of the younger students, "Their life is dormitory and classes; my life is suburbia, cooking dinner and seeing friends."

It is life-cycle differences rather than chronological age that re-entry women see as the greatest barrier to friendship with other students. That they have worked, married, and have dealt with many of life's problems leads these women to conclude that they have a better understanding of life than those who are younger:

> I tend to view them as being generally ignorant of life. I feel they have been sheltered by the university and have little understanding of the way life is outside of the classroom and the academic experience. I feel I know things that they don't know about life in general.

In addition, re-entry women typically have reached a point in the life-cycle where they have accumulated more material possessions and may have greater discretionary incomes than the younger student:

> I always feel I don't want the other students to see my house or the way I live or to be aware of how able I am to pay for this . . . I also remember a group of us taking a professor out to lunch after a seminar . . . It was quite apparent that they weren't used to eating out or spending much for dinner. Going to McDonald's for them was a big treat.

Life-cycle differences are also reflected in a lack of common history. Memories of shared triumph or of difficult times often serve as a basis for friendship between individuals. People also have a sense of their own position as a cohort within the unfolding of history (Strauss, 1969). These historical bonds can become so dear that generations tend to treasure their memories and resent those who intrude upon them (Mannheim, 1952). This pattern holds for the returning woman who discovers that today's students do not remember or perhaps have never experienced many of the events or happenings that are important to them:

> One freshman didn't even remember Kennedy and that was a big part of our lives. They didn't remember the picture from Kent State. We studied it in class. Half the class didn't recognize it, the other thought they knew what it was.

Another respondent spoke of these generational differences as creating a Rip Van Winkle effect. She explained that, "Being in a classroom with younger students is like waking up in another point in time."

Given the limited opportunity structure that exists for older women to make friends within the university, what does become the basis of friendship for the re-entry student? Obviously, one factor that must be considered is proximity (Simmel, 1955). Friendship can be maintained and even initiated through such conventions as letters and telephone calls, but some form of first contact is necessary. Yet physical contact alone is not enough to provide the sense of mutual commitment and shared experience that people associate with friendship (Weinberg, 1970). Within the context of friendship, then, proximity refers to a similarity of circumstance rather than a physical dimension. For the re-entry woman, course work and other duties required in meeting student role obligations provide an initial framework for interaction and a universe of discourse that can lead to other shared interests and possibly friendship.

THE BASIS OF FRIENDSHIP FORMATION ON CAMPUS

Like all students, re-entry women must study, complete homework projects, and pass various academic hurdles to stay in school. Class assignments and studying for exams provide a reason for returning women to get together with other students in work-related activities. In working together on shared projects and toward similar goals, work ties become established:

> When we worked on projects, I'd have the kids over to the house. I made a big spaghetti dinner when we worked on one project. It was fun, you were just one of them.

Bonds of camaraderie develop:

> It's sitting next to them and cramming for exams too, and when you say, 'Oh brother, is that professor a lemon,' you're experiencing what they are experiencing. That's a gap-closer more than anything.

And empathic ties emerge:

> I have far more sympathy now for college students who never work and go home in the summer and do nothing but sit at swimming pools. I applaud them and encourage parents to support them.

While these bonds encourage the formation of peer groups and perform a supportive role in helping students through their programs (Becker, *et al.*, 1961), purposive ties tend to create comrades of convenience rather than mutual friends. As Kurth (1970) observes, people develop many friendly relations in the course of meeting regular role obligations. These relationships make it easier and more pleasant for individuals to go about their daily lives. Yet friendly relations are not the same as friendships. These latter relationships are based upon shared intimacy and voluntary choice rather than forced circumstances and polite interaction. To understand friendship formation for re-entry women, we must look to additional factors besides those of work roles that encourage intimacy. We consider four: status identification, interpretive commonalities, reciprocal exchanges and personal circumstance.

Status Identification

In general, status positions based upon characteristics such as age, marital status and race, not only structure the social roles individuals enact but also strongly influence friendship choices (Mehrabian and Ksionzky, 1974). From earliest childhood, individuals are socialized to draw their friendships from a pool of like individuals. Within society, certain mechanisms exist to increase the likelihood that people of similar circumstances will be drawn together. One traditional function of universities has been to ensure that young people meet others of comparable background and family traditions (Waller, 1937). Once students enroll in college, fraternal organizations, religious foundations, and special minority programs provide students with access to readymade networks and friendship opportunities based upon religion, ethnicity and other status membership. Even though they are atypical students, re-entry women identify with organizations and groups composed of individuals with whom they share a similar status:

> I see a lot of my friends through school-connected activities. I'm connected with the Program on African Studies, that crowd is sort of my crowd.

Yet clubs and special studies organizations generally are limited in their friendship offerings for the older woman student. Informants explain that although these groups provide them with someone to "pal around with" between classes, age differences and family circumstance make it difficult to form friendships that carry over into other contexts. For this reason age, although a status not formally recognized by an organized group, becomes a natural basis for friendship when re-entry women encounter one another:

> When I heard about another woman who had returned, I especially sought her out to ask questions about what she was doing. I wanted to talk to someone who was going through the problems of learning to cut out family noise in order to be able to sit down and think.

Graduate departments in substantive areas that traditionally draw women students often have several returnees as recruits. These re-entry women create their own networks which provide one another with mutual encouragement and support.[4] One respondent recalled:

> I was in a fortunate situation in that there were a couple of re-entry women in my program and it was a real sense of community. It was loose but it was helpful.

In one instance, an association spanned several departments to form a larger network with a rudimentary ranking system based upon tenure as a student. A woman who had entered the university at a time when admission policies were less favorable to older students, served as a link between departments. She also acted as informal adviser to those re-entry women who needed counseling and other information. There was some suspicion among the returnees, however, that the woman exaggerated her accounts of her experience as a re-entry pioneer in order to solidify her position in the group. Nevertheless, returnees who entered the university under more open admissions policies looked up to such trailblazers wherever they appeared on campus and credited them with reducing the age bias toward older women.

Interpretive Commonalities

Although sharing a common status can bring people together, status commonalities do not automatically lead to friendship between individuals or even promote feelings of rapport. People of the same religion or social background, for example, do not necessarily feel a loyalty to one another and may attend to different characteristics when selecting a friend. Friendship, therefore, is influenced by an interpretive process in which people sort out aspects of themselves and others and assess their potential in providing a basis for friendship. Elements of this judicial process can be seen in the re-entry woman's interpretation of how various statuses enhance or inhibit friendship formation. The reports of re-entry women suggest that the difficulties surrounding a status like divorce, which can make it difficult for individuals to maintain close friendships, are subject to interpretation. For some re-entry women, divorce is seen as a barrier that separates the divorced woman from other students on campus:

> There are few people I can talk to about the divorce and my life circumstances. Most of those I have rapport with are so much younger, they have no idea what it is like to rear children, to leave a man after living with him for 17 years, or any of the problems I have.

Yet another divorced woman remarked that divorce created a circumstance that made it easier for her to make friends with younger women on campus:

> We gossip like teenage girls must. As a matter of fact, we are going through many of the same things . . . I'm getting used to seeing men on an adult basis, just as they are. Men problems are the same, whatever age you are.

Other status characteristics are subject to similar conflicting interpretations. For example, some informants reported that marriage enhances the ability to relate to young men on campus because the dating games that occur between singles do not enter into these relationships. But, other women felt male students to be disinterested in friendship once they find out the re-entry woman is married and unavailable for romantic involvement. These conflicting interpretations of status opportunities suggest that characteristics such as age, marital status, parenthood, and social class are not in themselves barriers or facilitators to friendship formation for re-entry students. Rather, definitions of their importance within the context of friendship may be critical.[5]

Personal Characteristics

An ability to make friends is a basic skill some returning women appear to possess. Among the returnees, past experience in forming friendships enhances the likelihood that a woman will become friends with someone on campus. Those women who have traveled extensively or moved from one neighborhood to another already have practice in integrating themselves into their surroundings. Wives of military men or corporate managers, for example, are likely to adjust easily to the college community because of a previous familiarity with moving into a new social world.[6]

Having just moved to the community can also prove advantageous. Without previous ties to the community, re-entry women tend to rely on the university to provide friendship. At the same time, women who have just joined the community don't have the problems of other re-entrants in forming new friendships while maintaining older relationships now outgrown. Need, therefore, can become a strong factor in the formation of friendship.

Reciprocity and Exchange

Friendship also includes components of self-interest and felt obligations (Daniels, 1979). In contrast to "fair weather friends" who shirk their responsibility, true friends help one another in times of adversity and are expected to be there when needed. On a daily basis, "norms or reciprocity" bind individuals together and create expectations of future involvement (Gouldner, 1960). Friendship can be seen as a symbiotic relationship based upon mutual gratification and dependency. Among re-entry women, the reciprocal aspects of friendship can be seen in the exchange of special services that occur between themselves and others on campus.

One important service people typically provide in friendship is validation (Chambliss, 1965). People tend to choose as friends those individuals who agree with their opinions and uphold their values. One re-entrant commented in this regard:

> I couldn't figure out for a while what the younger people saw in me as a friend. I knew what I saw in them. My daughter pointed out it's because you agree with so many of their opinions and attitudes . . . By agreeing with them, you validate their opinions.

Returning women often find themselves serving as validators for faculty members and teaching assistants as well as other students. A professor, for example, in discussing a presidential election in which most of the class were too young to vote, may turn to a re-entry woman to verify what was said concerning the issues. These types of exchanges form a basis for friendly relations that can become a first step toward friendship outside of class.

Other exchange forms develop as well. Re-entry women often play mother or sister to lonely students, drive classmates about, or act as a bridge to other relationships.

> I am a party person and I like to give parties. I often have parties and invite faculty to them. Some of the students who are shy about meeting the faculty come and I'm able to introduce them and get them started in conversation. In this way I have been able to help students who are academically bright but socially inept and unable to get to know people.

A drawback to these transactions is that they have certain costs. In this woman's case, her performance as expert and adviser made it difficult for her to discuss her own problems with student colleagues. Consequently, she was cut off from a valuable source of advice on student matters. Nevertheless, special services are generally useful in helping women to "learn the ropes" of being a student and are an important aid in meeting school obligations. These reciprocal services are summed up by one woman who says of a young student, "She showed me the library and in exchange, I listened to her problems."

The Unaffiliated

Not all re-entry students, of course, make friends or become part of the social world on campus. Some individuals have selves so strongly attached to alter statuses that these "sticky identities" (see Stone, 1966) prevent them from entering into new social relationships. Among returning women, these are individuals who typically define themselves as mothers or workers who happen to be taking courses. In their own words, they are not "really" students. They arrive promptly at the beginning of class, then leave quickly at the end. They report little interest in knowing other students or becoming part of the campus world. It is typical for them to say:

> I like going my way anonymously. There were people that you see from class to class and I would talk to them but I didn't feel the need to be part of them. I had a life outside of the university.

As students, these women limit their role performance to meeting work requirements but seldom get together with other students to talk after class or to study. While these women reap none of the benefits of mutual sharing, they also pay none of the cost of investing in a friendship. Women who have been lifelong loners tend to continue this pattern by not seeking out friends on campus. Because they are used to doing things without the support of a companion, a lack of friends is not seen as being problematic. Perhaps as Lowenthal (1965) suggests, it may be less personally disruptive to go through life situations without friends than to attempt friendship and fail.

Other re-entry women are prevented by heavy work or home responsibilities from joining into campus activities or seeking out friends. These women are unable to rearrange their lives to include the personal investment required to be sociable or to meet the demands of friendship. For women who want to be part of campus relationships, their frustration at being denied aspects of the student life can result in feelings of anger and regret:

Sometimes I yearned to have the freedom the younger students have. I used to
fantasize that I didn't have kids or a husband. I'd be free to study in the library
when I needed to. I'd be free to do all the things I saw others doing.

In sum, getting into a friendship requires social proximity and a basis
of commonality, but staying in a friendship requires an investment of
time and other resources. The willingness of re-entry women to meet
this commitment varies. One critical problem is that the management of
friendly relations and friendship on campus often cuts into other relationships that exist outside the university. In the next section, we examine the impact of school and campus based affiliations on roles, friendships, and network affiliations lodged in noncampus worlds.

INTERSECTION OF SOCIAL WORLDS

Because of their traditional role as wife and mother, women's opportunity
for friendship throughout history has been primarily confined to kinship
and locality rather than the larger social territories open to men (Simmel,
1965). Prior to returning to school, those re-entry women who did not
work outside of the home had little opportunity to expand their friendships beyond neighborhood, family networks and volunteer groups. En-
capsulation within the homemaking role not only restricted their pool
of possible friends but also resulted in a homogeneity of friendship circles.
Friendship behavior consisted of neighborhood exchange in services
(e.g., babysitting, borrowing), service on community committees, kaf-
feeklatsches, and the like. Children were often instrumental in bringing
families together and women formed friendships based upon shared child-
care responsibilities (see Lopata, 1971). When the re-entry women returned to school, the opportunity for friendship based upon personal
interest rather than circumstance expanded. The result is a lessening of
former friendship ties and greater feelings of personal freedom:

Before I came back to school, I had the feeling any friendships I had should involve
my husband. Now I feel my friendships are my own and if they like each other
fine, if not, then that's not important. So I've broadened out on different levels.

New friends and a new social world also provided the re-entry woman
with the opportunity to construct new identities. One informant remarked
that for her this process involved "peeling off layers of socialization"
that had prevented her from being the person she wanted to be. She
expressed her new self in more up-to-date hair styles and casual clothes.
Being around younger people also gave women the opportunity to engage
in what Guemple (1969) refers to as "renewal activities" or the privilege

of a younger cohort. This opportunity was satisfying to those women who had married young and felt deprived of the fun they perceived younger students were having.

Freedom from former identities and relationships is not without limits, however. Some friendships and roles have to be maintained despite personal inclination. Many re-entry women, for example, are engaged in two-person careers (Papanek, 1973) that require them to assist their husband's work as helpmate and hostess. In these marriages, business contacts have to be nurtured and entertaining is an important service that wives provide. The wife of a corporate vice president remarked:

> I get criticized all the time. I'm not doing the job for my husband I'm supposed to do. I'm supposed to help the junior wives but I just don't have the time any more.

Other women are pressured by similar obligations. These demands upon their time require women to develop indicators that cue them about critical and important social obligations that must be met. For example, one respondent explained: "When my husband says it's important to him, I go. Whenever he says that, I go no matter what." Typically, informal negotiations take place and symbolic personal contracts are drawn up to regulate these social demands. Another informant explained: "My husband and I agreed that I wouldn't drag him to my social functions if he didn't make me go to his business functions." Re-entry women commonly promise to make it up to their husband for a truncated social life if they will be patient until graduation.

Besides creating conflict over social life, tension also occurs when the women's schooling challenges the social order of the neighborhood or conflicts with the values held by their friends. Although friends and neighbors appear to feel it is all right for women to be in school, the re-entry woman is not supposed to take her schooling too seriously. When the returnees are perceived by friends as working too hard or when they earn a higher degree or show the potential of earning a better salary than their husbands, the re-entry woman's education falls outside the structure of a conventional relationship where husbands hold superordinate status (see Stiehm, 1976). This contradiction in traditional gender appropriate behavior calls down considerable attention, curiosity, and even ridicule upon the re-entry woman and her mate. One graduate student whose husband's education ended with a bachelor's degree remarks:

> It only became an issue in our lives because other people made it an issue. My husband doesn't have a Ph.D. so there was all this business about is it Dr. and Mr. so and so? . . . A woman with a degree that is higher than her husband's is seen as castrating him.

From this perspective, the price of education for the re-entry student can be quite steep.

Similarly, women from working class backgrounds discover that relatives and friends often have little understanding of what they are attempting and are at times suspicious that the re-entrants are using school to shirk adult responsibility:

> They can't understand why it's taking so long to get a Ph.D. They think that a bachelor's degree is enough to do what a typical poor family thinks one should do. You can buy a better home. You can have a car. They think that's enough.

Like Hoggart's (1957) scholarship boy who must leave his lower-class ties behind when education propels him into a higher class, the socially mobile re-entry student has conflicting loyalties. Although each spoke of wanting to retain their old friends, newly acquired values and the desire to enter a higher social class or to have a professional career created a widening gap between the women and their former friends.

Marginality for the re-entry woman goes beyond class boundaries. Women commonly find that the transformation in identity that accompanies their education places them between competing social worlds. Unable completely to join the world of the traditional student and no longer completely comfortable in former friendship circles, re-entry women tend to be caught between both:

> I really don't fit in with the students. I don't fit in any more as a PTA mother. I don't know many people in the neighborhood. I'm sort of an odd ball. I feel like an odd ball.

These feelings of marginality are in part produced by two factors—the esoteric nature of college work that makes it difficult for the woman to share her schooling with people outside the university and time pressure that prevents her from seeking out nonuniversity friends.

The Friendship Problematics of Dual Worlds

Re-entry women report over and over again that since they have come back to school they hardly see their old friends and cronies. Although these relationships have been important to them in the past, re-entry women often find that they no longer have much in common with those they know off-campus. With newly acquired knowledge of Renaissance history or the intricacies of advanced calculus, the student's universe of discourse has shifted. Re-entry women find it easier and often more satisfying to be around university people who share a common knowledge and similar concerns than to re-enter the social worlds of neighbors and friends whose lives center on different things. When women try to integrate their home and school network of friends, the result can be quite unsatisfactory. An informant explains:

> If I have a party, the two worlds have so little in common that it would be two groups at opposite ends of the room. Also there is the language barrier. In the French department, it's understood that at parties one only speaks French. None of my friends in town speak it. They are from the business world and not interested. On the other hand, friends I know in the department are not interested in the business world.

Women typically resolve the problem by keeping the two spheres separate. It is often easier for re-entry women to move between networks than to try to integrate the two.

Bringing home a school chum can present similar difficulties to those involved in bringing two worlds together. Among middle-class couples, husbands typically initiate and determine who the best friend of the couple will be (Babchuk and Bates, 1963). While the re-entry woman may develop a special camaraderie with a young student she has met in English, her husband does not have the benefit of a shared role. Without a basis of common experience, the 50-year-old businessman may find it quite uncomfortable to try to form a peer relationship with a young man of nineteen. When conversation turns to school happenings and other topics relevant to campus, the re-entry woman's spouse may become even more of an outsider. Value conflict can exacerbate the problem when the re-entry woman's role as a student gives her a perspective not shared by her husband:

> I was never around people who smoked pot before. And I found that I have now changed my feelings about that. I'd be surprised if my own kids didn't experiment with it. It would seem as if it were strange since I know it is something that all kids do. This is something my husband and I are in disagreement about. He can't understand how I could condone it and with what I know, I can't understand how he could object.

Nevertheless, finding something in common can provide the husband and school friend with a basis for interaction that may eventually lead to the discovery of other commonalities and perhaps friendship. "My husband likes to drink beer," one respondent remarked, "so he gets along fine at parties and with my friends."

Couple relationships can also be difficult for the re-entry woman to forge. Ideally, the husband should like the friend his wife has made and also the friend's spouse or date as well. Each of the participants requires a similar permutation. When there are complications such as age differences and opposing values, couple friendships become even more complicated and are likely to bog down. One respondent remarks:

> I think to have a social life with a couple that's 20 to 25 years younger is difficult. Their problems are different problems. They have problems getting a babysitter, not a problem for me. Also, we live in different worlds.

But as with the dyadic relationship, finding something in common between couples results in friendship bonds. An informant explains:

> There is one woman in the department in graduate school who is my age. She also has a condominium and has money and is on the level of sophistication that my husband and I enjoy, so we do a lot with her and her husband.

In sum, the experiences of the re-entry woman suggests that mutual interest and common concerns are a necessary ingredient for integrating friendships across multiple worlds. Yet returning women, for the most part, choose to move back and forth between school and neighborhood relationships rather than try to merge the two together. Although changing interests and network disjunctures are a critical component in this, so are the time pressures involved in managing numerous friendships.

Time Pressures

Every social setting has its own rhythm, pace and schedule of activities that place a constraint upon individuals who enter their boundaries (Gerson, 1976). Membership in multiple settings and social worlds may result in conflict when the demands of one setting infringe upon the obligations of another (Strauss, 1969). In this regard, re-entry women find it difficult to meet the daily assignments required in going to school and still maintain their home or work responsibilities. School and work obligations also leave them with little time to see off-campus acquaintances. Preferring to invest their energy in school, the women relinquished many of their former relationships and social activities. One respondent who gave up a coveted position in a woman's civic group remarks:

> If I could have done both, I would have but the provisional year in the _____ is really busy. And I couldn't do that and balance a family and go to school at the same time.

School also changes the kinds of contacts that occur between re-entry women and their friends. Spontaneity is considerably reduced and get-togethers typically become planned events organized around school timetables. Location of contact shifts as well. Re-entry women find it easier to entertain in a restaurant or go to a movie than have people to their home for dinner. Vacations become important catch-up times. Re-entry women mend fences by inviting people over for dinner and plan special events as an attempt to make up for their neglect.

Time pressures and the need to restructure their lives leads re-entry women to define friendship in terms of others' tolerance for their own behavior. One re-entry woman explained:

> Real friends are those who understand if you call and say, 'I can't go to the library.' Real friends also put up with infrequent telephone calls and broken luncheon engagements.

Or as another respondent said:

> Good friends understand the problem and will accept it . . . it's sort of a mutual thing in that this is the way it is for me and I understand that this is the way it is for them.

It is this understanding that the re-entry woman feels is the greatest barrier separating her from her neighbors and non-school friends. Unless you're in it, women explain, "you just can't really know what it's like."

The woman at home engaged in the traditional woman's role is perceived as being the least capable of understanding and also the most likely to display resentment. One respondent reported about a former friend:

> When I started going to school and tried to balance everything, our friendship just went by the way. I was conscious of not meeting her needs. She pouted and bitched at me about that. It got to the point where I just couldn't take it any more. She seemed jealous and competitive.

Women interpreted some of this resentment to the changing attitudes surrounding women's roles and the ambiguity they perceived that women feel over the part society expects them to play. "Women," according to one respondent, "are beginning to feel they should be doing something and those who are not feel uncomfortable when they are around those who do." Another informant remarked:

> It's the little women, the ones who trot alongside their husbands who are the main criticizers. Sometimes they'll say things to me like, 'Oh, we saw your husband at the party last night and he was all alone.' 'What do you think of Sandra, she's always working.' Then they [the wives] wait for the barrage of insults.

Respondents who were satisfied with their choice were tempted to proselytize women who were still homemakers and this coaching could add to the tension:

I tried to push her along the same direction but I think that it really plagued her that I had decided to step out a bit. I had to say to her, 'I'm going to do it, I'm going to make the difference. Are you going to too or are you going to live your same old way the rest of your life?'

Other women were more sensitive, however:

There's such a difference in their lives and what I am trying to do and I try not to let them know how busy I am or to make them feel inadequate or that I might feel that they're boring. But I find that the ladies in the suburbs lives are so very different from mine.

Nonetheless, the women's accounts suggest that traditional home-makers are not without a defense against such challenges. One neighbor, listening to a respondent talk at some length about what she was studying in class, finally silenced her by remarking that "since you've returned to school, you have become the most boring person I know." Such interchanges between returnee and friends suggest why another respondent explained, "You learn to hide what you are doing from those you know outside the university."

Of course not all friends and neighbors are negative or resentful of what the re-entry woman is doing. Informants report that they have friends who are also encouraging. Often support is drawn from women who are themselves waiting for children to get older or changed family circumstance to return to school or enter the work force. Similarly, friends who work or are in school are likely to show strong approval. Again, it is feelings of common concern and identity that transcend status and circumstantial differences between neighborhood and re-entry women and which helps to bind them together despite membership in other worlds of interest.

SUMMARY AND CONCLUSIONS

The experience of re-entry women raises an important question. Can individuals move in different social worlds and manage personal change without serious disruption either to the worlds or to the social self? The data on re-entry women suggest that major transformations of identity or role change create circumstances in which the loss of valued rela-tionships appears likely. Successful and continued performance within new roles and settings requires individuals to turn themselves into the kind of person the situation demands (Becker, 1964). Despite personal inclination, the investments entailed in assuming a new role and the change of perspective that accompanies this process, forces the returning student to choose between friendship embedded in the past and those that represent the present and possibly the future. Certainly there are aspects of self-interest involved in maintaining or rejecting friendships as people undergo change. Daniels (1979) observes that as long as a friendship circle offers advantages, it is comfortable to see people within it as genuine and likeable. But once circumstances change and common understanding and interests no longer cement us together, these same people lose some of their charm and glitter. Thus, it becomes easier to move into more rewarding relationships than to hold on to the old.

Among re-entry women, those friendships that are retained tend to be ones where the other party can understand and accept a relationship based upon limited time and personal resources. This understanding is most likely to occur when the friend is also experiencing a role change in returning to work or school. Perhaps as Foote (1963) suggests, friendships flourish and die as interests wax and wane; a constant stream of common interests is what keeps friendships stable.

Besides pointing to problems involved in maintaining relationships in the face of change, the re-entry data also remind us that friendships do not always transfer well from one situation to another. As Mead (1934) observes, settings call out different selves. When people build their expectations on one form of self-presentation, difficulties can arise in other settings when other selves emerge. One re-entry woman tells a poignant story of a friendship that developed between herself and a younger student on an archeology dig. After the field course was over, the student came to visit her at her home. When the young student saw the re-entry woman without her digging hat and old jeans, she was dismayed at the change in her appearance. Later when the two went to the grocery store, the younger student followed the re-entry woman about—much as she used to follow her mother when she lived at home. Although both women wanted to retain their friendship, they found these new aspects of the relationship disconcerting. It was the selves lodged in another setting that were close, not the ones situated in their present circumstance.[7] Thus, we see the power of situations to transform and change personal relationships as well as their role in creating or withholding a foundation for further interaction.

As more women enter the work force or return to school to finish their education, this change can be expected to have a strong impact on the friendship of those around them. The experience of re-entry women suggest that commitment to community service and the social relationships of the neighborhood decrease as women find new interests. For the women left behind in traditional roles, there are increasingly fewer women available to them as friends and their opportunities to find someone they want to spend time with diminishes. The custom of the neighborhood centered kaffeeklatsch may even be disappearing from the

American scene. Children can also be expected to feel the change. Re-entry women who once had been active in school and community organizations stopped baking cookies or participating actively in groups such as the PTA. Because men's ties to the neighborhood typically are expressed through their wives (Useem, *et al.*, 1960), men too may be facing diminishing neighborhood involvement. Finally, the women themselves may be losing many of the benefits of community and family social ties. Re-entry women discover they can't ignore neighbors' overtures for friendship and then draw upon these women as a resource for last minute babysitting or other neighborly services. Thus, women's return to school or work can provide a new world of friendships and affiliates but often at the cost of valued relationships and useful friendly relations.

ACKNOWLEDGMENTS

This paper is drawn from a study of re-entry women sponsored by the Program on Women at Northwestern University and funded by the National Institute of Education (NIE–G–79–0003). I would like to thank Arlene Kaplan Daniels, principal investigator, for her direction and help as well as Helena Lopata and David Maines for their comments on an earlier draft of this paper. Esther Benjamin deserves special thanks for her suggestions and assistance in collecting and thinking through the data.

NOTES

1. "Rate busters" are a problem in any labor situation where there are group norms governing the pace and output of work. For an excellent account of this phenomenon see Roy (1953), "Work Satisfaction and Social Reward in Quota Achievement: An Analysis of Piecework Incentive."

2. "Passing" is recognizable as a tactic commonly used by many marginal groups of individuals. Langston Hughes' (1970), "Who's Passing for Who?" is a classic tale of mistaken or incorrect identity placement. Strauss (1958) points out that all individuals occasionally find themselves in circumstances where they are unwittingly forced to pass because they have been taken for someone or something they are not. Re-entry women, therefore, are not alone in adopting this behavior.

3. See Stone (1970) who regards age and sex as a "universe of discourse" which bounds many of our possible relations.

4. Spady (1970) suggests that less conventional students typically have a narrower range of peers than their more traditional counterparts. Integration into the university, however, is more dependent upon finding a compatible subgroup of individuals than conforming to dominant values and interests (Tinto, 1975).

5. Blau (1961) suggests that the structural context for friendship strongly influences how a particular status affects an individual's position within a group. She found that widowhood is only a deviant status for widows when everyone else they know is married. In the later stages of the life cycle, widowhood may become the more normative status in female social groups. In the case of re-entry women, respondents reported feeling far less deviant if there were other re-entry women in the classroom alongside of them.

6. Many studies suggest that wives of corporate executives, diplomats and military personnel suffer feelings of displacement and loneliness when forced to move to new

communities as the result of their husband's work (see Maines, 1978:255). Yet the wives that were interviewed in this study appeared to have adjusted quickly and with little personal disruption. It may be that universities draw those wives who are active in finding new social worlds for themselves.

7. Maines (1978) observes that bodies often migrate at a different pace from personal identity. Individuals may move to a new location but their identities as expressed in thoughts and sentiment remain behind. Similarly, people can project their identities into the future through daydreams and discussions of anticipated happenings yet their bodies are lodged in the present. These two re-entry women shared identities from the past but a physical proximity in the present.

REFERENCES

Babchuk, Nicholas, and Alan P. Bates
  1963   "The primary relations of middle class couples: a study of male dominance." American Sociological Review 3:377–84.
Becker, Howard S.
  1964   "Personal change in adult life." Sociometry 27:40–53.
  1976   "Art worlds and social types." American Behavioral Scientist 19:703–719.
Becker, Howard S., Blanche Geer, and Everett C. Hughes
  1968   Making the Grade. New York: Wiley and Sons.
Becker, Howard S., Blanche Geer, Everett C. Hughes, and Anslem L. Strauss
  1961   Boys in White: Student Culture in Medical School. Chicago, Ill.: University of Chicago Press.
Benedict, Ruth
  1938   "Continuities and discontinuities in cultural conditioning." Psychiatry 1:161–67.
Berk, Barnard
  1977   "Face-saving at the singles dance." Social Problems 24:530–544.
Blau, Zena Smith
  1961   "Constraints on friendship in old age." American Sociological Review 26:429–439.
Brandenburg, Judith B.
  1978   "The needs of women returning to school." Personnel and Guidance Journal 53:11–18.
Bucher, R., and Anselm Strauss
  1961   "Professions in process." American Journal of Sociology 66:324–34.
Burns, Tom
  1953   "Friends, enemies, and the polite fiction." American Sociological Review 18:654–662.
Chambliss, William J.
  1965   "The selection of friends." Social Forces 43:370–380.
Daniels, Arlene Kaplan
  1979   "Self-deception and self-discovery in fieldwork." Conference on Ethical Problems in Fieldwork, Coolfront Conference Center, Berkeley Springs, West Virginia.
Davis, Fred
  "Deviance disavowal: The management of strained interaction by the visibly handicapped." Social Problems 9:120–132.
Fisher, Claude
  1976   The Urban Experience. New York: Harcourt Brace Jovanovich.
Foote, Nelson N.
  1955   "Matching of husband and wife in phases of development." Pp. 15–21 in Marvin B. Sussman (ed.), Sourcebook in Marriage and the Family. Boston, Mass.: Houghton Mifflin Co.

Gerson, Elihu M.
1976   "On quality of life." American Sociological Review 41:793–806.
Gouldner, Alvin W.
1960   "The norm of reciprocity: a preliminary statement." American Sociological Review 25:161–78.
Gross, Edward, and Gregory P. Stone
1964   "Embarrassment and the analysis of role requirements." The American Journal of Sociology 70:1–15.
Guemple, D. L.
1969   "Human resource management: the dilemma of the aging Eskimo." Sociological Symposium 2:59–74.
Hoggart, Richard
1957   The Uses of Literacy. New York: Oxford University Press.
Hughes, Everett C.
1945   "Dilemmas and contradictions of status." American Journal of Sociology 50:353–359.
Hughes, Langston
1958   "Who's passing for who?" The Langston Hughes Reader. New York: George Braziller, Inc.
Kurth, Suzanne B.
1970   "Friendship and friendly relations." Pp. 136–170 in George J. McCall, Michael McCall, Norman K. Denzin, Gerald D. Suttles and Suzanne B. Kurth (eds.), Social Relationships. Chicago, Ill.: Aldine Publishing Co.
Levitin, Teresa E.
1975   "Deviants as active participants in the labeling process: The visibly handicapped." Social Problems 24:548–57.
Lofland, John
1971   Analyzing Social Settings. Belmont, Cal.: Wadsworth Publishing Co.
Lopata, Helena Z.
1971   Occupation: Housewife. New York: Oxford University Press.
Lowenthal, Marjorie Fiske
1964   "Social isolation and mental illness in old age." American Sociological Review: 54–70.
Maines, David R.
1978   "Bodies and selves: notes on a fundamental dilemma in demography." Pp. 241–265 in Norman K. Denzin (ed.) Studies in Symbolic Interaction, Vol. I. Greenwich, Ct.: JAI Press.
Mannheim, Karl
1952   "The problems of generations." Pp. 276–320 in Essays in the Sociology of Knowledge. New York: Oxford University Press.
Mead, George Herbert
1934   Mind, Self and Society. Chicago, Ill.: University of Chicago Press.
Mehrabian, Albert, and Sheldon Ksionzky
1974   A Theory of Attribution. Lexington, Ma.: D. C. Heath and Co.
Neugarten, Bernice L., Joan W. Moore, and John C. Lowe
1965   "Age norms, age constraints, and adult socialization." American Journal of Sociology 70:710-717.
Papanek, Hannah
1973   "Men, women and work: reflections on the two-person career." Pp. 90–110 in Joan Huber (ed.), Changing Women in a Changing Society. Chicago: The University of Chicago Press.

Riesman, David
1954 Individualism Reconsidered. New York: The Free Press.
Roy, Donald
1953 "Work satisfaction and social reward in quota achievement: an analysis of piecework incentive." American Sociological Review 18:507–514.
Schein, Edgar H.
1968 "Organizational socialization and the profession of management." Pp. 134–148 in Henry L. Tosi and W. Clay Hamner (eds.), Organizational Behavior and Management: A Contingency Approach. Chicago: St. Clair Press.
Schutz, Alfred
1944 "The stranger: an essay in social psychology." American Journal of Sociology 49:499–507.
Shibutani, Tamotsu
1955 "Reference groups as perspectives." American Journal of Sociology 60:562–568.
Simmel, George
1955 Conflict and the Web of Group Affiliations. Glencoe, Ill.: Free Press.
Spady, W.
1971 "Dropouts from higher education: an interdisciplinary review and synthesis." Interchange 1:64–85.
Stiehm, Judith
1976 "Invidious intimacy." Social Policy, March–April:12–16.
Stone, Gregory P.
1962 "Appearance and the self." Pp. 86–118 in Arnold M. Rose (ed.), Human Behavior and Social Processes. Boston, Mass.: Houghton–Mifflin.
1966 "Review of roles: an introduction to the study of social relations" by Michael Banton. American Sociological Review 31.
1970 "Sex and age as universes of appearance." Pp. 227–237 in Gregory P. Stone and Harvey A. Farberman (eds.), Social Psychology Through Symbolic Interaction. Waltham, Mass.: Xerox College Publication.
Strauss, Anslem L.
1969 Mirrors and Masks. San Francisco: The Sociology Press.
1978 "A social world perspective." Studies in Symbolic Interaction 1:119–128.
Suttles, Gerald D.
1970 "Friendships as a Social Institution." Pp. 95–135 in George J. McCall, Michael McCall, Norman K. Denzin, Gerald D. Suttles, and Suzanne B. Kurth (eds.) Social Relationships. Chicago, Ill.: Aldine Publishing Co.
Tinto, Vincent
1975 "Dropout from higher education: a theoretical synthesis of recent research." Review of Educational Research 45:89–125.
Unruh, David R.
1979 "Influencing common sense interpretations of an urban setting: The freeway coffee shop." Symbolic Interaction 2:27–42.
Useem, Ruth Hill, John Useem, and Duane L. Gibson
1960 "The function of neighboring for the middle-class male." Human Organization 19:68–76.
Van Dusen, Roxann A., and Eleanor B. Sheldon
1976 "The changing status of American women." American Psychologist 31 (Feb.):106–116.
Waller, Willard
1937 "The rating and dating complex." American Sociological Review 2:727–734.

Weinberg, S. Kirston
  1970 "Primary group theory and closest friendship of the same sex: an empirical analysis." Pp. 301–319 in Tomotsu Shibutani (ed.) Human Nature and Collective Behavior. Englewood Cliffs, N.J.: Prentice-Hall.
Wiener, C.
  1980 The Politics of Alcoholism. New Brunswick, N.J.: Transaction.
Young, Anne M.
  1973 "Going back to school at 35." Monthly Labor Review (Oct.):39–42.

THE ORGANIZATIONAL AND CAREER CONTEXTS OF FRIENDSHIP AMONG POSTDOCTORAL STUDENTS

David R. Maines

INTRODUCTION

In the social psychology of George H. Mead (1934) and the interactionist tradition fostered by his thinking is found the contention that human conduct cannot be fully understood unless the social matrices in which that conduct takes place are first specified. That general position is central to this paper, with the more specific argument being that the meaning of friendship relations, perhaps to a greater extent than other categories of social relationships, are especially subject to contextual determination. Previous research lends support to the view of the situated meaning of friendship: Giallombardo's study (1966) of social roles in a women's

prison; Little's analysis (1964) of buddy relations among combat infantrymen; Liebow's investigation (1967) of street corner black men; and
Whyte's classic study (1955) of slum boys indicate a portion of that body
of literature. All contribute to the proposition that friendship and sociability relations take on shape and meaning in terms of the social contexts
in which they are formed and maintained, and that they must be viewed
in light of those contexts if they are to be properly understood.[1]

Analyzing friendship relations is a particularly troublesome topic of
study. For one thing, friendship is a generic category of social behavior
and contains within it a great number of sub-types. A number of sociologists recognize these varieties, as do people in the course of their
everyday lives, and accordingly take them into account in their research
and writing. Hiller (1947, pp. 107–110), for instance, distinguishes friendship and acquaintanceship from the standpoint of differential personal
identification, while Weinberg likewise deals with the varieties and degrees of friendship by restricting his empirical analysis to ". . . one type
of friendship, closest friendship . . ." (Weinberg, 1970, p. 301). John
Lofland (1969, p. 8), though not directly investigating friendship relations,
also makes these necessary distinctions in a more substantive vein by
noting that acquaintanceships are perhaps safer for us insofar as strangers
and intimates, who represent the practical boundaries of friendship, are
most likely to do us personal harm. Suzanne Kurth (1970), though, provides us with a very useful distinction by differentiating "friendship"
from "friendly relations." Kurth convincingly argues that it is the friendly
relationship which is the more prevalent in our society. As will be shown
later in this paper, it is the friendly relationship also which is found to
be the most possible among postdoctoral researchers. The point to be
made here, however, is that these varieties and sub-types slide into one
another and become transformed situationally and biographically, thus
making it difficult to specify the exact nature of the relationships under
investigation.

The second source of difficulty in analyzing friendship pertains to the
actual use of the terms "friend" or "friendship." These are terms which
can be invoked by a person to describe to himself and to others any
number of differing relationships with others. What is being referred to
here is the existential property of communicating to someone that another
is a friend, or the act of saying, in effect, "this person is my friend."
This other can be a neighbor with whom an across-the-fence relationship
exists, a school chum, a political ally, a favorite teacher with whom one
would like to establish an interpersonal relationship, an instrumental
"contact," someone you've met only once in your life but would like
to see again, or any number of relationships. They all can and in fact
are referred to as "friendship" relationships.[2] In this sense, it is a catch-

all term which is conventionally understood and recognized as having no fixed relational referent outside of the situation itself. Given such built-in elasticity, it becomes even more clear that an understanding of how the term is being used at the time depends upon the context of its use, and it becomes imperative that the study of friendship relationships systematically take the social context into account. However, I should like to interject a word of caution. There is also the general understanding that there are such things as "true friends." This notion seems to be at odds with the suggestion that friendship is inherently elastic. We need only to think for a moment about this notion of true friend, though, to realize that it also is made meaningful on a situational basis. We usually regard others as true friends when they come to our aid in a crisis situation. Such crisis situations can vary tremendously, ranging from community disasters, to conditions of financial need, to such everyday circumstances as needing a baby-sitter for an hour or two. The "you're a true friend" response acknowledges that another has been useful and has acted instrumentally on our behalf. But true friends can change dramatically and surprisingly fast as in those situations when we feel that the person's "true nature" has been finally revealed. Thus there is the common phrase, ". . . and I thought you were a true friend . . ." There is another meaning of true friend, however, and that meaning exists in a relationship with another we regard as a true friend, regardless of circumstance. This is the person who is a friend no matter what, and these relationships seem to be highly prized in our society because they seem to be so hard to come by. Important in this relationship is what Harry Stack Sullivan calls "person building"—literally the interpersonal creation of the other. Concretely, what goes on is a dynamic process of discounting. When we build up special relationships with others we invest ourselves in those persons so that what happens to them in effect happens to us. They become cherished relationships and in preserving them we mutually discount information about the others which threatens them, or we define and regard that information in a way which is compatible with the relationship. Such true friendships, therefore, become private relationships with special meanings, and insofar as both friends continue to engage one another in this special way, the relationship can become transsituational. But that continuing engagement is essential for the joint meaning to remain stable. For our true friendship to persist, we must continue to interact (obviously, not necessarily in a face-to-face manner) and treat one another as friends. Without sustained activity, even the meaning of this type of true friendship can be lost. "He's still my best friend, but it's different from the way it used to be." Thus, the assertion regarding the elasticity of friendships remains viable. Even our true friendships can take on a wide variety of meanings and can be described in a number of ways. This view brings us back to the earlier contention in this paper that to understand the meaning of friendships, the contexts of those relationships must also be specified and understood.

In the following pages, I shall be discussing friendship relations and the contexts of those relationships among postdoctoral researchers.[3] I will restrict my analysis to the work lives of postdoctoral researchers and will proceed along the following lines. In pursuing the perspective of the contextual meaning of friendship relations, I first will present what can be taken as the circumstances of postdoctoral life. What are the typical social arrangements found in the work lives of postdoctorals? What structures their day-to-day lives? This discussion will establish a framework for an examination of postdoctoral friendship relations. The central question here is, given the conditions and constraints of post-doctoral life, what kinds of interpersonal relationships are possible? Can postdoctoral researchers be friends?

My discussion is based on information obtained during a two-year study of postdoctoral students in the physical and biological sciences at the University of Minnesota. The first year was spent in making obser-vations of postdoctoral work activities and settings primarily in the de-partments of physiology, biochemistry, physics and pharmacology, and in conducting in-depth interviews of forty-four postdoctoral students. The aggregate characteristics of the sample show that they are young (83 percent under age 32), male (91 percent), and American-educated (97 percent). These distributions conform closely to those found in the postdoctoral population at Minnesota as well as in the U.S. postdoctoral population. The second year of the study entailed a comparison of flexible and inflexible postdoctoral training programs from the standpoint of the impact of those types of programs on postdoctoral success. In this phase, fifteen complete career histories were obtained by re-interviewing the first year postdoctoral students from the previous year. Both distribu-tional and longitudinal data were generated by these multiple information gathering devices.

THE CIRCUMSTANCES OF POSTDOCTORAL LIFE

There are two categories of circumstances of the postdoctoral world which I shall propose as constituting the context for postdoctoral con-duct. The first, the social organizational circumstances, consists of the typical arrangements of roles and organizational positions which form the latticework in which postdoctoral students do their work, pursue their goals and careers, and establish identities and social relationships. The second, the social psychological circumstances, involves the indi-vidual postdoctoral student as he becomes a situated object to himself;

the meaning of others as they become implicated in the courses of action which he must carry out in his capacity as a postdoctoral researcher; and the meaning of the organizational career matrices as they serve to mobilize his personal career. Friendship relations among postdoctorals must be seen as existing at the intersection of these circumstances, bounded by the imperatives of work and career demands and by the process of expanding professional networks and interpersonal activity.

Social Organizational Circumstances. A structural circumstance of major importance is the fact that postdoctoral students are neither faculty members nor matriculating students. In a sense they are between careers, having already finished their career as a graduate student but not yet starting that of faculty member. Postdoctoral "neither-norness" should, therefore, be seen as a special case of career ambiguity, perhaps as a type of marginality that is created by the university. It is the ambiguity itself, however, that is significant here rather than the mere fact of "neither-norness." In contrast to the circumstances of faculty and graduate students, the university as a whole has little to do with postdoctoral education and little to offer the postdoctoral researcher.[4] There are no deans for postdoctorals, no formal or informal postdoctoral organizations, and no institutional forms of status passage signaling the completion of postdoctoral training. Moreover, they have uneven and limited access to university services such as parking space, health services, and insurance programs. They are members of that category of university personnel which Kerr (1964) has termed the "unfaculty." They are present, often in large numbers, but institutionally unnoticed and unaccounted for. As Mayntz puts it, "he is a temporary fixture at the host institution, but he is not a member of it" (Mayntz, 1960, p. 737).

Postdoctoral researchers can be thought of, then, as existing not only at a career stage structured by this "neither-norness," but also as being wedged between two subcultures. There is evidence, however, which suggests that it would be inappropriate to think of them as embedded in a postdoctoral culture. There is no postdoctoral culture in the usual sense of student subculture.[5] A minimal requisite for the development of a culture, for example, is the communication among persons who would constitute the culture. Little such communication or contact was found among the postdoctoral researchers studied. In response to the question, "Do you know other postdoctoral students in other departments?" seventy percent responded that they did not, and of those who did have such contact, half of them did so only for purposes of work. Consider some of the statements made by the postdoctorals themselves.

I haven't had a chance to get to know anyone else even if I wanted to. First of all, I have all I can handle right here and the work just seems to pile up, so it really gets to be a rat race. No, I don't know any of the others—don't have time.

No, not really. I met one once in the Pathology Department when my boss consulted on a project, but mostly I just come in in the morning and stay in the lab until it's time to go home at night. I don't get out much.

Obviously, social contact increases when considering only postdoctorals within the same department, but even here the identification with one another, a phenomenon characteristic of subcultures, is weak or missing.

I've only been associated with two postdocs since I've been here two years and we all had the same adviser. We used to talk about him and the way he ran the lab and the way he approached science and such things as that.

Q. Are there other postdocs in your department?
A. Yes there are. I know one for sure.
Q. Do you ever interact with him?
A. Very minimally. Only in the hallways but not socially. If there are some other postdocs here I don't know of them.
Q. Do you have any sort of "we" feeling with the other postdocs?
A. No, not at all. No bonds. If there is a common denominator with my interaction with other people it is age—same age. One of the young staff men here is the same age and we play hockey together and go to hockey games together. Things like that, but postdocs aren't really in it.

The mutual identification with one another, the social bonds, norms and standards particular to postdoctoral lives are thus lacking. From the standpoint of the person, there is no over-arching social mechanism outside of the work itself serving to bond one to another.

What is there then? How is meaning and social order possible among postdoctorals? The answer to this question requires an analysis of the settings in which postdoctoral work is carried out and the types of identities and role relationships found in those settings.

There are three settings in which the postdoctoral student can meaningfully place himself as a social object within the university. Perhaps the most conventional, but certainly the least important of the three, is the academic department. The limited importance of this setting lies only in that it is here that the basic pool of persons with whom the postdoctoral student will work and associate in his daily work life is found. This structure and bureaucratic function of the department, however, rarely enters into postdoctoral routines. The fundamental reason for this is that the postdoctoral is not a matriculating student; he does not register for classes, take examinations, receive grades, confer with graduate advisers, and the like. Thus, the administrative functions of the department do not apply to him and he finds himself out of timing with the rhythm of the department.

The two remaining settings, however, bear directly upon the social locating of postdoctoral students. The first is an organizational unit usually referred to as a "research group." This collectivity is a loosely organized cluster of faculty, postdoctoral students, graduate students, and technicians all working in a given specialty area in an academic discipline. The drug metabolism group in the Pharmacology Department and the nuclear physics group in the Physics Department are examples of such clusters. The mechanisms holding research groups together typically consist of common research interests, the borrowing of instruments and often of technicians, direct or indirect support from large research grants often totaling millions of dollars, informal discussions of one another's research, and group seminars. These bonding mechanisms serve to focus and coordinate the energies and activities of the participants, and while not all postdoctorals are in such groups (about half of my sample were so located) they function as a significant base of operation and as a significant organizational context for the lodging of postdoctoral selves.

The other postdoctoral setting is the laboratory. Whereas the research group refers to a "pure" organizational unit, the laboratory refers to both the organization of personnel and of space. Spatially it consists of the rooms, instruments, benches, desks, and storage areas in which the actual research is done. From the standpoint of the personnel, it can be seen as a sub-unit of the research group (there can be several laboratories in a given research group) or as an organizational unit in its own right. In either case, it is here that the postdoctoral finds his most sustained activity and his most persistent relationships. It is common, for instance, to refer to someone as "working in Dr. Jones' lab" or, when meeting someone for the first time to ask in whose laboratory he works. When postdoctorals are trying to decide where to take their postdoctoral training, they, in fact, often use as their criterion the research that is currently being conducted in a particular faculty member's laboratory.[6] This choice is a critical one, for it serves not only to commit the postdoctoral student to a substantive specialty area in which he will carry out his research, but it establishes the initial network of personnel with whom he will be more or less intimately associated in the course of that work. Thus, there is a fate-like quality in the selecting of a laboratory.

Having indicated these settings, we know where postdoctorals are most likely to find and establish socially meaningful relationships. The next task is to indicate whom they encounter in these settings, and briefly to describe the basis of the relationships which are established. These relationships will be described from the standpoint of the extent to which another enters routine postdoctoral life.

University and departmental administrators *as administrators* hardly ever enter postdoctoral worlds. When they do it is in a highly specific and routinized context such as the request for and issuing of a library card. Departmental secretaries, although being many times more visible, also come in contact with postdoctorals on a situational basis. A typical point of contact here would involve the secretary making flight reservations for transportation to professional meetings and then handling the post-travel reports usually required by the university. Postdoctoral relationships with people in these positions, therefore, tend to be highly instrumental and non-continuous or continuous, but highly ritualized.

Another category of persons could be included among those who touch only the edge of postdoctoral work lives. This category is composed of nonrelevant faculty, graduate students, and postdoctoral students—those who are in the department but are working in other specialty areas and in other laboratories. These individuals are rarely or never seen (or they may be seen but unnoticed) although they may be heard of. Of course, the composition of this category will vary depending upon the laboratory or research group in which the postdoctoral is working, but the point is that they are of little consequence to a given postdoctoral student.

Identities which are relevant bear a direct relationship to the main task of "postdocing"—research—and, bearing such a relationship, they become central participants in the postdoctoral world. In a roughly descending order of importance, they are postdoctoral advisers, technicians, relevant postdoctoral students and relevant graduate students.

All postdoctoral researchers have faculty advisers. The adviser is the faculty member with whom the postdoctoral works and his basic importance rests in the fact that it is his laboratory in which the postdoctoral conducts his work, it is the adviser's grant money which supports the research, and the fact that the adviser is the initial and primary link between the postdoctoral and the rest of the department. It is the adviser-postdoctoral student relationship that comprises the fundamental research unit in the postdoctoral world. Research problems and procedures are discussed, findings are evaluated, and research papers are co-authored in these units. They focus research activity and to a large extent define the quality and quantity of that activity. Advisers, however, do less of the actual experimentation than do the postdoctorals. With other professional obligations competing for their time, advisers tend to assume the role of an overseer. That is, they coordinate research efforts in the laboratory, especially when there are large numbers of graduate students and postdoctoral students involved. This feature of the adviser-postdoctoral student relationship is interesting insofar as postdoctorals often select laboratories in order to work with a particular faculty member, and this is especially true when the faculty member is nationally or internationally prominent. What actually happens, though, is less of a working relationship and more of a structural relationship. As expressed in the actualities of these relationships, then, a disjunctiveness is found between the career desires of the postdoctoral student and the circumstances of the laboratory.

While advisers play a crucial role in the postdoctoral's professional career, the centrality of technicians is based on their practical utility in the daily research routines. They perform those tasks which enable the postdoctoral researcher to carry out the primary experimental activities. Technicians thus perform "enabling roles." They make solutions, do preparatory surgery, set instruments in place, inject animals, order needed materials for research projects, kill research animals, and the like. They are universally regarded as indispensable. A nuclear physicist says, "If I can't get him to build a piece for me, I don't do the research. It's as simple as that." A physiologist remarked, "They really run the whole show." And when a technician in one of the Pharmacology laboratories quit before a replacement arrived, activities got bogged down to the extent that ". . . I haven't accomplished hardly anything . . . it's been so messy around here." Not only are technicians indispensable, they actually gain a considerable measure of control—a control based on their indispensability and their on-the-job familiarity with the range of tasks involved in the laboratory.

Advisers and technicians, then, constitute the two most significant persons for postdoctoral students from the standpoint of the degree to which they penetrate the very core of everyday work routines and career processes. But they perform very different functions. The adviser is primarily a coordinator, a discussant, a co-author and the provider of a "home" for the postdoctoral student, and this value lies more in the context of the scientific community. Technicians are helpers, the ones who do the dirty work of research, and their value to the career of the postdoctoral student lies in their accuracy and competence in carrying out the daily tasks of experimental research. The bulk of postdoctoral work and time involves one or both of these persons.

The basic relationships that postdoctorals have with other postdoctoral students and graduate students can be considered together although there are certain differences. Postdoctorals who get to know each other usually do so because they have some common research interest. The research group and the laboratory are important here insofar as they serve as the context for this acquaintance process. An illustration of this factor is provided by a nuclear physicist.

. . . there are other people, particularly people in theoretical physics that I interact with quite a lot because of my interest in theoretical physics although I'm really an experimentalist. I have an office in the nuclear physics lab down by the river that I share with the other postdocs and I see them quite a lot down there, although this is really by accident.

The extent of interaction with graduate students seems to depend upon the particular laboratory. In one of the large biochemistry laboratories and, generally, in nuclear physics, there are large numbers of graduate students, and part of the implicit postdoctoral responsibility is to oversee the graduate students. Relationships tend to be sociable in these situations, but they are basically functional in nature. In nuclear physics, for example, a given experiment goes on for twenty-four hours a day for three or four days, so they are thrown together because of the imperatives of work. In general, graduate students are viewed by postdoctoral researchers as "being in the way of my research." Graduate students engage in considerable laboratory work, but they are too committed to other tasks such as doctoral examinations and doctoral theses to be of any concerted, consistent help to the postdoctoral.

The situated importance of other postdoctoral and graduate students in the department, then, depends not so much upon the specialty area as it does upon the specific research project. Postdoctoral work is bound to the experiment and in this binding process, only those others who have something to contribute enter into the center of the postdoctoral world.

Social Psychological Circumstances. In focusing upon the elements which circumstance the *postdoctoral as a person,* I necessarily must employ a career perspective for two reasons. First, the conditions and elements change; and second, interpersonal relations must be seen as a process. Three social psychological elements will therefore be considered here: motives for engaging in postdoctoral training, the career of felt ambiguity, and the process of social constriction of time. Each of these elements bears a direct relationship to the process of friendship establishment and maintenance.

The responses given to the question "Why did you want a postdoctoral position?" reveal a great deal about the sentiments and anxieties of postdoctoral students as they find themselves at this particular career juncture. Sixty-four percent indicate that they felt they needed more research experience, 57 percent stated they needed time to conduct research and publish some papers, 39 percent felt that postdoctoral experience was expected in their discipline, 32 percent were responding to a tight job market in taking the postdoctoral position, 23 percent wished to avoid the nonresearch duties of the faculty position, and another 23 percent didn't yet feel ready to be a faculty member.[7] Strong commitments to the discipline, to science, and to research are implied in these responses and exist at the center of the careerist perspective held by postdoctorals. They are forward looking and concerned about their careers as scientists. Permeating this, however, is career anxiety, perhaps even a sense of desperation. Note the following:

When I was finishing the Ph.D. I wanted to find a permanent position where I could teach and do some research. But I couldn't find anything suitable and I began to realize really how provincial it was at West Virginia. So somewhere along the line someone mentioned a postdoc—so I looked into it and I ended up here. Since getting here, though, I'm really glad I did it. I'm sort of repenting now. You know, I really want to learn. Like the University of Minnesota will never hire me, so I think that I can really open up and learn.

Similarly,

For the first time in my whole graduate career, this is the time for me to learn. It's not for a grade—I've *got* to learn. So, I can't fake it. He's (the adviser) going to know if I'm stupid so I might as well let him know it and if he's going to kick me out then let him kick me out. But I want to learn it. I'm tired of not knowing things. I don't want to go through my life and when they say something, just shake my head and hope that they change the subject.

Institutionalized, conventionally accepted, and legitimized motivations which center around matters of career and competence, then, are often laced with more intimate and personal reasons having to do with self-regard and career anxiety. Together they provide a tremendous push to "make it."

The structural property of "neither-norness" was noted earlier in a consideration of the social organizational circumstances of postdoctoral life. Here I wish to consider the personal dimension of that circumstance. Do postdoctorals feel this "neither-norness?" Does it matter to them, and if so, how does it enter into their lives?

It first should be noted that the neither-nor circumstance is widely recognized. One faculty member I interviewed expressed it as, "postdocs are neither fish nor fowl" while another commented that "they are in no man's land."[8] Likewise, postdoctoral students themselves are aware of these circumstances. One commented, "I understand what you're talking about. You don't do what the graduate students do and you don't do what the faculty do." So the question arises, exactly how do postdoctoral students see themselves? The interview data indicate that 36 percent see themselves as being closer to graduate students, 28 percent see themselves as being closer to faculty status, and another 36 percent find it difficult to make a choice. It is this third category of responses which is interesting, for when comparing first and second year postdoctoral students, the percentage increases from 25 percent to 35 percent with over 60 percent of postdoctoral students with more than two years of experience falling into that category. The same pattern exists in the responses to questions regarding whether postdoctorals are treated more like graduate students or faculty members. Twenty-five percent of the first year students found it "hard to say" compared to 50 percent of

those with more than two years experience. The pattern, then, is that
the longer a person occupies a postdoctoral position, the more difficult
it becomes to specify his own sentiment toward himself regarding this
"neither-norness," as well as his perception of how he is acted toward
by others. Postdoctoral ambiguity, therefore, increases through time.
The following quotes illustrate postdoctoral sentiment toward their "neither-norness."

> . . . postdocs are a dime a dozen and are just here—they are just part of the
> machinery of the department.
>
> . . . postdocs are non-entities. They come and go without ever being missed. When
> I first came, Dr. T showed me around and introduced me to some of the faculty,
> but now when we see each other he doesn't even say 'hi' to me.
>
> It's actually a pretty ambiguous situation. I'm so close to being a faculty member,
> yet I'm not. I want to be friends with some of the faculty members, especially some
> of the younger ones. But the postdoc is such a temporary status . . . and the
> prolongation of temporary status is bad. Your salary is inconsistent with your ability.
>
> I didn't enjoy it the first few months—not at all. Trying to figure out where in the
> hell I stood because it was so unnerving not to have any of the staff benefits and
> not really exist in the eyes of the university. Even not to have my name in the
> directory. So far as the university is concerned, I don't exist. You know, I felt that
> I was without a country.

The neither-nor circumstance enters the selves of postdoctoral students
and is consciously felt. One consequence is that they must work at
establishing identities. In dramatic and pervasive terms, they must answer the question of who they are and how do they want others to regard
them. The "I am a postdoc" is insufficient because that designation itself
is one of ambiguity. Thus, postdoctoral students must manage their relationships with others. If, as they view it, their futures in science hinge
on their postdoctoral success, they cannot leave the determination of
their professional selves and identities up to chance.

One of the distinguishing features of the postdoctoral career is that
at its inception the postdoctoral student can envision or see its end. It
should be remembered that a pervasive reason for taking a postdoctoral
position is the establishment of more respectable professional credentials
through which a better academic appointment might be secured. Within
this personal framework, postdoctoral students are not only able to des-
ignate the terminal point of the postdoctoral career, but they are able
to look beyond it to the time when they are faculty members. Thus, the
two years usually involved in postdoctoral training, perhaps long chron-
ologically, become constricted from the standpoint of the person going
through the career. In addition to and involved in this socially constricted

perspective is a series of contingencies which must be effectively dealt with. These contingencies take the form of demands or requirements and serve to remind the person that his career as a postdoctoral student is indeed a short one.

The first contingency occurs within two or three months after the postdoctoral student arrives on campus. For administrative purposes, the adviser must know if the postdoctoral intends to stay for the next year. So, from the start, the postdoctoral researcher must commit himself and is forced into thinking in terms of a year ahead. Now, the anticipation of the "next year" is not an uncommon occurrence, especially for the ambitious person, but for the postdoctoral, it means the anticipation of the last year. During the latter months of the first year, many postdoctoral students and advisers begin considering potential job placements for the postdoctoral for the fall one year ahead. Thus, the temporal frame of reference is shifted to the end of the postdoctoral career. This further constriction of time becomes all the more dramatized and perhaps traumatizing by the necessity of having completed some research during the first ten months. If research papers are to be presented at annual spring professional meetings, it is necessary to have sufficient laboratory success within the first six months so that research papers can be written and submitted in time to meet winter deadlines. All of this is contingent upon several factors, including the establishment of a workable relationship with the adviser and having instruments working optimally. The ways in which these matters are worked out form the core of the postdoctoral's perspective regarding the significance of the end of the first year. This is the time when the adviser sends the postdoctoral's curriculum vitae to his colleagues at other universities. If publication reprints or abstracts of papers or forthcoming articles can be included, the employment potential of the postdoctoral student is enhanced. Of course, the process of the postdoctoral attempting to secure employment can extend for several months or even a full year. However, the point is that the necessity of being productive within a real, but importantly, perceived restricted time span exerts a great deal of pressure on the postdoctoral researcher. This pressure is felt and manifested in various ways including differential definitions of researchable ideas and problems, definitions of what constitutes publishable data, cutting corners in laboratory experiments, and moonlighting by conducting side and/or "quickie" experiments.

These contingencies and activities, therefore, force the postdoctoral researcher into feeling a sense of urgency. Unlike the prison inmate, the person going through the postdoctoral career perceives time, deadlines, work and interpersonal relationships in a constricted, pressurized perspective.

These last several pages dealing with the circumstances of the post-doctoral world can now be summarized into a profile of the essential and relevant elements of the context of friendship relations among postdoctoral researchers. Without the supporting and directing norms and standards of an active subculture, the postdoctoral student is socially left to fend for himself. He is largely restricted to those settings in which he must "prove" himself scientifically, and most of the relationships he eventually forms come from persons directly implicated in the activities of these settings. But he is subjected to a pervasive ambiguity regarding who he is and what is expected from him, which often is accentuated and transformed into a general anxiety which overlays an anxiety particular to the postdoctoral career stage. This element combines with career commitment, ambition, and the contingent imperatives of laboratory research to form a personal perspective in which daily research details are viewed as crucial to the progress of the scientific career. This, in turn, increases the tendency toward forming instrumental and pragmatic relationships.

FRIENDSHIP AND SOCIABILITY IN THE POSTDOCTORAL WORLD

What is of interest sociologically and the issue under examination in this paper, are the conditions under which postdoctoral students are friendly. As shown earlier, postdoctorals share a uniqueness derived from the particular combination of elements of work circumstances and the postdoctoral career stage. So, the specific issue is on how and the extent to which these elements impose boundaries on the frequency and meaning of friendship relationships. In reflecting upon this issue, attention will be given to the degree of interpersonal accessibility, forms of friendliness, and the function of friends in the postdoctoral world.

Ralph Waldo Emerson defines a friend as "a person with whom I may be sincere. Before him I may think aloud." This is a particularly sensitive conception of friendship because of what it implies about interpersonal relations among friends. By "thinking aloud" in one another's presence, they become accessible to one another, and they voluntarily create vulnerability. They lose their "front," and this loss makes easier the discounting of outside information which would threaten the relationship. The participants in the friendship can reject alternative interpretations of whom the other "is" and what he is like, because, by virtue of the accessibility, they are convinced that they know the truth about the other. Thinking aloud, therefore, provides not only private information, but also an ongoing indication that the friendship and personal accessibility continues to exist. Friendship is thus a process, at the heart of which lies the process of identity establishment and maintenance.

Such accessibility is not likely to occur among postdoctoral researchers. Postdoctoral training is recognized as a springboard to better and more prestigious jobs. To manage this springboard, these postdoctorals must establish themselves first and foremost as competent and serious scientists. Because of the "neither-nor" circumstance, they are forced to establish these identities in the everyday process of research and scholarship. Thus, they must construct and maintain a "scientific face." One postdoctoral student, for example, commented that, "You'd better *look* busy, whether you are or not." This defined requisite of maintaining face intrudes into the relaxed spontaneity which presumably is a component of friendship. A heightened awareness of self and others permeates postdoctoral worlds and enters into the interaction.

Before considering the central relationships involving postdoctoral researchers—the postdoctoral-adviser, postdoctoral-technician, and postdoctoral-postdoctoral relationships—it should be pointed out that upon entering the postdoctoral career, there is less friendliness than expected.

I expected to be more visible when I came here and have more status. I thought it would be warmer and more friendly.

Well, I came here knowing I'd have a hell of a lot of work to do, but I really didn't anticipate the coolness around here. I don't know what it is, but people just aren't friendly.

It must be part of being a postdoc. Postdocs are at a place for only a short time, so I guess that they (others) don't feel any impulse to get close with them. It's OK but I'd like it better if I didn't have to be a scientist all the time—you know, a little friendlier.

Part of the initial postdoctoral perspective involves a view of others not being interested in creating friendships. This is not too surprising. Postdoctoral students get to know others initially in work roles in highly productivity-oriented settings where conventional expectations regarding the display of competence operate. From the beginning, then, there exist major strands criss-crossing the postdoctoral world which are not conducive to the formation of friendships. These can be described in more detail as they appear in specific relationships critical to the postdoctoral researcher.

As noted earlier, the postdoctoral student-adviser relationship is perhaps the most important relationship for postdoctorals. In addition to the part he plays in postdoctoral research, the adviser is the personification of career promise for the postdoctoral student, and through his higher reputation in the discipline the adviser lends a lustre and sense of credibility to co-authored papers. But, paradoxically, these very matters also present the adviser as a problem to the postdoctoral student because it is the adviser, certainly as seen by the postdoctoral, who controls his career fate. Since it is imperative that the postdoctoral establish an early working relationship with the adviser, he becomes someone to be "handled." This coping process involves the recognition on the part of the postdoctoral researcher that there are clear limits to their relationship. These limits can be defined in terms of a power or leverage differential. Although the postdoctoral student can gain leverage advantages, it is the adviser who controls the career mechanisms of the postdoctoral; namely, letters of recommendation and publishing.

> Q. Are the data coming out of this lab his (the adviser's) responsibility?
> A. Yes, very definitely. And if you want to publish anything it has got to be okayed by him. You've got to make him believe it—unless you want to publish it alone, but that would be crazy because you're here to get his name on some papers with you.
> Q. So you want to co-author with him?
> A. Well, that's the whole shot.

Even those who verge on violating these limits censure themselves. A biochemist who described himself as "not taking any of his (adviser's) bull" said, "Even I don't go all the way because when it comes down to it, he's the one who will be recommending me." With such constraint, personal accessibility is next to impossible. The postdoctoral student cannot "think aloud" with the adviser. The risk is too great. Commenting on the self-restraint in his relationship with his adviser, another postdoctoral commented. "It's like joking with God."

The elements constraining the postdoctoral-technician relationship are rather different and somewhat less clear cut than those structuring postdoctoral-adviser relations. The centrality of the technician to the daily research process has already been emphasized, but there are two additional elements which need mentioning from the standpoint of friendship. First, unlike postdoctorals and advisers, technicians can maintain a certain distance from the research process, although they are very near the hub of it. This distance is possible because their lives and careers are not so directly implicated in the results of the research. Their selves, in other words, are less defined and permeated by the experiment. They can provide technical assistance on a given project and maintain a certain independence from its findings. Secondly, there is often a tension between technicians and postdoctorals which takes the form of resentment toward postdoctorals by technicians. The source of this tension derives from a kind of disjunctiveness. Many technicians have dropped out of or have been terminated from graduate school and feel uneasy working for a new Ph.D who is about their same age or younger. The postdoctoral symbolizes the success so far denied the technician. Still other technicians may have the doctorate but have been unable for a variety of reasons to find satisfactory employment. This tension, combined with the differential meaning of experiment, results in a postdoctoral perspective in which a good technician is regarded as "someone who will take orders and not talk back." Postdoctoral-technician interaction involves the postdoctoral keeping a pressure on the technician to get things done and the technician not wanting to do too much.

As with advisers, then, postdoctorals find themselves in a situation in which they must devise adaptive responses. One response is taking a "superior" attitude toward the technician. This attitude in effect is a self-fulfilling ploy and involves the postdoctoral presenting himself as a person-in-authority in the anticipation that by conducting himself in this manner a pressure will be exerted on the technician to act toward him as if he is that kind of person. If the technician does, the postdoctoral's claims to and performance of authority are supported and a *de facto* authority relationship emerges. Thus, several postdoctorals say that the best way to deal with a technician is simply "to boss him around." But there must be palpable cooperative efforts as well, and therein lies a second kind of adaptive response. Part of the effective folklore of the laboratory is "don't get the technician against you." Once antagonisms are created, technicians can do a variety of things to make life miserable for the postdoctoral researcher. He can arrive late and leave early, work at a slow pace, complain to the postdoctoral's adviser (who actually is the technician's employer), or intentionally make mistakes, thus, subverting an experiment. Postdoctorals, therefore, often find themselves doing some of the technicians' work: helping them clean up, making calculations for solutions, setting up instruments, running errands, and the like. These activities reduce the scientific efficiency of the postdoctoral, but feed into the over-all efficiency of the laboratory.

Again, concerning the personal accessibility that one person has for another, it can be seen that rather imposing constraint exists in the postdoctoral-technician relationship. For quite different reasons than in the postdoctoral-adviser relationship, the postdoctoral student cannot allow personal vulnerability to become part of his relationships with technicians. He must be aware of the relationship and keep a perspective regarding the pragmatics of it. He must, in a very real way, step outside the relationship—objectify it—and manage his involvement. Thus, his involvement cannot include a "thinking aloud" dimension.

Relationships among postdoctoral students themselves have an element not present in those involving advisers and technicians. Postdoctoral students can view themselves as caught up in a similar set of circumstances, and from this, a certain degree of empathy emerges. They are able to place themselves in the attitude of other postdoctorals and, to an extent, feel what they feel. But a problem exists in this particular

empathic process. Being competitive, they know that other postdoctorals
are competitive; having to maintain "face," they know that others also
must do so; viewing their postdoctoral career from a constricted time
perspective, they understand that others share this perspective. So the
"content" of postdoctoral empathy establishes the basis for a wariness,
and a look-out-for-yourself attitude emerges.[9]

How does this attitude manifest itself? One way is through competition
for valued resources, and one such resource is scientific equipment.
When acted upon collectively, a piece of equipment becomes something
more than an object that measures, weighs, or transforms research material. Its meaning is tied to the routines, interactions, and appraisals of
its users. Laboratory research simply cannot be done without instruments, and some instruments, depending upon the discipline and type
of research, become more important than others. In the drug metabolism
group of the Pharmacology Department ". . . it is the centrifuge. If
you're a drug metabolism man, you use the centrifuge all the time. It's
your tool. Without it, you're just dead." There is a kind of tyranny that
the equipment holds over its users. That is, the scheduling of instrument
time, the efficiency of the instrument, and the competence in using it
loom large in the day-to-day work routines. A rigor and drama is introduced to the work relationships. A pharmacologist reflects this drama.

> The past week or so has been interesting in a way. The whole topic is the centrifuge.
> Everybody is centrifuging and we go around and make deals. We exchange heads
> for time and tubes for this and that. There are always some people who are cen-
> trifuging and it really gets hectic when someone like me comes along who centrifuges
> all the time.

Similarly, concerning the same instrument,

> Everyone wants prime time. We want to use it between eight and ten in the morning
> so we can get out of here by five. R, another postdoc, has been getting very upset
> lately because there has been so much competition. You know, scheduling and who
> gets what. He says he should quit because there is not enough material and equipment
> to work with. He wants another centrifuge but the people in his lab won't listen.

Moreover, the competition for equipment carries with it major implications for the efficiency of work. Consider the following dialogue between two postdoctorals.

> R: J is gone to Tulane so I have cancelled your time on the centrifuge because I
>   have some very high priority work.
> D: What do you mean? You can't take my time!
> R: V (a technician) needs it. She has to watch the scintillator later on.
> D: That's too bad!
> R: You can switch to my time and get your run in, can't you. I really need it
>   because this has got to get out.

D: No. I have been planning today's experiment for three days now and G (a technician) is set up and everything. No.
R: Well, I don't know. I'll see what I can do.
D: You can't have it no matter what . . .

R's attempt to take D's instrument time was not really malicious, but it was deliberate and intentional; and therein lies the social significance of equipment. The competition is less over the time itself as it is over an attempt to create personal order. The scheduling of instrument time allows a person to implicate others in a desired line of action. Technician's work, for example, is contingent upon certain materials being centrifuged at certain times, and in this sense, the instruments are the key to any anticipated plan of action.

Regardless of the form of cooperation, therefore, postdoctorals are out to gain an edge in their relationships with other postdoctorals. Sometimes this verges on hustling or polite exploitation. In any case, being a postdoctoral researcher includes the assumption that their careers are guided by a kind of zero-sum game: if another postdoctoral benefits more from the trade-offs, investments of professional judgment and time, and joint research efforts, then I lose. Symbiotic relationships, so common and essential in scientific endeavors, are partially defined by postdoctorals as threats. Yet they must engage in them; indeed, they are thrown together by virtue of the laboratory or research group circumstances, and in those circumstances they must attempt to actualize their career ambitions.

The possibility of friendship—interpersonal involvements which include personal accessibility—among postdoctorals and those with whom they most frequently encounter in sustained activity is thus constrained and limited. In one sense, postdoctoral researchers feel that they don't have time for it; in another sense, the organizational and relational imperatives of the postdoctoral world do not permit it.

What forms or varieties of friendship are found then? Certainly all is not a grim and manipulative existence. What forms of affectivity soften the often harsh edges of postdoctoral relationships, and what are the types of relationships to which the term "friend" is applied?

The structure, the "givens," of the postdoctoral world contains pressures against the formation of friendship, but as Kurth (1970) points out, friendly relations can and do typically exist in these types of circumstances. It is the friendly relationship which, in fact, is most likely to occur here. Therefore, two of the more prevalent forms of friendliness among postdoctorals will be presented to illustrate the structuring process as found in these settings.

Postdoctoral researchers become the most enthusiastic about one another when they are working together on a particular project jointly regarded as important. They both have a stake in the outcome and they both will benefit from its success, so they find it useful and even spontaneous in some cases to establish truly cooperative bonds. They may find themselves spending evenings together in the laboratory and in these situations they may engage in the more sociable forms of interaction: eating dinner together in a restaurant or having coffee together. Also, they are likely to go out and have a beer together and discuss the project. But there is a career to this enthusiasm which is linked to the career of the project. Just as the project brings them together in ways conducive to instrumental relationships becoming partially transformed into sociable or friendly relations, so also do these friendly relations tend to disappear as the project is finished. The work enthusiasm fades, and especially if the project fails, so does the personal enthusiasm. What is existentially taken as situated friendship in retrospect becomes a venture lost. New meanings are discovered as the participants reflect backward. Successful projects, especially those which eventuate in papers published in prestigious journals, however, can establish a framework for sentiment conducive to the persistence of the relationship. Such a framework is found in the following quote from a pathologist.

> Mike is my best friend around here. We have worked well together over the past few months and the work is turning out the way we want it, so I suppose we'll try some other projects together. I really don't know.

What made Mike a "best friend" was that an informal style was established. However, it was the *research* which was discussed informally and not the nonwork aspects of their lives. While postdoctorals can find friendliness in their work relationships, the very meaning of the friendliness is defined in terms of the work itself.

A second form of the friendly relationship is found in a kind of strategic style used by some postdoctorals. This can be called a "sociability style" and is very similar to what Oswald Hall (1949) refers to as a friendly career. This style can be conceived as a type of career perspective in which the postdoctoral student attempts to create relationships which will be beneficial to his career. In effect, they are busy trying to establish professional friends or "contacts." They are prone to speak of their friends in high places such as the National Institutes of Health or the National Science Foundation, or of leading scientists they met at the most recent professional meeting they attended. Characteristic of this sociability—indeed, as Burns (1953) points out, implicit in all sociability— is the simultaneous presence of fact and fiction. The "as if" or fictive element is most at work in the sociability style, consciously managed into a career strategy. In everyday postdoctoral routines, this style appears in the form of dropping by another's laboratory to chat, trying to get others to go out for beer, performing minor favors for persons in authority positions, and the like. But there are limits imposed upon the extent of this sociability. There is an unspoken standard regarding how friendly one can be. Staying too long in another's laboratory without the display of instrumental purpose is often met with a "I've got work to do," and wanting to go out for beer too often can create a backlash defining the sociable person as one who is not really committed to science. For hardworking, nose-to-the-grindstone postdoctoral students, they become people to be avoided. Thus, too much friendliness constitutes an impropriety.

But such sociability can be useful, for, unlike friendships, we can drift in and out of friendly relations. We can even be friendly with those we dislike so long as there is some other value to the relationship. Friendliness thus can become an opportunistic tactic, and if a sociability-oriented postdoctoral wants to hang around the laboratory and chat, the instrumentally-oriented postdoctoral will accommodate him so long as he can profit from the encounter, e.g., gain useful information relevant to his research. A fictive consensus overlays and masks an underlying tension and dissensus here, and in such situations occurs irony—playing at being friendly while intimating distance. Irony here functions as a situational safeguard and smooths over a certain insecurity deriving from vague or ambiguous identities (see Burns, 1953).

Before concluding this paper, I would like to briefly follow up the notion of friendly relations among postdoctorals as an opportunistic tactic. Allowing for the element of instrumentality, even in the best of true friendships, it is clear that friendships can be functional. They can be used, within limits, for our own individual purposes. This feature, in fact, becomes one of the criteria essential in differentiating friendships from professional contacts; the latter are socially courted through friendliness for instrumental purposes, while the former, those involving cherished friendship relations, must contain checks against the excessive display of instrumentality. Because of the transitory nature of the postdoctoral position and the personal sense of urgency experienced by postdoctoral researchers, interpersonal efficiency becomes a career imperative. A pattern within the postdoctoral career thus emerges which reflects the kinds of relationships which are instrumental at various points along the career. The clearest instance of the temporal placement of friendly relations is found at the beginning and ending points of the postdoctoral career. Succinctly, postdoctorals have beginning and ending friends—those relationships which help the postdoctoral get into the postdoctoral career and those which help him terminate it and launch him into his professional scientific career. These beginning and ending friends are differentiated by the extent to which they are useful or possess capabilities relevant to activities immediately anticipated by the post-doctoral. Technicians and other postdoctoral students, for instance, typically become beginning friends. Technicians are familiar with the every-day pragmatics of the laboratory and other postdoctoral students become sources of information regarding specific research problems engaged in by members of a research group. They also possess information regarding personal quirks and tastes of advisers and other faculty members. Advisers, on the other hand, tend to become ending friends. They sponsor the postdoctoral in his quest for a fulltime faculty position. Thus, there is a shift in significant others as the postdoctoral moves through his career and is faced with different friends which tend to persist beyond the postdoctoral career. Technicians may never be seen again; other postdoctorals may remain as professional acquaintances; but advisers continue, at least for a time, as instrumentally valued friends.

In conclusion, I should like to suggest that friendship is one of the most important but under-examined topics of direct sociological significance. Gerald Suttles (1970) attempts to sensitize us to its importance by assigning it the status of an institution, while William Goode regards friendship as one of the "four great control systems in all societies" (Goode, 1972, p. 507). The implications stemming from the central argument regarding the situated meaning of friendship as presented in this paper require that a necessary task in the investigations of friendship must be the determination of the conditions under which friendship exists and is maintained, the elements which give friendship relations their form and direction, and the concrete kinds of relationships variously referred to by the term "friendship." In short, we must put people and the situations in which they are called on to act into our analyses of friendship.

ACKNOWLEDGMENT

This paper is based in part on my doctoral thesis (18), the research for which was facilitated by a predoctoral research fellowship from the Midwest Council for Social Research on Aging, and on my own research as a NIMH Postdoctoral Fellow at the University of Minnesota. I am grateful to Robert W. Habenstein for his guidance in the original research and to Gregory P. Stone and William J. Goode from whom I greatly benefited in several discussions of friendship relations.

NOTES

1. Implied in this proposition is a fundamental opposition to sociometric studies purporting to investigate friendship choice or friendship clusters. [For examples of this literature, see Maisonneuve (1954), Lazarsfeld and Merton (1954), Hollander and Webb

(1958), Lanphier (1968), Krieger and Wells (1969), Laumann (1969)]. While such studies do have value insofar as they are able to descriptively indicate something about popularity and clique composition, there is little evidence that the mere act of selecting another as a questionnaire or interview response is the equivalent of selecting or designating a friend. A fact of major importance which is typically overlooked is that what constitutes friendship in these studies is largely set by the sociometric design itself.

2. Note how commercial advertising utilizes the theme of friendship as a commodity. United Airlines' "Friendship Service," the slogan "You've got a friend at Chase Manhattan Bank," Shell Oil Company's "We can be very friendly," and "G. Fried is your friend in the carpet business" all illustrate the transformation of the more affective elements of friendship into instrumental mechanisms of the marketplace.

3. Postdoctoral researchers, more often referred to as "postdoctoral students" or simply as "postdocs," are those recent doctoral recipients who seek temporary research positions where they may augment their research skills and gain additional experience before taking the more permanent faculty position.

4. In a survey of 140 universities hosting postdoctoral students, only three reported that they actively promoted postdoctoral work while another ten indicated that they had any degree of control over postdoctoral appointments (National Research Council, 1969, p. 146). The top-rated universities, of course, can offer prestige, but the point is that little in the way of active organization of postdoctoral experiences is provided.

5. See Becker, et al. (1971) for an excellent study of culture among medical students. My use of the concept of culture is not only consistent with theirs but with Shibutani's use of the notion of "social world" (1961, pp. 136–137). The essence of culture lies in the collective response to problems and circumstances shared by members of a group.

6. This is not always the case. Postdoctoral trainees, i.e., those whose financial support comes from a departmental training grant, select the department itself. After they arrive, they are given the opportunity to sample various laboratories in the department and then make up their minds regarding with whom they want to work. In any event, it is ultimately the laboratory which comes under specific consideration.

7. Each respondent gave more than one response to the question, thus the total percentage exceeds one hundred percent.

8. Writing about postdoctoral education, Richard Curtis notes that, "It is not clear to universities whether the postdoctoral is the most senior student or the most junior faculty" (1971, p. 192).

9. These comments are restricted to postdoctoral researchers who find themselves engaged in some form of cooperative effort. Such instances of joint action are obviously found in either laboratory or research group contexts, and typically not in a cross-disciplinary or cross-laboratory context. Thus, while this sharing might enter into a consideration of laboratory culture, it lies outside of considerations of postdoctoral culture.

REFERENCES

Becker, Howard S., Blanche Geer, Everett C. Hughes, and Anselm L. Strauss
   1961 Boys in White. Chicago, Ill.: University of Chicago Press.
Burns, Tom
   1953 "Friends, enemies, and the political fiction." American Sociological Review
       18:654–662.
Curtis, Richard B.
   1971 "Postdoctoral education." Pp. 188–192, The Encyclopedia·of Education 7 New
       York: Macmillan.

Giallombardo, Rose
1966   "Social roles in a prison for women. Social Problems 11:268–288.
Goode, William J.
1972   "The place of force in human society." American Sociological Review 37:507–519.
Hall, Oswald
1949   "Types of medical careers." American Journal of Sociology 55:243–253.
Hiller, E. T.
1947   Social Relations and Structure. New York: Harper and Brothers.
Hollander, E. P., and Wilse B. Webb
1958   "Leadership, fellowship, and friendship: an analysis of peer nominations." Pp.
       489–496 in Eleanor E. Maccoby, Theodore M. Newcomb, and Eugene L. Hartley
       (eds.), Readings in Social Psychology, New York: Holt, Rinehart and Winston.
Kerr, Clark
1964   The Uses of the University, Cambridge, Mass.: Harvard University Press.
Krieger, Leslie H., and William D. Wells
1969   "The criteria for friendship." The Journal of Social Psychology 78:109–112.
Kurth, Suzanne B.
1970   "Friendship and friendly relations." Pp. 136–170 in George McCall, Michal
       McCall, Norman Denzin, Gerald Suttles and Suzanne Kurth (eds.), Social Re-
       lationships, Chicago, Ill.: Aldine.
Lanphier, Michael
1968   "Clique and complementarity." The Journal of Social Psychology 74:53–64.
Laumann, Edward O.
1969   "Friends of urban men: an assessment of accuracy in reporting their socio-eco-
       nomic attributes, mutual choice, and attitude agreement." Sociometry 32:54–69.
Lazarsfeld, Paul F., and Robert K., Merton
1954   "Friendship as a social process: a substantive and methodological analysis." Pp.
       18–66 in Monroe Berger, Theodore Abel and Charles H. Page (eds.), Freedom
       and Control in Modern Society, New York: D. Van Nostrand Company.
Liebow, Elliot
1967   Tally's Corner, Boston, Mass.: Little Brown and Company.
Little, Roger W.
1964   "Buddy relations and combat performance." Pp. 195–219 in Morris Janowitz
       (ed.), The New Military. New York: Russell Sage Foundation.
Lofland, John
1969   Deviance and Identity. Englewood Cliffs, N.J.: Prentice-Hall.
Maines, David R.
1973   Encounters and Careers of Postdoctoral Students, unpublished Doctoral Disser-
       tation, University of Missouri, Columbia.
Maisonneuve, Jean
1954   "A contribution to the sociometry of mutual choices." Sociometry 17:33–46.
Mead, George Herbert
1934   Mind Self and Society. Chicago, Ill.: University of Chicago Press.
Mayntz, Renate
1960   "The visiting fellow: an analysis of an academic role." American Sociological
       Review 25:735–741.
National Research Council
1969   The Invisible University: Postdoctoral Education in the United States. Washing-
       ton, D.C.: National Academy of Sciences.
Shibutani, Tamotsu
1961   Society and Personality. Englewood Cliffs, N.J.: Prentice-Hall.

Suttles, Gerald
 1970 "Friendship as a social institution." Pp. 95–135 in George McCall, Michal McCall, Norman Denzin, Gerald Suttles and Suzanne Kurth (eds.), Social Relationships, Chicago, Ill.: Aldine.
Weinberg, Krison S.
 1970 "Primary group theory and closest friendship of the same sex: an empirical analysis." Pp. 301–322 in Tamotsu Shibutani (ed.) Human Nature and Collective Behavior. Englewood Cliffs, N.J.: Prentice-Hall.
Whyte, William F.
 1955 Street Corner Society, Chicago, Ill.: University of Chicago Press.

FRIENDSHIP PATTERNS OF THE AMERICAN CATHOLIC CLERGY

Thomas M. Gannon

"Friendship," as Simmel (1950:325, 138) observed, "aims at an absolute personal intimacy . . . based entirely on the individualities of its elements." But friendship is also a relationship that grows within limits set by culture, social structure, and social change. Friendships among Roman Catholic priests in the United States well illustrate the profoundly social nature of this intimate relation.

Compared to the population at large, the clergy are a fairly homogeneous group. Variations in friendships derive more from the social structure of the priesthood than the personal backgrounds of priests. This social setting includes, first, an action system or way of life based on clerical status, and second, structural differences within the priesthood arising from characteristics like age, work, and affiliation with the diocesan or religious order clergy. This chapter will examine how friendships grow within this action system and how the pursuit of friendship varies with structural position.

The priesthood today is not static. Indeed, given the major shifts within Roman Catholicism since the Second Vatican Council (1962–65), the priesthood has become a profession in transition, experiencing some degree of crisis (Gannon, 1979). The data to be considered here do not measure change. They do, however, demonstrate its effects. Younger clergy, with only brief experience as priests in the pre-Vatican II church, differ from older clergy with longer familiarity with traditional church life. Those with less traditional religious perspectives and less exclusively priestly jobs differ from more traditional priests. Thus, even though the data of this chapter were collected at a single point in time (1970–71), they reveal something about the fundamental changes in Catholicism and the priesthood that have affected priests' friendships.

THE PRIESTHOOD AS AN ACTION SYSTEM

One approach to understanding the Roman Catholic priesthood is to conceptualize it as an integrated action system (in the Parsonian sense).[1] Historically, the priesthood has been seen as a "state" of life and the priest as a "man set apart." The priesthood is more than an occupation; the priest is a member of a community whose claims on his daily existence extend well beyond his official duties. Any profession which performs crucial "life and death" tasks develops such claims, especially when these tasks belong to the realm of the sacred. We should expect, therefore, that a priest's profession will be reinforced by a constellation of cultural norms and structures, including those that define friendship.

Two features of this action system are particularly important. First, in the traditional society in which the priest's role developed to the definition still prevailing, most functions—especially those involving authority—were assigned by right of birth or by virtue of some sort of sacred investiture. Both types of assignment were felt to give the individual an essentially different character by virtue of which the individual acquired a certain "power" and the right to demand obedience from others. This power and concomitant right were not granted for some specific and demonstrated competence, but because of the character that was "innate." This character conferred a "universal" or "general" competence on the king, the nobleman, and the priest. For the priest, this investiture was demonstrated at his ordination, when he was empowered by the church to celebrate the Eucharist and certain other sacraments.

Second, the priesthood is essentially an *expressive* role, in contrast, for example, to the primarily instrumental role of the business executive. A priest works to meet man's need for meaning and love, for approval and esteem. What the priest does, he does in the name of the diety. His is not a role that can be achieved, since by definition its special and sacred powers and rights are beyond human achievement.

This non-instrumental character of the priesthood appears when we try to describe the qualities of the ideal priest—qualities everywhere related not so much to what the priest does in terms of skill or knowledge or efficiency, but to what he lives and witnesses. The priest, in other words, is a special person. Church law reinforced this special quality by regulating priests' lifestyle, garb, and seminary indoctrination.[2] In large measure, this regulation was effective because priests lived and worked in a relatively closed Catholic environment. In turn, the style of priestly life contributed to the self-consciousness and self-assurance of the priest himself.

What happens to men formed by such a system in an era that is increasingly professional, empirical and instrumental? To be effective in the contemporary world, a priest must modify his work and adapt his lifestyle. Does the priest join this world through his friendships as well as through his work? If so, how do these friendships affect his commitment to the traditional action system of the priesthood?

THE CHANGING ORGANIZATION OF THE PRIESTHOOD

The essential characteristics of the priesthood as a profession call for strong bonds of solidarity among those who assume the priestly role. While the ultimate ground of this solidarity is a commonly shared vocation, a "received calling" (in Weber's term) that transcends personal qualities or demonstrated competence, the solidarity also derives from three additional factors: the organizational structure of the priesthood (specifically, the existence of two generically distinct types of priests—diocesan and religious order), a shared status in the Catholic community, and clearly defined functions in the church structure. Each of these factors merits attention because of its relation to friendship patterns of the clergy. Moreover, not only have the status and function of the priesthood undergone significant alteration over the past ten years, but these changes seem likely to have an impact on the organizational reality of the Catholic priesthood itself.

Catholic priests either work directly under the diocesan bishop as parish priests or in some other task related to the "care of souls," or live in a religious community under rule and work primarily under the superiors of these communities. The "primary type" of diocesan priest is the parish priest or pastor. However, the large and complex modern church has required that an increasing number of diocesan (or "secular") priests also be engaged in more specialized work as administrators, teachers, scholars and chaplains. The development of the specialized diocesan priest has been spontaneous rather than planned, although the tradition of the priest-scholar goes back at least as far as the fourth century.

Men who wish to become diocesan priests, therefore, are principally trained to be pastors; occupational specialization comes later. Indeed, even as occupational specialists, these priests may preach sermons, administer the sacraments, and perform limited parish activities. Candidates for the diocesan clergy enter a seminary (most after grammar school, some after high school, and a small proportion at a later age) administered by the local diocese solely to train men to serve the needs of the church within that diocese. Diocesan priests normally expect to spend the rest of their lives within this diocese, living and working with others who have been trained at the same seminary. This model not only determines the kind of general and specialized education they receive, but also who their close friends are. The diocesan priest should be expected, then, to choose his friends from among the clergy and seminarians with whom he lives and works, the "client" parishioners whom he serves, the family which raised him, and perhaps teachers from the parish school or a few others he might meet when performing his duties.

Although the religious order clergy often assist with parish and diocesan tasks, these priests have a wider scope than serving local parishes and meeting diocesan needs. The traditon of religious orders in Catholicism dates from about the fourth century. These orders originated as charismatic movements that responded to new or unfulfilled needs in the Catholic church and came to embody both a set of ideals and an evolving institutional style of life that underscored (with varying emphases) the need for protest, prayer, solitude, renunciation and supra-diocesan activity. Hence, these groups provided a safety valve for those who wished to be priests but who sought a more intense pursuit of the Christian life. The order clergy represented a break with past institutional clerical forms and thus offered the possibility of new patterns of priestly community and work-style. At the same time, they functioned as a flexible and mobile work force in the church. Since orders were neither bound by the territorial limits of a parish or diocese nor operated entirely under the jurisdiction of a local bishop, they could be used by the papacy to provide important and specialized services, e.g., education, social work and missionary activity, for the church throughout the world.

In contrast to his diocesan counterpart, the religious order priest enters at a slightly older age (i.e., usually after high school or later), and is a member of an order or congregation which is often international in scope; he goes where his order sends him, lives in one of its religious communities, and performs the special kind of work designated by the group.

He is most likely, therefore, to choose friends from among fellow priests of his group (whether those he lives with or others assigned to different religious houses), his family (if he lives near them), the people with whom he works and those he serves. Clearly, then, the organizational structure of the priesthood creates different contexts for diocesan and religious order clergy and these contexts necessarily influence the friendships priests form.

Priests' friendships are also circumscribed by the changing situation of the priest in American Catholicism. Historically, the priest was not only the religious leader but also the best educated person in a group of lower-class faithful, often immigrants, who depended on him for guidance in American ways, as well as in religious matters. This traditional relationship between priest and people had at least two major consequences. First, the American Catholic priesthood emerged as a profession of great influence and dignity. By default and by abrogation, the priest was "all things to all people"—not merely in a religious-expressive way, but also in an instrumental sense. Put simply, a large measure of the priesthood's cohesion derived from the fact that membership in the fraternity represented a *total status* which served not merely to promote solidarity, but created an environment which understandably produced a healthy supply of recruits. Second, a well-knit but relatively isolated clerical subculture developed. The rewards of this subculture were the respect and support of the larger Catholic milieu for priests, who were almost a separate caste.

The priest moved away from these structures at his own peril. The very tightness of the Catholic and clerical worlds helps to explain the strong reactions to anyone who left the seminary or priesthood. The exseminarian, even more the ex-priest, had sinned against tribal unity and was viewed suspiciously ever after as a "spoiled priest."

Even though there still exists a priestly community, as well as norms and expectations regarding proper priestly behavior, it does not operate as strongly as it did in the past. One of the significant features of the present situation is the fragmentation of the American Catholic population and the consequent weakening of the clerical subculture. The breakdown of the clergy's social isolation strains the effectiveness of traditional mechanisms designed to maintain priestly identity and cohesion. As the former structure of Catholic authoritarianism grows ineffective, the authoriarian aspect of the clerical subculture necessarily collapses with it. Moreover, these changes are occurring just as the church itself, once the potent symbol of unity and certainly for all its adherents, is rapidly becoming polarized by sudden developments in theology, worship and devotional practice.

It is important to investigate the ways in which these changes have affected the social integration of the priestly profession. New patterns of integration and personal relationship are essential for the new roles that religious professionals are now called upon to perform. How have shifts in the value-orientations and normative standards of the church and the clergy affected friendship relations within the profession, and the priest's supportive ties with the laity and "outsiders" generally? To what extent does a "clerical subculture" continue to exist? Are there pressures toward more diffuse friendship patterns among the clergy? What influence does the internal differentiation of the clergy profession (i.e., diocesan versus religious order) have on the structure of priests' interpersonal relations? What evidence is there of dissatisfaction with the priestly role and of a serious problem with loneliness? How is the incidence of these problems related to the priest's friendship patterns and supportive relations?

DATA AND RESEARCH STRATEGY

In answering these questions, I will draw on the data from the 1970–71 National Opinion Research Center survey of some ten percent of all Catholic priests in the United States.[3]

Focusing on the friendship patterns of the clergy has demanded that I take the individual priest as the basic unit of analysis and consider clergy-group membership as one of the structural properties of the profession. This strategy assumes that a priest's selection of friends, as well as the source and level of his perceived affective support, are related to the structural properties of the organization to which he belongs, to his personal and social background, and to the normative standards (derived from his religious beliefs and value-orientation) that govern appropriate behavior and affective relations. It is further assumed that the structure of a priest's interpersonal relationships will have consequences for his happiness, role satisfaction, feelings of solidarity with the church, and commitment to the priesthood. Age will probably be the most important structural variable for explaining different patterns of friendship. Not only do those of similar age generally share similar experiences, but, given the changes in Catholicism and the priesthood over the past decade (including the large number of priests who have resigned from the active ministry), older priests were socialized into an entirely different world than were their younger colleagues. Type of job is expected to be the next more important factor influencing these differences.

Four hypotheses follow upon these assumptions: (1) the friendship patterns of diocesan priests will differ substantially from those of religious order priests; (2) The kinds of close friends a priest has and the amount of colleague-support he perceives will be significant to his general morale—level of work satisfaction, experience of loneliness, and happiness in the priesthood[4]; (3) The kinds of close friends and associates a priest has and the amount of colleague-support he perceives will significantly affect his level of commitment to the normative structure of the church and to the priestly profession[5]; (4) The continuing existence of a clerical subculture (as indicated by a priest's number of priest friends, the number of priests with whom the respondent lives, and his feelings of closeness with other priests) will directly influence the patterns of priests' friendships. It is anticipated that priests who experience a weakening of the clerical subculture will be more likely to extend their interpersonal relationships to include Catholic laity and non-Catholic friends. However, where the clerical subculture remains strong, it will reflect the structural properties of the organization to which the priest belongs (diocesan or religious order), with order clergy more likely to report experiencing strong clerical ties.

CLOSE FRIENDS, ASSOCIATES, AND COLLEAGUE-SUPPORT

The social solidarity and the expressive relationships of the clergy are grounded in a peculiar occupational fact. Separation between place of work and place of residence, characteristic of most other urban occupations and professions, is virtually absent. Over 90 percent of American priests, in fact, live either in parish rectories or in religious houses (cf. NORC, 1972:183–185). Only bishops are likely to have quarters of their own, and even three-fourths (74 percent) of them report that they live in rectories or religious houses.

The priestly community has been relatively closed, with professional and residential life normally intermingled. In this, the clergy are not unlike some other highly specialized professions, like the military and certain groups of artists and writers. Nevertheless, the fusion between work and residence means that the realities of the profession pervade both public and private life. Historically, this has resulted not only in a certain social isolation—priests tend to have more contact among themselves than with outsiders—but it has also contributed to a powerful *esprit de corps* among the clergy.

On the surface, priests show little evidence of serious dissatisfaction with this intermingling of work and residence. Indeed, 73 percent of the diocesan clergy and 80 percent of the order priests say they consider the place they live to be their home, "a place where you can be yourself, relax, or entertain as you wish." Although this satisfaction constitutes the majority opinion among all age groups of priests, the level of satisfaction decreases as priests grow older (NORC, 1972:185). The feeling that one's residence is "home" is only slightly affected by the size of residence (i.e., the number of priests living and working together), and is unrelated to the number of close friends priests report among their living companions or among those doing the same kind of work.

It is true, however, that fewer order than diocesan clergy live alone (11 percent versus 28 percent), and more order than diocesan priests live in larger priest-communities. This difference in residential patterns has observable consequences. Priests living in larger residences are more likely to consider these places as home; they are also more likely to report experiencing colleague-support and to have more priest friends. Also, priests in more specialized jobs tend to live in large communities.

The lack of sharp separation between work and private life, plus the segregation of traditional seminary training and the restrictions of celibacy have led some observers to postulate severe intimacy problems as a basic factor in the present clergy crisis.[6] Although this assertion cannot be totally disregarded on either theoretical or empirical grounds, the data provide evidence that priestly relationships constitute a more complex and nuanced phenomenon.

In the first of the NORC items geared to measure the friendship patterns of the clergy, respondents were first asked to think about all the people with whom they felt free to discuss personal matters and then were asked if they thought they had many close friends. About one-third of the priests (31 percent for diocesan; 36 percent for religious) thought they had many such close friends, and these proportions remained stable in all age categories. Very few (2 percent) felt they had no close friends. That such a proportion report many close friendships seems to indicate considerable and continuing capacity for intimacy among priests, despite their living situation, seminary training and celibate state. People may, of course, over-estimate both the number of their close friends and the degree of closeness. But the fact that priests perceive themselves as having close friends is itself a reality quite independent of its objective accuracy. Certainly there is no evidence that clergy perceive themselves as cut off from human contact.

The friendships (beyond the limits of their own family) most frequently reported by the clergy are with other priests. As can be seen in Table 1, less than half the priests say they have close friends among laymen in the parish or connected with their present work, and less than one-third with laywomen with whom they work. Finally, half the diocesan priests (51 percent) say they have close friends among laymen not involved in their present work, just over one-third (37 percent) with laywomen not involved in their present work, and one-fourth (24 percent) record close friendships with women religious. Order priests have most close friends among members of their religious group; they are somewhat

Table 1   Classification of Close Friends and Frequent Associates

Group	Per Cent Having Close Friends in Each Group		Per Cent Associating Most Often with Each Group as Close Friends	
	Diocesan	Religious	Diocesan	Religious
Members of my immediate family or other relatives	70	70	46	32
Fellow priests with whom I was in the seminary	69	52	45	23
Fellow priests from my religious order or congregation	a	86	a	72
Fellow priests whom I met after leaving the seminary	68	44	50	26
Laymen from the parish where I am now, or connected with my present work	46	39	31	28
Laywomen from the parish where I am now, or connected with my present work	32	28	20	18
Laymen from outside my present parish, or whom I met while involved in other work	51	44	28	24
Laywomen from outside my present parish, or whom I met while involved in other work	37	35	19	19
Women religious	24	29	11	12
Ministers from non-Catholic churches	11	10	5	4

a Not applicable.

less likely than diocesan clergy to report close friends among the laity. Moreover, although younger clergy are more likely than older to report close friends among laymen and women and with women religious, they still report most close friends among the clergy.

This pattern of friendship preference is confirmed by other data in the NORC survey. Although the different social situations in which diocesan and order priests live and work make comparisons difficult to interpret, it is clear that significantly more religious order clergy list priests in their own organizational group as close friends and friends with whom they most often associate. Further, when asked about the total number of their close priest friends, half the diocesan priests say they have six or more close priest friends. But over three-fourths of the order priests report the same number of priest friends and almost twice as many order as diocesan priests say they have one or more close friends among the clergy with whom they live. (Note that none of these proportions varies significantly with age.) In part, the higher proportion of priest friends among religious order clergy can be understood as a function both of the emphasis on community explicitly characteristic of religious life and of the larger numbers of people residing in religious order communities. This interpretation is borne out by the positive relationship between having many priest friends and living with a larger number of priests (.14), and the satisfaction priests report from living a common life with likeminded colleagues (.2).[7] Clearly, then, the higher incidence of close friendships with other priests constitutes a major generic organizational difference between American diocesan and religious order clergy.

Another aspect of clergy friendship is reflected in the quality of the social relations which encourage and support their professional life. Beyond the question of friendships, in what way does the interaction with colleagues provided for by priests' living situations offer expressive support? How does differential organization of living situations affect the amount of support priests experience?

Although a slightly larger proportion of diocesan clergy report that they find only low or medium support among their colleagues, the differences in each category are not substantial (cf. Table 2). The major difference lies in the much greater proportion of religious priests who report high levels of colleague support (30 percent versus 18 percent). Diocesan priests who experience a high degree of colleague support are somewhat less likely to live with more priests (− .13); for religious order clergy, colleague support is unrelated to the number of priests with whom they live. It is true, however, that priests who experience a high degree of colleague support are likely to have more priests who they feel are close friends (diocesan = .23; religious = .24). Again, age is related to colleague support (.21) as it is to the number of kinds of friendships priests develop; older priests are much more likely to experience colleague-support than do younger clergy.

PARTICULARISTIC, INCLUSIVE, AND DIFFUSED FRIENDSHIPS

Although the dominant friendship pattern for priests is friendship with other priests, as the data reveal, clergy also form friendships with other people. In an effort to uncover the *clusters* of close friends that priests develop, it is necessary to distinguish those friendship groups which are tightly linked to a priest's social background and Catholic identification. I have called *particularistic* friendships, friends who come only from a priest's family, seminary friends, clerical friendships made after the sem-

Table 2 Degree of Supportive Colleague Relationships by Affiliation
(Percent)

Degree of Colleague Support	Diocesan	Religious
Low	36	31
Medium	46	39
High	18	30

inary, and Catholic parishioners. I have called *inclusive* friendships, friendship groups that include family, priest friends, and parishioners, but which also extend to Catholics outside the parish and to women religious. A friendship group that includes the entire or "universal" range of close-friend choices listed in Table 3 (extending to Protestant ministers and non-Catholics), I have called a *diffuse* friendship pattern.[8]

As can be seen in Table 3, over one-fifth (22 percent) of the religious order priests, as compared to only seven percent of the diocesan clergy, can be characterized as having friendships that are primarily particularistic. Whereas over one-third (37 percent) of both diocesan and religious order priests display a friendship pattern that is basically inclusive, over half (54 percent) the diocesan clergy—as compared with 38 percent of the order priests—can be classified as having developed a diffuse cluster of friends. Clearly, the friendship pattern for order priests is more restrictive and particularistic than the friendship choices of diocesan clergy.

Using this friendship typology allows us to understand more precisely the effect of age on priests' friendships. The proportion of priests with primarily particularistic friendships steadily increases with age; older clergy, in other words, are much more likely to have restrictive friendships than are younger priests (Table 4). For diocesan clergy the proportion of men characterized by diffuse relations is greatest for middle-age priests, somewhat less for young priests, and least for older priests. For order clergy diffuse relationships steadily and noticeably decrease with age. There is little difference between diocesan and religious priests in the proportion of older or younger men whose friendship patterns are primarily inclusive.

Table 3 Types of Friendship Clusters by Affiliation (Percent)

Typology of Friendships	Diocesan	Religious
Particularistic	7.2	22.1
Inclusive	36.6	36.8
Diffuse	53.9	37.8

Table 4   Types of Friendship Clusters by Age* (Percent)

Typology of Friendships	Diocesan Priests			Religious Priests		
	Young	Middle-Age	Older	Young	Middle-Age	Older
Particularistic	5.3	6.3	10.4	17.0	22.2	27.2
Inclusive	35.0	32.3	42.6	34.9	37.7	38.2
Diffuse	57.6	60.0	43.7	46.3	37.9	28.6

* In this table (and in Table 5) age is defined not in terms of chronological years, but in terms of a priest's year of ordination. Thus, priests ordained from 1902–1945 were placed in the "older" category; those ordained from 1946–1958 were considered "middle-aged;" young priests were defined to include all those ordained between 1959 and 1970. Diocesan priests' median age at ordination was 26; the median age at ordination for religious priests was 28.

It was also hypothesized that the kind of work priests do would influence the friendships they develop, although it was expected that job would influence friendship less than age. For purposes of analysis, priests' jobs were grouped according to six principal work categories: parish-pastoral, pastoral work outside the parish context, administration, education, chaplain work (in a hospital, prison, or the military) and social action. Priests were then assigned to the category which corresponded to the job to which they devoted the largest proportion of their time per week.

As expected, type of job is significantly related to priests' friendship patterns. Priests involved principally in parish work (the majority of whom are diocesan priests) tend to report fewer close friends who are priests and experience the least colleague support among all the respondents. Priests whose major work is outside the parish—particularly those in administration and education—have significantly more close priest-friends and are among those who rank highest in colleague support. Age does not affect the relationship between type of job and number of close priest-friends, but degree of colleague support is significantly related to both age and job for diocesan priests. Older diocesan priests in special assignments report experiencing a slightly higher level of colleague support then middle-age diocesan priests in similar jobs; in this regard younger diocesan clergy more closely resemble older priests than they do their middle-age colleagues. Likewise, priests whose work brings them into contact with a wider range of non-clergy are more likely to have developed a diffuse pattern of friends; particularistic clusters of friends are most characteristic of order priests. The kind of work priests do, therefore, operates as a critical intervening variable through which friendships develop that reflect the structural properties of the priestly profession (age, organizational affiliation, and type of residence).

CORRELATES OF FRIENDSHIP

At the outset of this study, it was hypothesized that the kinds of close friendship a priest develops and the amount of colleague support he perceives will be significant factors in his general morale (measured in terms of work satisfaction, loneliness, and level of happiness), as well as his commitment to the normative structures of the church (i.e., his attitudes toward celibacy, relationships with women, and the exercise of authority in the church), and his commitment to the priestly profession (i.e., whether he plans on resigning or remaining in the priesthood). It was expected that priests with primarily particularistic friendships would have high morale, a sense of normative solidarity with the church, and strong commitment to the priesthood.

Such was not the case. Whether friendships are particularistic or diffuse appears to have little predictive value for morale and commitment either for diocesan or order clergy. What, then, accounts for differences in level of morale and commitment?

It has already been demonstrated that the proportion of priests with primarily particularistic friendships steadily increases with age. Among diocesan clergy there was no significant relationship between the tendency to develop particularistic friendships and any measures of morale, except for a moderate decrease in work satisfaction among older priests ($-.25$). However, young order clergy with a primarily particularistic cluster of friends do experience significantly less loneliness than either older confreres or diocesan priests generally. The pattern of friendship for young order men with diffuse friendships appears unrelated to loneliness. Similarly, young order priests with particularistic friendships report few problems with the way authority is exercised in the church. Conversely, young diocesan priests who have extended their friendships beyond the clerical subculture, report serious problems with the church's exercise of authority.

Because of their wider circle of relationships, we might expect that priests with diffuse clusters of friends would be more likely to have positive attitudes toward social relations with women and to report having greater problems with celibacy. This pattern was clearly discernible for both order ($-.13$) and diocesan ($-.17$) priests. Finally, there appear to be significant associations for some age groups between types of friendship and priests' commitment to remain in the profession. Younger diocesan and older order priests with mainly diffuse and inclusive friendship patterns are somewhat more likely to report having seriously thought of leaving the priesthood. In contrast, the only group for whom particularistic friendships relates to a higher level of commitment to the profession is the older order clergy.

Assuming that the movement from more restrictive, particularistic friendship patterns manifests a weakening of the clerical subculture, then the differential effects of diffuse friendships become clearer. Young diocesan priests moving away from the clerical subculture are more likely to experience greater problems with the church's exercise of authority; young order priests also report greater problems with celibacy. Neither group appears to decline in work satisfaction, but the support they might have derived from a more particularistic cluster of friends for their commitment to the priesthood is diminished. Given the tradition of community life and the generally restrictive patterns of friendship more characteristic of order priests, any breaking up of the clerical subculture appears to have a stronger adverse effect on them than it does on diocesan priests.

At the same time, although age does influence the strength of particularistic clusters of friendships, the combination of these two variables is only minimally related to morale and commitment within the profession. The weakness of the relationship raises a question about the quality of affective support which these friendships provide for young clergy, if different friendship patterns have little noticeable effect on priests' satisfaction and professional commitment. It could be that these friendships—whether particularistic, inclusive, or diffuse—are simply not meeting the priests' need for love, esteem, and approval so necessary to morale and strong commitment. Perhaps priests do not generally perceive that their friendships do (or should?) function in this way. If this suggestion is correct, then it may be that clerical friendships comprise mainly *instrumental* relationships with little strong expressive content that would influence morale and commitment. In social psychological terms, the movement from particularistic to diffuse friendships may thus represent an increasing compartmentalization of the affective (or expressive) and instrumental aspects of a priest's life.

In order to explore the expressive aspect of priests' interpersonal relations, it was hypothesized that those relationships which in some way support and reflect the norms of the church will be related to high morale and strong commitment; relationships which do not support or reflect these norms will be associated with lower morale and weaker commitment. Further, the effect of such norm-related friendships will be intensified with age, so that younger priests will be more acutely aware of their effect than older clergy.

One aspect of the normative structure of the priestly profession most directly related to the area of affective relations is celibacy. Pursuit of the celibate life is a basic social characteristic which distinguishes the Roman Catholic clergy from non-Catholic clergy and the laity, and which reinforces the clerical subculture. As the changing role and work-style of Catholic priests brings them into increasing interaction with the larger society, the norm of celibacy limits the kinds of relationships priests may legitimately develop and influences a priest's general attitude toward women as colleagues, companions, and friends. For this part of the analysis, priests' jobs were categorized as (a) those jobs in which a priest could be expected to relate to women primarily as "clients" (e.g., parish pastoral work, counseling, religious instruction and chaplain work); (b) jobs which involve greater interaction with women as co-workers and in which priests could be expected to develop "colleague" relations with women, as in university teaching; and (c) jobs in which contact with women would be minimal and, hence, would involve no particular kind of personal relationship with women (e.g., diocesan administration and chancery work; administration within a religious community; teaching in a seminary; military chaplaincy).

It was hypothesized, first, that priests involved in jobs that encouraged colleague-type relationships with women would also show a preference for more diffuse and universalistic clusters of friends, whereas priests working in jobs that fostered client-type relationships with women would tend to have particularistic friendship groups. Second, priests whose jobs encourage colleague-type relations with women would be more likely to see the priest as a "minister among the people," whereas those with jobs characterized by client relationships with women would define the priest as a "man set apart." Third, priests with colleague relations with women would display a less conservative attitude toward relationships with women generally, be less committed to the norm of celibacy, have lower morale (i.e., greater feelings of loneliness, unhappiness, and lower levels of work satisfaction), and be less committed to remaining in the priesthood.

As can be seen in Table 5, order priests are more involved than diocesan clergy in jobs that encourage colleague-relationships with women; this distribution is clearly related to the fact that order priests are more likely to be involved in specialized kinds of work. At the same time, order clergy are also more likely to have jobs that involve no particular kind of personal relationships with women. Among both order and diocesan clergy, however, young priests are more likely to have jobs which encourage such kinds of colleague relationships, whereas jobs that involve no identifiable relationships with women are relatively evenly distributed among all age groups. Jobs characterized by client relations with women increase with age, particularly for diocesan priests who, independently of age, are more likely to occupy these jobs generally.

Although the priest's self-image as a "minister among the people" is positively related to colleague-type jobs (diocesan = .25; order = .12) and the image of the priest as a "man set apart" is more common among

Table 5 Types of Work Relations with Women by Age and Affiliation (Percent)

Work Relations With Women	Diocesan Priests				Religious Priests			
	Young	Middle-Age	Older	Total	Young	Middle-Age	Older	Total
Colleague-type Relations	51.0	32.2	18.7	34.6	69.3	51.8	39.2	53.3
Client-type Relations	39.6	53.6	64.8	52.2	13.5	21.2	31.5	22.0
Neutral-type Relations	8.8	12.9	8.6	10.1	13.5	24.7	23.0	20.4
Other	.6	1.2	8.0	3.1	3.7	2.3	7.2	4.4

those whose jobs foster client-type relations with women (diocesan = .21; order = .11), the "minister among the people" role is related to more diffused friendship clusters *only* for middle-age priests. Therefore, to the extent that the relationships associated with a priest's job do affect his morale and commitment, this effect does not operate through the diffuse and universalistic friendship cluster any more than through the particularistic pattern. Rather, the effect of work relations with women on morale and commitment seem more attributable to whether or not these relationships generate conflict or support with the normative structure of the priestly profession. The following findings support this interpretation.

First, compared to order clergy, diocesan priests experience fewer problems with loneliness as they get older and loneliness is less a problem for diocesan priests involved in jobs associated with client-relationships with women. For order clergy, having colleague-type work relations with women and experiencing loneliness as a significant problem are unrelated. Second, younger diocesan priests with colleague relations with women experience greater problems with the way authority is exercised in the church than do older priests or those involved in client relations with women. Third, priests whose work tends to foster colleague relationships with women are more likely to consider leaving the priesthood, regardless of age or whether they belong to the diocesan or order clergy. Fourth, among both diocesan and order priests, regardless of age, clergy having colleague-type work relations with women report higher work satisfaction.

When diocesan priests, therefore, are involved in occupational roles which encourage relations with women as colleagues, they—more than order clergy—are likely to experience conflict with those normative expectations of the profession which emphasize client-type attitudes toward women. Such conflict is positively related to greater problems with loneliness and authority in the church, but also to greater work satisfaction. For both diocesan and order priests, work contact with women as colleagues is positively related to the likelihood of their thinking about leaving the priesthood.

The general attitudes priests hold toward associating with women also exert a significant influence on morale and commitment. Priests with more positive attitudes toward these associations are more likely to experience loneliness, unhappiness and low work satisfaction, and to have considered leaving the priesthood. Priests' attitudes toward celibacy operate in a similar way. Those who would like to see the norm of celibacy revised are more likely to experience the same negative effects noted above. Age is important because younger priests are more likely to hold liberal attitudes toward women. Similarly, middle-age and older clergy who seriously question the norm of celibacy also report lower levels of morale and commitment to the priesthood.

CONCLUSION

Friendship patterns of the clergy are a complex social reality. Though the intermingling of professional and residential life which grounds the social solidarity of the priestly profession is the normal pattern for most priests, this has not created a situation of clerical isolation. Understandably, the fusion of public and private life has helped to maintain a distinct clerical subculture introduced by seminary training, supported by a closely-knit Catholic community, and reinforced by the mores of clerical etiquette (e.g., regulated lifestyle and distinctive garb) and celibacy. Negatively, there is little indication of general dissatisfaction with the integration of work and private life. Positively, this arrangement appears to contribute to the development of closer friendships within the priestly community and greater colleague support. In fact, a high incidence of inter-clerical friendships remains the dominant pattern for the clergy, regardless of the number of confreres priests live with.

Despite the strong tendency for clergy to associate more frequently with other clergy, priests are certainly not isolated from a varied pattern of relationships with non-clergy. This variety is especially noticeable among younger priests who tend to have more close friends who are not priests. Nevertheless, even among younger clergy, the majority indicate their closest associations are with other priests. Furthermore, as far as can be judged from priests' relationships with those with whom they live, the priestly community does provide some measure of colleague support.

Religious order clergy, however, are more likely than diocesan priests to report close friendships with other priests in their own group and less likely to have close friends among the laity (Catholic and non-Catholic). Order priests tend to develop particularistic friendship patterns, but these friendships do not account for their substantially higher levels of colleague support. For both diocesan and order clergy, younger priests form more diffuse friendships. The incidence of diffuse friendships, however, is also related to the kind of work a priest does. Especially for middle-age priests, those with specialized work-roles are more likely to develop diffuse clusters of friends. Nevertheless, diffuse friendship patterns appear to exert little influence on priests' overall morale and the strength of their commitment to the priestly profession.

There is also evidence suggesting that priests may compartmentalize their personal relationships into those which are basically instrumental— i.e., relations which they perceive as directly contributing to their work or fulfilling their role as sacred "experts" and religious leaders—and those which are basically expressive—i.e., those which meet the priest's personal needs for love, recognition, and esteem. Instrumental relationships appear to have little or no effect on morale or professional commitment. But interpersonal relationships which support the norms related to priestly friendships (particularly those regarding friendships with women and commitment to celibacy) are associated with higher levels of morale, less loneliness, fewer problems with authority, greater work satisfaction, and commitment to the priesthood. If interpersonal relationships conflict with these norms, the subsequent conflict generates lower levels of morale and commitment. But if priests' relationships neither reflect nor conflict with such norms, they remain at the instrumental level with little or no effect on loneliness, work satisfaction, problems with authority, and questions about remaining in the priesthood.

Finally, at least in terms of friendship patterns, a clerical subculture does exist. Its persistence and effect is, in part, a function of age, affiliation, and job, but is also affected by the kind of work relations (especially with women) and friendship clusters priests develop. Where there is evidence of a weakening of a priest's ties with this subculture, there are also signs of decreasing morale and commitment to the profession.

In summary, then, the general hypotheses underlying the present study were confirmed. Even though the data on which this confirmation rests come only from clergy, they do provide a basis for continuing research and analysis. Further study should not only add greater depth and nuance to our present understanding of friendships in the priesthood, but also advance the basic argument development here. The priesthood should be conceived not only as an occupation, but also as an action system, and an action system undergoing significant shifts in orientation and perspective because of the profound cultural changes occurring in contemporary Roman Catholicism. Friendships in the clergy, therefore, will not only be different from those formed by members of ordinary occupational groups, but will also reflect the strains and changes within the action system and its wider socio-religious context. Significant factors affecting changes in friendship will be: the structural properties of the profession (age, organizational affiliation, and type of job); a priest's participation in the clerical subculture (i.e., number of priest-friends, number of priests he lives with, and amount of colleague support he perceives from confreres); and the kinds of work relationships he develops. These interpersonal relationships will also be influenced by priests' conformity to or deviance from the normative structure of the profession (especially those norms related to celibacy and general attitudes toward relationships with women). In turn, these will significantly influence priests' morale (work satisfaction, loneliness, happiness) and commitment to the profession.

NOTES

1. For Parsons (1951:4–5), "action" refers to any behavior that involves an awareness of a goal and a choice between alternative means of attaining that goal. Thus defined, action does not consist only of ad hoc "responses" to particular situation "stimuli." Rather, it has the fundamental property that through action individuals develop a system of "expectations" relative to the various physical and social "objects" of the situation. These expectations become organized around the meanings, signs, and symbols which serve as media of communication between persons interacting in the same action system.

2. Regulations concerning clerical lifestyle are extensive. Church law (Bouscaren, et al., 1963:118–22) prohibits a long series of actions regarded as unbecoming for the clergy. If all these structures were enforced in any one place, the list would be quite comprehensive: going to the theater, the opera, the movies, sports events (especially racing), restaurants and bars; riding in an automobile with a woman of any age, using public beaches, going anywhere after sunset except for an urgent summons for priestly ministry (which usually means death actual or impending). The list is reminiscent of the prohibitions associated with British or American Puritanism. While many of these prohibitions are widely ignored, particularly in the United States, a structure which clings to laws of alleged importance that have become meaningless is not in the best of shape. Further, where these prohibitions are enforced, the clergy are so distanced from the laity, that they are, therefore, distrusted.

3. A 46-page self-administered questionnaire was sent to 7,260 of the 64,000 U.S. clergy (including bishops and those American priests living and working abroad); 5,155 usable questionnaires were returned, thus yielding a response rate of 71 percent. The sample design used in the NORC survey may be described as a stratified two-stage cluster sampling with probabilities proportional to size; individual responses were weighted for the analysis. In the first-stage sample 85 of the 155 American dioceses were chosen, plus 91 of the 253 self-governing units of religious institutes. In the second stage, 7,260 of the 64,000 American Catholic priests were drawn—35–70 from each primary sampling unit (NORC, 1972:317–23).

4. The source for the measures in the NORC questionnaire was question 81 (NORC, 1972: 419, see also, 346–47). The sources for the measures of work satisfaction, loneliness, and happiness were questions 11, 36J and 79 (NORC, 1972:379, 392, 419).

5. The source for the data on colleague support is a specially constructed index from the responses to question 69 (NORC, 1972:344–45). Normative commitment was measured in terms of conformity with the present norm of celibacy for all Catholic clergy (q. 36F), attitudes toward women (q. 53), and extent to which respondents indicated that the church's exercise of authority presented them with a "serious problem" (q. 36D). Commitment to the priestly profession was measured in terms of the respondent's response to the question (q. 74) whether or not he planned to resign from or remain in the priesthood (NORC, 1972: 392, 416, 391, 417).

6. See, for example, Charles Davis (1967). For a critical discussion of explaining priestly resignations in terms of intimacy problems, see Schneider and Zurcher (1970:197–200).

7. Two measures of association are used consistently throughout this study: the gamma statistic for cross tabulations of ordinal data and Cramer's V for cross tabulations involving nominal-ordinal data. Unless otherwise indicated, the coefficients present in the parentheses are gammas.

8. The friendship typology presented in Table 3 was constructed from the response to question 57A (NORC, 1972:410). Applying techniques of scaling to these data yielded a

Guttman Scale with a coefficient to scalability of .68 for diocesan and .52 for religious priests. I wish to acknowledge the valuable contributions of Zondra Lindblade, who constructed this scale and provided reliable assistance with the additional statistical analyses used in this chapter, and of Elizabeth Freidheim, who offered valuable suggestions for improving the exposition as a whole.

REFERENCES

Bouscaren, T. Lincoln, Adam C. Ellis, and Francis N. Korth
   1963   Canon Law: A Text and Commentary. 4th ed. rev. Milwaukee, Wisc.: Bruce Publishing Company.
Davis, Charles
   1967   A Question of Conscience. New York: Harper and Row.
Gannon, Thomas M.
   1979   "The impact of structural differences in the Catholic clergy." Journal for the Scientific Study of Religion 18 (December):350–362.
National Opinion Research Center
   1972   The Catholic Priest in the United States: Sociological Investigations. Washington, D.C.: United States Catholic Conference.
Parsons, Talcott
   1951   The Social System. New York: Free Press.
Schneider, Louis, and Louis Zurcher
   1970   "Toward understanding the Catholic crisis: observations on dissident priests in Texas." Journal for the Scientific Study of Religion, 9 (Fall):197–200.
Simmel, Georg
   1950   The Sociology of George Simmel. Translated, edited and with the introduction by Kurt H. Wolff. New York: Free Press.

PART III
SITUATED FRIENDSHIP:
COMMUNITIES

FRIENDSHIPS IN THE MILITARY COMMUNITY

Roger Little

Few occupational groups are marked by the significance of friendship as is the military organization. The unique nature of the interpersonal bond is derived from the intensity of mutual experiences in combat, the isolation of the family of military members from their kinship groups, the frequency of interaction required by an almost continuous group context, and the insulating effects of a unique occupational culture. It is all the more remarkable that friendship should have such significance in an institution that is viewed by many as the epitome of bureaucracy. Yet in no other occupational community is there a tradition of "comradeship" comparable to that of the soldier, sailor or airman.

This article is an attempt to combine published reports of research on friendships in the military community with the author's observations during a military career which included positions as an infantry private and platoon leader during World War 11 and as a psychiatric social worker and sociologist during the following years. The basic data are those collected for a doctoral dissertation during the Korean conflict. Later, the author participated in studies of the relationship between American military bases and Japanese and German communities. This included helicopter evacuation of casualties in Vietnam. (The latter studies, conducted under military sponsorship, are unpublished.)

Most empirical studies of friendships in the military organization have concentrated on the primary group in combat. Shils and Janowitz (1948) were the first to identify the significance of primary groups in the German Army in resisting Allied psychological warfare. On the basis of interviews with German prisoners of war captured during the last months of the war, when Allied victory was apparent, it was concluded that the individual combat soldier continued to be effective to the extent that the primary group "met his basic needs, offered him affection and esteem from both officers and comrades, and adequately regulated his relations with authority." Earlier, Marshall a military historian, had observed (1947) that only 15 percent of American combat troops fired their weapons at either personnel or positions, and that the small proportion of effective "fighters" were usually in small groups working together.

The most extensive and widely cited study is the two-volume work, *The American Soldier* (Stouffer, *et al.*, 1949), a collection of attitude surveys of World War II Army personnel on a variety of topics. Some data are relevant to friendships, especially those dealing with the significance of primary group loyalties in maintaining combat motivation. For example, in response to the question, "Generally, in your combat experience, what was most important to you in making you want to keep going and do as well as you could?" Thirty-nine percent answered "ending the war"; 14 percent "solidarity with the group"; nine percent "thoughts of home and loved ones;" ten percent "a sense of duty and self-respect"; and 28 percent miscellaneous factors. As indicated by Stein (1959), these data hardly suggest the primacy of primary group affiliations in combat. A more pervasive theme in Stouffer is the significance of the stratification of officers and enlisted men and the resentment expressed by enlisted men toward this system. Resentment was highest among garrison (non-combat) troops and least among combat men where junior officers were more socially integrated with enlisted men and shared their material discomforts as well as the risks of survival. This theme was extensively and brilliantly depicted by Mauldin, the cartoonist for the service newspaper, *Stars and Stripes,* in a series featuring the intimate relationships between two front line infantrymen, Willie and Joe.

Thus, at the beginning of the Korean Conflict, friendships in combat, as primary groups, had not been studied directly but only incidentally as research for other purposes. This author had the opportunity to make such a study as a participant observer with a rifle platoon in Korea for six months in 1952–1953. It was assumed that the informal—or primary—groups of riflemen would be comparable to industrial work groups, except that the relationships would be intensified by the effects of risk and functioning in a continuous group context. Some norms were found to be identical with work groups; for example, the regulation of exposure to risk was comparable to the restriction of production. Friendships—or buddy relationships—were defined at two levels. Like workers, riflemen were loyal to one another as status peers in a specific relational context, mediating the demands of the organization for their combat performance. But at a deeper level, friendships represented specific interpersonal choices in a system of mutual dependency essential for survival. Ideological factors were significant only to the extent that they were mediated by some credible element of the larger society, such as the family. (Little, 1965)

During the Vietnam War, Moskos (1970) conducted a similar study and detected a greater degree of self-interest in the maintenance of primary group ties, combined with "latent ideological factors." Ideological factors operated as ". . . a widespread attitudinal context of underlying value commitments; most notably, an anti-political outlook coupled with a belief in the worthwhileness of American society." Comparing his observations with previous studies he asserts that "rather than viewing soldiers' primary groups as some kind of semi-mystical bond of comradeship, they can be better understood as pragmatic and situational responses." He asserts that the differing explanations from the primary groups described by Stouffer, and Janowitz and Shils in World War II—what he interprets as "two man relationships" reported by Little during the Korean Conflict, to the "essentially individualistic soldier" he observed in Vietnam—suggests a trend toward increasing individuation in combat friendships.

None of the studies cited above were concerned with the military community in the larger sense. Indeed, they resemble markedly studies in industrial sociology which concentrate on the work group while ignoring the larger organizational and societal context in which the worker lives. Three studies did this.

During the years between World War II and the Korean Conflict, two studies of the Air Force Base Project utilized a larger perspective. Hunter's (1952) study of an "Air Force Base and Host Community" analyzed the relationship between base commanders and local community elites with particular reference to housing policies. Lindquist (1952) studied the family life of officers and airmen in a unit of the Strategic Air Command, including family roles, housing patterns, income and spending, and the impact of periodic absences from home (temporary duty) on family life. Unfortunately, neither of these studies was ever published, although they are available as government documents. The most significant study was *The Professional Soldier* (Janowitz, 1960). Although primarily concerned with the professional socialization of the officer corps of World War II and earlier, the process is analyzed in the context of the military community, the significance of etiquette, and the "gentlemanly code of honor" which regulates friendships among officers and their families. A comparable study, though less extensive, of enlisted men is *The American Enlisted Man* (Moskos, 1970). His analysis of the enlisted culture is especially insightful.

One final study, used extensively in this article, is the author's chapter, "The Military Family and Community" (Little, 1971), which consists of a secondary analysis and interpretation of a large number of surveys conducted by Armed Forces agencies for other purposes. No single report was sufficient for a publication, but viewed as a whole, the information provides a useful profile of the military family and community.

BASES FOR MILITARY FRIENDSHIPS

In this article, friendships in the military community will be analyzed in three phases: entry relationships, career friendships and friendships in retirement. A theory of friendship in the military organization is based on the following propositions:

1. Substantial interpersonal bonds are assumed to be necessary for the attainment of organizational goals and, hence, friendship among peers is deliberately fostered as an objective of training and personnel policies. The initial or "shakedown" cruise of a naval vessel, for example, is not only for the purpose of testing its mechanical fitness but also to enable crew members to develop functional interpersonal bonds or "esprit de corps." Similarly, the air crew and infantry unit are not considered "combat-ready" until such relationships are demonstrated in operational effectiveness.
2. The relationships are regulated by an extensive code of etiquette and ceremonial norms which exemplify the importance of friendship to the organization as well as standardizing the modes of conduct which are required. Thus, the gentlemanly code of the officer applies not only to the individual member, but extends as well to the behavior of his spouse and children. (Janowitz, 1959) The code is especially salient among officers; it is apparent also among enlisted members.

3. The unique conditions of life in the military community accentuate the importance of friendship. The absence of the husband-father during periods of field service, at sea, or during tactical maneuvers, leaves the family dependent on a network of interpersonal bonds and mutual aid with others in the military community to mitigate their isolation. Similarly, frequent changes of residence require an aptitude for the rapid establishment of new friendships.

4. The military community provides a set of common institutions such that the round of life is carried on in the same social context, using the same facilities, economic (the exchange and commissary), education (the dependents' school), medical (the dispensary or hospital), religious (the chapel) and domiciliary (the barracks or family "quarters"). This commonality of institutions reinforces friendship by providing a set of mutual experiences and identifications of enduring value. Even after retirement, former military members continue to use some of these facilities (especially the exchange, commissary, and medical facility), thus maintaining their identification with the social context of the military community.

ENTRY RELATIONSHIPS

Entering the armed forces always involves a sharp rupture of existing friendships and imposes an immediate necessity for establishing new relationships in a strange and distant environment and an esoteric occupational culture. Basic or "boot" training is indeed a rite of transition from youth to adulthood. Friendship at once becomes a necessity for survival rather than a purely social activity.

Several factors facilitate this transition. First is the fact that all recruits are "in the same boat," a condition in which all of their pre-service statuses and identities are declared irrelevant. They are immediately confronted with an enormous amount of material to be "learned"—not only the technical aspects of their military roles, but also a vast number of customs and traditions which have little immediate meaning or utility.

Second, most of the learning experiences occur in a group environment and require recruits to "team up" with one another for specific tasks: rifle marksmanship involves a "coach and pupil," physical training requires pairs of relatively equal size and agility, and the bivouac pup tent is one of the few occasions when men are required to sleep together in intimate proximity. The development of friendships is hastened.

Third, basic training fosters solidarity of the recruits in opposition to the "cadre" of training instructors and officers. There is a unique status stratification, therefore, between those who have already "made it" and have apparently committed themselves to a military career and those who are entering. This solidarity takes the form of fighting "the orderly room"—the military equivalent of City Hall. Preparation for inspections, for example, requires frantic and elaborate cooperation in cleaning the barracks, aligning the beds, and warning fellow recruits of the approach of the inspecting officers. This too fosters a range of intense friendships unlike those encountered in the peer group of youths but more like those of an industrial work group.

Finally, there is so little environmental privacy that individuals can find relative privacy only by developing friendships with a few persons who have similar needs and interests. This is the prototype of the combat buddy, without the danger that promotes the intense emotional bonds of that relationship. These friends are the ones to whom the recruit can confide in moments of homesickness, disappointment, anger, or fatigue, or to share the highly prized momentary escape from the training context: the week-end pass or liberty.

At the officer academies the entry process is even more elaborately organized to insure that friendships are developed. Periodic "peer ratings" are used by the academies to determine class standing and "aptitude" for an officer career. The cadets with the greatest skill in establishing a wide range of friendships are ranked highest in their class and selected for the most important leadership roles. Those cadets without such skills either learn them quickly or are eliminated from the Corps. Even after graduation from the academy, the social rank persists as an indicator of the officer's potential for prestigious assignments.

The novice enlisted wife has a more difficult entry experience—unlike the recruit or cadet—there are no institutional mechanisms for insuring her socialization into the military community. She usually resides in a strange civilian community close to the military base, completely isolated from the kinship and other pre-marital relationships which facilitate adjustment to the marital role in civilian life. Since the recruit or trainee is on duty for long periods during the day and night, and often prohibited from leaving the base except on weekends, the wife is alone for correspondingly long periods. She is dependent on other wives in similar conditions for friendship and access to the base facilities—the commissary, exchange, and hospital—where wives can establish friendships and participate in a common round of activities.

The adjustment of the officer's wife is less difficult. If she enters by marriage to an academy graduate, she will have experienced some anticipatory socialization by "dragging" (dating) while her husband was a cadet. Her entry is then elaborately celebrated by marriage during "June week" (graduation) at the academy chapel. The couple leave the ceremony through a corridor of arched sabers held by the peers of the groom which formally recognize their entry to the military community as a pair. Thereafter, she will probably live in quarters on the military post. Since the officer's wife is an almost essential component of her husband's occupational role, she is consistently incorporated in the social activities of the military community so that the establishment of friendships is simplified. An elaborate code of etiquette for her behavior is promulgated in numerous "guide books" and manuals, all of which emphasize the persisting importance of friendship in the military community and its effects on the career of the military member. (Little, 1971)

Entry relationships in the military community are based on the group context of activities, the stratification of recruits and cadre which promotes solidarity, and the institutional stress on the importance of friendships for organizational effectiveness—for both the military member and his spouse.

CAREER FRIENDSHIPS

During the longer period of a military career, other factors affect the establishment and maintenance of friendships. Residence on the base is more likely to result in the regulation of friendships by the norms of military organization. A basic division is that between officers and enlisted men, a distinction which is extended with equal significance to the spouse and children of the service member. This division affects the range of their potential friendships. However, normative regulation of officer friendship relations is more effective than that of enlisted men.

Enlisted men and warrant officers were three times as likely in 1968 to be married to foreign-born wives (20 percent and 22 percent) as were officers (six percent). Officers were more apt to have been married prior to overseas duty and the more integrated officer and family sub-community was more apt to favor marriage to Americans than was true of enlisted men and warrant officers. The latter frequently moved up from the ranks to their current position rather than receiving officer training. Twice as many enlisted men's wives were employed outside of the home as were officers' wives (32 percent to 16 percent). The officer's wife is less likely to work because her occupational role might put her in a subordinate relationship to the enlisted man or his employed wife. When officers' wives did work, they were more likely to be employed as teachers, nurses, or supervisors—roles which were identified with officer status and did not risk subordination. (Little, 1971).

Thus, friendships among enlisted men and their spouses could be established with less concern for normative regulation. Indeed, the regulation of marital choice created one of the most significant bases for friendships—that of foreign-born wives and their spouses. This friendship set transcended the officer, enlisted boundary and involved spouses of all ranks. But the friendships of officers and their wives were more visible: they were more likely to entertain at such public places as the officers' club. Furthermore, the nature of the friendship and its conformity to the norms could be interpreted as potentially affecting the officers' career, more often negatively than positively. (Little, 1970)

The only institutional setting for friendship relations which was relatively free of status distinctions was the chapel. Religious and church groups provided the major form of social participation by base residents. Wives were more active than military members, and the wives of junior officers and enlisted men were the most active. The church was the one familiar institution in the military community to which preservice behavior patterns could be easily transferred. Entry was readily granted and participation minimized the status distinctions prevailing elsewhere and dominating social life in the military community. But friendships established in religious activity were confined to the chapel and rarely transcended the rigid boundaries separating officers and enlisted men and their families.

The uniqueness of the occupational culture which prevails in the military organization tends to separate them from members of the larger society (or "civilians") and to correspondingly intensify friendships within the military community. Thus, garrison life brings couples together in a continuous round of social activities: to welcome new members and to bid goodbye to those departing ("Hail and Farewell"), to receive new commanders and their wives, to mark anniversaries of significance to the organization, and to mourn the departure or celebrate the return of spouses for or from training maneuvers, a long distance cruise, or a tour in a combat area. Each of these events provides an opportunity to establish—and suggests the need for—friendships within the organization (Little, 1971).

But the organization also intrudes by activities which require periodic separations of the marital pair, consequently forcing each spouse to turn to their sexual peers for mutually supportive relationships. When the husbands depart for the sea or field, wives are drawn into more intensive relations of mutual dependency based on present or past organizational affinity. Foremost as the basis for these friendships are the practical needs of sharing transportation to post facilities—the commissary, exchange and hospital—because a prolonged absence of the military member requires the remaining family to vacate military housing and to move into the adjacent civilian community. Secondly—and often emerging from this dependency—are the emotional and communicative needs of persons in the same relative plight, to share reactions about the affective deprivation of their mates, to compare correspondence from their absent spouses about their experiences in foreign areas, and to reassure one another of their spouses' probable continued marital fidelity. Common organizational membership is the primary focus for friendship relations in this period (Lindquist, 1952).

The friendship relations of the detached member of the marital pair are also changed. Separated from his wife and family, his circumstances are like those of a bachelor. Marital status declines in significance in friendship choices and persisting relations are almost exclusively with sexual peers. Such periods of detachment from family life—on a cruise or period of field service—have many of the characteristics of a prolonged bachelors' party. The long idle hours after the brief excitement of a flight or tactical exercise, or the brief interlude ashore after a monotonous cruise, are tempting opportunities for escape from the constraints of marital status and for reverting to the behavior patterns of pre-marital status. Friendship relations are intensified by the need for maintaining secrecy among peers about the nature of their activities, especially those which are sexual in fact or by implication.

The most intensive friendship relations among adults in the military community are those which develop among "buddies" in combat. All of the traditions of military comradeship are related to the intensity of these relationships. They seem to be functionally essential for the combat unit to operate effectively. They are induced by close and continuous spatial proximity and mutual exposure to hazards which threaten their lives and deprive them of comfort. Four norms of the buddy relationship have been identified (Little, 1965):

1. The buddy was a *confidante*. They were expected to "understand" one another so that they could tolerate any deviant emotional reactions such as expressing a fear of imminent death in combat or while on patrol. Thus, they engaged in long, rambling conversations about their pre-service lives, so that they became familiar with each other's pasts. This familiarity was reinforced by exchanging letters they had received from wives or girl friends so that they entered into each other's lives to a very real extent.

2. The relationship was subjective and secret, rather than overt and public, thus preserving the integrity of the small unit—the squad or platoon. A public display of friendship choices might have revealed some members to be unchosen, a frightening prospect on the battlefield when the integration of every member was essential for their survival. Such a display might also have made the friendships vulnerable to manipulation by the organization, by either ex-

ploitation—requiring the friends to go on patrol together, or by dissolution—transferring one friend to another unit so that distance would interfere with their relationship.

3. The combat role was subordinated to the friendship relation most of the time. Boastful talk about individual combat skills was suppressed. Persons who insisted on such talk were stigmatized by such negative labels as "heroes" or "war daddies" until they conformed to the norm. Persons who carried such labels were thought to be the ones most likely to forget, when in a combat crisis, that every man had a buddy and that they depended on each other.

4. Buddies tried to avoid situations where they would be forced to choose between loyalties as friends and their obligations to the organization as infantrymen. But if forced to make a choice, their loyalty to a buddy would come first. Thus, one buddy would avoid volunteering for hazardous tasks such as patrols because to do so would compel his buddy to reciprocate. But in a crisis where such a choice was unavoidable, the buddy would come first and the organization second. If a man was wounded he expected his buddy to stay with him until the medical aid man arrived, even though his organizational role required him to continue in the attack. Even in the extreme situation when one man would be overwhelmed by fear and "bug out" or flee the field—the most stigmatized kind of combat behavior—the remaining buddy would tolerate the behavior and not think less of him, even though the organization would impose severe sanctions.

However intensive the buddy relationship was in combat, it quickly dissolved when the necessity of mutual survival was over. Even when buddies were in the reserve bivouac rather than "on the line" in direct contact with the enemy, they became more contentious and less mutually supportive. When they left the unit they always promised to write to their buddies about life in "the world" (the United States), or to visit one another when both had returned, but they rarely did. Departure from the battlefield terminated the relationship (Moskos, 1970).

While buddy relationships were most characteristic of friendships among enlisted men in combat, there was one officer—the platoon leader—whose proximity to the enlisted men in combat hazards as well as living conditions would make him also a potential object of friendship relations. But such a relationship—between officers and enlisted men—was considered dysfunctional for the organization because it would jeopardize the officer's willingness to give orders essential to achieve organizational goals. Consequently, platoon leaders—who were Second Lieutenants by rank—were integrated ceremonially with other officers of equal and higher rank. On those occasions when they came together, their conversations were more often concerned with the ideals and traditions of the organization and its activities, than the rambling, intimate banter of the enlisted buddies in their bunkers within the range of enemy fire. Friendships were more difficult for officers to establish and maintain because they were isolated from their status peers most of the time. When they did come together, there was always a pervasive sense of hierarchy—whether of rank or of awards for exceptional valor—which made their relationships more formal. It inhibited the development of the intensive solidarity epitomized by the riflemen in the buddy system.

There were other enlisted men, not in combat, who developed friendships on different bases. These were men who worked at clerical tasks or "headquarters men." They were an elite, having some attributes lacked by men of the line, the riflemen: either more years of education or service or more specialized skills. Because of these factors and often because of social class origins, they were more like the officers. Headquarters men worked in a safe, comfortable environment so that their friendships were not as essential to survival as those of combat buddies. Indeed their working environment was so much more pleasant than their living space in the tent or barracks that they often returned to the office at night—to play cards, read, or talk. Their conversations were more sophisticated, less intimate, and more often concerned with their plans for the future, than those of the riflemen or even the officers. They were often cynical about military customs and traditions. Officers were viewed with more detachment and less awe than by riflemen because they worked in close proximity to them and shared secrets about their evaluations made by superior officers. Their friendships were more likely to be based on such criteria as common educational level or pre-service region of residence than by the mutual risk shared by riflemen. Because they had ready access to transportation, they were more likely to maintain earlier friendships by visiting them in the headquarters of distant units. But these relationships were also terminated by separation from the service area (Little, 1956).

Thus career friendships were based on recurrent experiences of military life. A basic division which regulates the range of friendships is that between officers and enlisted men. Social relationships among officers are more explicitly regulated than among enlisted men; thus enlisted men are more likely to marry foreign wives than officers, and officers' wives are less likely to be employed outside of the household than enlisted men's wives. Organizational activities require periodic separation of spouses; during these interludes friendships with members of their own sex are intensified. The most intensive friendships are between buddies in combat—riflemen in direct contact with the enemy.

LEGITIMATING CONDITIONS IN CAREER FRIENDSHIPS

Career friendships in the military community are typically relationships among relatively young adults. A usual characteristic of such relationships is that they are dependent on earlier and later institutional affirmations. In the civilian community, this occurs on such major kinship-related occasions as weddings, christenings, or funerals. Thus, young, adult friendships more often "pay off" in a sense as potential guests at the wedding of the friends themselves, or as "friends of the family" who can be invited by the parents. The number of guests at a wedding is often interpreted as a "score" of the social integration—or range of friendships—of the couple and their parental families. The invitation to the wedding as well as the participation and "gift-giving" ritually reaffirms friendships, not only at the wedding ceremony but throughout the duration of the marriage. Later, the guest list for the wedding ceremony constitutes the "mailing list" for the first birth announcement.

However, since most members of the military community are married either prior to entry, or in the civilian locale of the bride (with the single exception of the academy wedding), this institutional affirmation of the friendships of the couple does not have the same long-range significance because they are quickly isolated from the social context in which they were meaningful. Even when weddings do occur in the military community, the guests are predominantly the military peers of the groom, so that organizational relationships are substituted for friendship obligations.

The funeral provides a comparable occasion for the affirmation of friendships when it occurs in a community which extends through the entire life cycle. But death rarely occurs in the military community of young adults, even though it is a major contingency of a military career. When it does occur, the funeral is conducted at the pre-service place of residence where the deceased military member or his spouse are taken for burial. Most deaths occur after retirement when career friendships have been weakened or dissolved.

Other factors tend to limit the depth and persistence of career friendships. The personnel policy of rotation—from one post to another, and from home bases to overseas stations—precludes the establishment of an enduring neighborhood. It produces constant interruption of friendships and requires that they be established with other persons at other places. The uncertainty of the duration of residence at one base limits the degree of commitment to the friendship and fosters cynicism about the enduring value of such relationships. Finally, the fact that the military organization itself so dominates the military community, and that the occupational role of the military member is so much more significant for his placement in the community, fosters a greater investment in organizationally related friendships that will "pay off" for his career (Little, 1971).

FRIENDSHIP IN RETIREMENT

Military retirements are unique because they occur relatively early in the life cycle—after 20 to 25 years of service, or ages 40 to 50 years—when the service member's civilian peers are well-established in their occupations and communities. Consequently, entry to existing friendship sets, voluntary associations, or other forms of informal organizations, is difficult. This point also coincides with the period in the family cycle when the children of the retiree are in late adolescence or early adulthood and financial needs are greatest. Unless the retiree has a military occupation with a civilian equivalent (such as one of the professions) resettlement as a civilian involves a sudden decline in both occupational prestige and income level. These factors tend to foster reliance on—and attempts to maintain—career friendships.

One pattern is largely vicarious, and that is the continued utilization of such military facilities as the exchange, commissary and hospital. Although there are some economic "savings" in using these facilities in preference to their civilian equivalents, the social factor is probably the greater. They constitute a familiar environment in which the pre-retirement status is still relevant—the courtesies extended to active duty officers, for example, are extended equally to those in retirement. But they also provide opportunities for renewing career friendships, or for establishing new friendships based on pre-retirement experiences: common service in a foreign or domestic post, former membership in the same organization, or mutual loneliness in the civilian community.

Another pattern is the establishment of satellite communities of retirees in the immediate vicinity of military posts (Monterey, California; San Antonio, Texas; and Columbus, Georgia). Such communities facilitate the persistence of career friendships, access to the facilities and amenities of the military community, and often participation in the affirmation ceremonies of weddings of their children and funerals of their peers. They also mitigate the loneliness of the retired status and the problems of entering existing friendship groups in the civilian community.

A third pattern, often in combination with the preceding two, is the process of "keeping in touch" with friends after separation by retirement, through Christmas notes, and the graduation and wedding announcements of the children. Service newspapers are also scanned for retirement notices and obituaries. These activities maintain the military community and career friendships in fantasy and also mitigate the alienation of the retired status.

CONCLUSION

The "loneliness" of the retired status is a "cost" of the intensity of friendships during active service, the dominance and pervasiveness of the organization in the military community, and the lack of segregation of occupational roles and friendship relations. It also suggests the principal theme of friendships in military organization: their instrumental rather than expressive quality. There is a similarity between the friendship of an enlisted rifleman who would risk his life, or even die, to save his buddy (but does not maintain the relationship after his brief term of service) and the retired career officers on the officers' club golf course: their friendships are meaningless without the group context of military life.

REFERENCES

Hunter, Floyd
    1952   Air Force Base and Host Community. Chapel Hill: Institute for Research in Social
           Science, University of North Carolina.
Janowitz, Morris
    1960   The Professional Soldier. New York: Free Press.
Janowitz, Morris, and R. W. Little
    1965   Sociology and the Military Establishment. New York: The Russell Sage Foundation.
Lindquist, Ruth
    1952   The Family Life of Officers and Airmen in a Bomb Wing. Chapel Hill: Institute
           for Research in Social Science, University of North Carolina.
Little, Roger W.
    1956   "Headquarters soldier." Army 7(4):58–65.
Little, Roger W.
    1964   "Buddy relations and combat performance." In M. Janowitz, (ed.), The New
           Military. New York: Russell Sage Foundation, 1964.
Little, Roger W.
    1970   "Dossiers in military organization." In S. Wheeler, (ed.), On Record: Files and
           Dossiers in American Life. New York: Russell Sage Foundation.
Little, Roger W.
    1971   "The military family and community." Pp. 247–270 in R. W. Little, (ed.), Hand-
           book of Military Institutions. Beverly Hills, Calif.: Sage Publications.
Marshall, S. L. A.
    1947   Men Against Fire. New York: William Morrow and Co.
Mauldin, Bill
    1945   Up Front. New York: Henry Holt and Co.
Moskos, Charles
    1970   The American Enlisted Man. New York: Russell Sage Foundation.

Shils, Edward A., and Janowitz, M.
   1948   "Cohesion and disintegration in the Wehrmacht in World War II." Public Opinion
          Quarterly 12, Summer: 280–315.
Stein, Maurice R.
   1960   "World War II and military communities." Pp. 175–198 in The Eclipse of Com-
          munity. Princeton, N.J.: Princeton University Press.
Stouffer, Samuel, *et al.*,
   1949   The American Soldier: Studies in Social Psychology in World War II. Princeton,
          N.J.: Princeton University Press.

THE PUBLIC SOCIETY OF INTIMATES:

FRIENDS, WIVES, LOVERS AND OTHERS IN THE DRINKING-DRIVING DRAMA

Joseph Gusfield, Joseph Kotarba
and Paul Rasmussen

The affinity of the role concept to dramaturgical usage has been repeatedly pointed out in sociological discussion (Manning, 1978; Brissett and Edgley, 1975, Introd.). This paper is less an addition to such analyses than an exercise in its application to a specific area of behavior—drinking-driving originating from bars. The material is drawn from an ethnographic study of public bars conducted as part of a study of drinking-driving. Our focus here is on the interaction among bar patrons who act in the roles of intimates—friends, wives, husbands, lovers or significant others in some relatively recurrent relationship.

The bar is a specific context within which role behavior takes on particular, situated characteristics. As a stage, it is a theatre whose rules are not the same as those of some other theatres. Many analysts of bars and drinking behavior have pointed out that public drinking places are areas of unusual accessibility to social interaction (Cavan, 1966, Ch. 3; LeMasters, 1975; Clark, forth.). Unlike private homes, they are public places, formally open to anyone of legal age who decides to enter. But they are also accessible in a way different from private homes and from many other public places such as restaurants, stores or theatres. In Erving Goffman's phrase, they are "open regions"—places where unacquainted people have the right to engage each other in social interaction (Goffman, 1963, p. 132). Just by taking the role of customers, people can engage others in conversation without being obtrusive or ill-mannered. This prescriptive right to "invade" social privacy does not preclude differences in levels and types of sociability between and among types of customers, such as "regulars" and "transients." Nevertheless, it does turn the public arena of the bar into some of the private aspects of a home, a matter of the continuing appeal of the "pub" to its patrons and to field workers bedeviled by problems of entry.[1]

Since Goffman's *Presentation of the Self in Everyday Life*, it has been an axiom of dramaturgical analysis that actions "front stage" differ from those "backstage" (Goffman, 1956, pp. 66–86). Because behavior occurs before a mixed audience of strangers and acquaintances it takes on a public display considerably different from the private. The housewife prepares the living room for company; the sergeant gets the platoon in order before inspection; the drinker displays competence in drinking before the audience of the barroom. "Stage" is itself a metaphorical expression—a site for appearing in public. Much depends on who constitutes the audience and what their relation is to the actor.

Intimacy, as we use it here, is less a matter of physical closeness than of openness to embarrassment. As the many accounts of the shyness and strain of the wedding night constantly attest, the man and woman who make love for the first time to each other may be acting "front stage" and in public as are the theatrical performers. Between human beings there are layers of defensiveness and performance-orientation which can be shed between intimates as the Victorian woman shed her petticoats on retiring. It is this quality of "moral stripping" which enable intimates to act in the public situation of bars in a manner of particular relevance to the phenomena of drinking and driving.

ETHNOGRAPHY AND THE STUDY OF CULTURE

In order to present the material, we too must set the stage. The central material of our paper is one scene among the several that make up the complete drama of our study. Something of the first act must be conveyed.

This is *not* a study of the public problem of drinking-driving. It is a description and analysis of the phenomena and behavior of drinking-driving. Our intention has been to investigate this subject matter as sociologists would study other forms of social life, such as getting married, crossing the street, or playing tennis. The research has proceeded on the assumption that drinking-driving, like other social phenomena, is organized and responsive to shared understandings and rules. The aim of our ethnography has been to discover the rules and understandings which govern the experience and behavior of drinking-driving.

This is an ethnographic study. The data have been obtained through observation, participant-observation, conversation and quasi-interviews conducted in four public bars in San Diego County. Two of the bars were neighborhood bars and two were transient in type. The data represent more than 100 hours of observation of interaction in these public facilities. This is a study of the drinking-driving phenomenon as it emerged in the naturalistic setting of barrooms—as a topic of conversation, as behavior, as a response to queries initiated by observers.

Underlying the choice of an ethnographic method are assumptions regarding the nature of social life and the object of this study. While we do seek to uncover the rules of action, such rules are not as clearly discoverable as law is to lawyers—through examination of definitive statements. Most rules of social behavior are tacit and unstated. Frequently they arise in interaction and can only be recognized after the fact rather than *a priori*. They are, however, the rules used by participants, not those imposed by others—legal officials, managers, or social observers. An ethnographic analysis is preoccupied with understanding the orderliness in behavior, not with predicting it. In observing behavior, including conversation, our intention is to capture the rules and meanings by which drinking-driving is defined and observed by participants. It is also to understand the cultural categories and meanings through which drinking-driving is assessed, understood and seen as appropriate or inappropriate, and the ways in which such categories are applied in different circumstances. Whatever the system of organization derived from our observations, the result is a set of assertions of how people expect each other to behave within that culture (Mehan, 1980, Ch. 5).

Frake has expressed the same idea in another fashion, likening the ethnographer to the linguist:

> . . . it is not, I think, the ethnographer's task to predict behavior per se, but rather to state the rules of culturally appropriate behavior. . . . In this respect the ethnographer is again akin to the linguist who does not attempt to predict what people will say but to state the rules for constructing utterances which native speakers will judge as grammatically appropriate. The model of an ethnographic statement is not:

'if a person is confronted with stimulus X, he will do Y,' but: 'if a person is in situation X, performance Y will be judged appropriate by native actors.''' (Frake, 1969, p. 124)

Collecting Data

The virtue of ethnography is that social behavior is observed in its natural scene. If, as we assume, social rules are complex and take account of specificity of situations, then efforts to observe them in retrospect are both too general and too much distorted by the character of the setting in which they occur. Responses to questionnaires are affected by both of these difficulties: they cannot cover the multifold and highly specific contingencies in which action occurs, and they are not responses to the situation to which questionnaires are addressed. Responses consist of behavior occurring within the situation of question-answer. They are behavior addressed to the question-answer situation rather than to the situation in which the drinking-driving behavior occurs.

More significantly, the attempt to derive the rules and meanings used by participants is limited by the investigator's lack of experience or observation of participant's behavior. Put in another way, the sociologist cannot know what questions are sensible, significant and relevant to the participant's social organization without a prior exposure to it.

Thus, the principle of ethnographic data collecting is to derive the data as much as possible from the naturalistic settings in which it occurs. This is not always possible, and departures from it were made, but the effort was to keep as close as possible to the setting which was under observation.

More specifically, three units of data were obtained:

a. Naturally occurring participant observation: Here the observer either perceived behavior or heard conversation in which he was or was not a participant as a barroom customer. Example: The observed discussion between a bartender and a customer over continuance of service.

b. Conversation, and in a few instances, behavior initiated by the observer on matters of interest to him but introduced as part of the action of him as barroom customer. For example, "steering" a conversation toward topics relevant to drinking-driving.

c. Quasi-interview: Here the observer identifies himself as someone "interested in studying drinking behavior" and elicits conversation about previously observed bar behavior or other matters of interest to him. This was only used in the case of bartenders or "bouncers." An example of this is a query to a "bouncer" about whether he has experienced any troubles from drinking-driving in his work recently.

In this account of different units of data, the role persona of the observer undergoes change—from observer to participant-observer to interviewer. In all of these postures, the observer assumed a continuous role—that of customer in the bar. In that role is found the reason for selecting bars as the setting of this study. Simply by virtue of appearing as a customer, the observer can engage in conversation without seeming to be obtrusive. This characteristic of bars is the feature which makes them especially useful to the ethnographer. The relation between bars, drinking, and driving also makes them excellent sites for the study of drinking-driving but so too do parties in private homes. What the bars possess, however, is greater accessibility to observation and to participant-observation.[2]

The system for recording data used in this study is much like that used in many other bar studies and other field research in contemporary societies (Cavan, 1966). We call it the "stool system," because of the key role of the public toilet in it. The observer functioned as a cusotmer, talking with other customers and/or the bartender. He observed his interaction and other interaction within his perception. He had to rely on his memory to "record" significant conversation and events as they occur. Every possible moment socially acceptable, he left the scene of interaction and went to the men's toilet. Using the toilet stall as a place of privacy, he made quick, mnemonic notes of the previous interaction. On arriving home, or in the car, after the observational period, the short notes were expanded. The expanded version was put on tape and transcribed by secretarial service. It is these expanded versions which constitute the data of the study. The frequency with which the observer was able to make the original, short notes depended upon the interaction taking place and his judgment that it could be missed. This variable also included the risk that too frequent absences would occasion suspicion among fellow-customers. Note-writing approximately once an hour appears to have been the norm, although we did not keep a record of it. A reputation for weak kidneys is one of the risks of this kind of field work.

MANAGING COMPETENCE: THE PUBLIC DEFENSE OF THE SELF

The observations and analysis were particularly attentive to how the phenomena of drinking-driving was talked about in the context of the bar. Perhaps the major conclusion of the ethnography was that drinking-driving was assumed to be the normal, anticipated behavior of adult male drinkers. The deviating, problematic act is not drinking and driving. That is the behavior which has to be explained to others. The fully competent person is assumed to be able to participate in the drinking culture of the bar and to be able to manage his automobile as well. When his driving becomes problematic, as a topic of conversation through his appeal for help or through the intervention of others, that is taken as an attack on his competence as a member of the immediate group. (We use the male term because in the bars studied, females are not bound by the same rules, as explained below.)

Competence display is a first order of understanding. In a number of situations people did ask for help or intervention did occur. Customers did limit their drinking and/or their driving, and openly admitted it. It is the systems of accounts for behavior that interested us (Scott and Lyman, 1968). Admissions of incompetence do occur against the backdrop of the usual maintenance of a "front" of competent drinking which includes competent driving as well. Instances of conflict between the actor's protestations of competence and the other patrons' claims of his incompetence do occur. However, in many instances the display of competence is maintained through a secondary order of competence—the open recognition of one's incompetence. What this paradox involves is acceptable excuses, what in law are called "exculpatory defenses" for committing otherwise criminal or civilly liable actions (Hart, 1968). Self-defense is such an excuse to the charge of murder. The use of exculpatory defenses is an aspect of much of daily life and speech. Illness, for example, is an acceptable defense for incompetence in many areas of behavior (Parsons and Fox, 1952).

It is permissible for the patron to ask for help or to avoid or curtail drinking and/or driving when the drinker can present an acceptable excuse, such as the need to be at work exceptionally early or the currently poor state of his automobile. These explain away the charge of incompetence.

There is a further level of paradox. Competent drinkers are also presumed to recognize when they have become incompetent. This is a second order in maintenance of the display of competence before an audience. There is a rationale behind the triteness of "*I* know when *I've* had enough." The self is rescued from the status of a flawed person when the departure from the norm of drinking-driving can be explained as a special circumstance or is a result of the actor's own recognition. The expectation of adult male competence is one of self-management and drinking. Within the bars we studied, especially the neighborhood bars, that display of self-management was most in danger of being undermined when the patron had others define him as "too drunk to drive."

Certain categories of people are defined as already less than fully competent and their admission of limited drinking or non-drinking-driving is accepted and/or intervention more readily offered. Women and old people have a license to refrain from the modal adult male norm; to ask for, to accept and to be offered aid which would be embarrassing or insulting to modal males. Similarly people defined as "alcoholics" have excuses to display less competence. These categories of people are perhaps already "failed" persons and less self-management is expected, although the issue of the role of women is more complex and will be examined in detail below.

Accident or arrest are not profoundly operative risks. These are seen as the "normal risks" of drinking in daily life. When the risk is greater than usual or the responsibility of management is greater, the occasion exists for defining otherwise incompetent behavior as quite competent in this situation. The drinker who has been arrested for drinking-driving and thus faces a stiffer penalty if rearrested can excuse his use of taxis. Men who are accompanying women can use that relationship of greater responsibility to excuse their limited drinking.

To sum up the conclusions derived from one phase of our observations, drinking and driving is the behavior expected of competent males, although a range of excuses for not adhering to this norm are culturally available. Within the arena of the bar and the groups who serve as relevant audiences, the actor attempts to manage his self-presentations so as to conform with that model.

The following colloquy illustrates the system of norms at work in a situation in which others both challenge the self-display and help the actor maintain it:

First Man: You're sure as shit driving home tonight.
Second Man: No, I ain't . . . You're the one who's drinking Seven-up. You gotta take care of your buddy, even when you don't have the balls to take care of him by drinking with him.
First Man: Don't worry, I'll get you home. I wouldn't strand you on the street at this time of night, would I?

THE ROLES OF FRIENDS, WIVES, LOVERS, OTHER INTIMATES AND PEERS AND THE MANAGEMENT OF COMPETENCE

The disposition to act competently has its most compelling impact where the drinker confronts an audience whose judgment of him depends, to some degree, on its view of his competence. The public interaction of friends, lovers, spouses or other significant people is complicated by the degrees of intimacy between them. They may be part of the audience before whom competent display is called out. Yet as they are close to the drinker—peers, friends, intimates—they can, and even should, feel the responsibility to intervene when they judge the drinker to have passed the point of competence.

The more intimate the relationship, the more the members can accept the drinker as incompetent, can tear down the front of competence with no regard for the tissue of exceptions, excuses and defenses by which the self is dramatized as competent to cope with the world of drinking and driving. It is the essential character of family and primary relationships not only that the person can be hated, excoriated, embarrassed and insulted without the relationship being necessarily destroyed. Husbands and wives, lovers and mates, or close associates, can say things to each other that would make other relationships shrivel and die. That is also what it means to be "backstage" rather than "on-stage."

Both aspects of the staging of the self—its being "onstage" and "offstage" must be perceived if our account of how the peer group operates is to be understood. Despite the modal norm of the self-competent drinker and driver responsible for his own actions, there *is* intervention; there *is* criticism; there *is* advice and embarrassment. The self is not permitted to exist in a world of its own script.

Borrowing two terms first used by Everett Hughes to described the rights and responsibilities of professions, we are saying that when the drinker is in a society with intimates, that group has the mandate to preserve his display of competence but also the license to destroy it where it seems to threaten him or themselves (Hughes, 1958). Mandates imply obligations; licenses imply liberties. This is the point of this paper.

We use the term "intimate" rather than "peer" in order to emphasize the character of the relationship rather than the status of the parties involved. However, below we will refer to "peer intervention" as the general process by which others attempt to influence or control the drinker. The basis of legitimate rights and/or duties rests on the degree of intimacy between the two people involved, rather than on an official, legal or managerial one. The test is a practical one: imagine what the interaction would signify were it between two "strangers." In fact we have seen similar "insults" between comparative strangers in a bar result in fist fights.

In one sense the bar is itself an arena within which relations between customers are defined in terms of closer intimacy than exists in non-drinking situations in American society. The major reason we selected the bar as a research site was the easy availability of people to each other, the lack of strong restraints against engaging each other in conversation, and the role of alcohol in dissolving reserve between strangers. It is a place where self-expressiveness is quicker to reach action and display than in soberer places. If it is a place where friendliness can be fostered, it is also a place where hostility and antipathy are closer to expression. Both help and abuse are there as tangible possibilities. It is the presence of other people formed into a social group that sets the scene for possible interventions. As one customer at a transient cocktail lounge put it, in discussing the constraints on his drinking and his driving when with a date or when alone: ". . . just having someone there to tell you when to stop and having someone there to do the driving at the end of an evening."

The neighborhood bars studied encourage and develop groups of "regulars"—people who come into the bar several times during the week and come to constitute a recurrent group. One of us estimated that at most times in one such bar (Al's) customers were fifty percent regulars. The group of regulars at another (The Club) were the base of much of the observations there. At The Club the pattern of each member buying rounds not only acted to control the amount of drinking and put pressure on members to drink, but it also was the means by which the drinker created the solidarity with others that defined him as "in" the group. "Rounds" are tangible obligations to stay and to uphold one's duties to others.

Peer Intervention: The Mandate to Help

In the vernacular of American language the incompetence of the drunk is a test of the charity of his intimates. It is noteworthy that people bolster their claim to intimacy with others by statements such as "I diapered you" and "I held your head when you'd too much to drink." George's roommate, embarrassed by the behavior he displayed when drunk at The Club, is "even sort of mad at George for letting him get that drunk."

The mandate to help your buddies is two-fold: a mandate to help with the driving and a mandate to help preserve the display of self as competent. George's roommate was embarrassed by his behavior when drunk and feels his buddy, George, should have helped to prevent it. We saw friends help drinkers protest they were not too drunk to be served, to define the situation as bartenders' obstinacy. We saw three regulars help a drunken fourth by carrying him to his car to sleep it off.

The canon of mutual aid can be called upon by the drinker, by his intimates and even by bartenders to help one of "their bunch." One of us recorded an incident at The Club in which five men came in, already visibly drunk. The oldest was about 35. There was a younger man with him, about 27 or 28. Both were evidently "smashed" but the younger one even more so. They were buying rounds; the first by one of the soberer of the group. The young one wanted to buy the next round but the bartender wouldn't let him because he'd had too much to drink.

It was one of the few times I'd seen Frank actually refuse drinks. The older guy who was a little bit soberer but not a whole lot, claimed that he would take care of the 'kid' and drive him home. . . . Frank then allowed him to buy a round of drinks for everyone. The direct quote from Frank earlier was "you already have enough to drink. Let it ride for a while. Besides, you're already drunk on your ass." His friend's direct quote was "Frank, I'll take care of him, Lord knows he has taken care of me often enough." (Gusfield, 1981)

The "kid" (note how he has been turned into an object of obligation and also legitimately lessened competence) has not only been permitted to continue drinking, but also to preserve his display of competence by holding up his end of the rounds-buying obligation. Further, he is to be helped in getting home.

Bartenders can utilize the mandate to help by calling on customers to help transport fellow regulars. This was pointed out earlier in the ways in which women and old people are special obligations. Bartenders at Al's have been observed to ask fellow patrons to take someone home. Frank did this with George one night:

Richard (age about 50) came in, sat down at the bar and kind of went into a sleep, would occasionally wake up but go back into his sleep. Frank served him a beer but commented about how he'd had enough to drink and definitely would not drive home. ". . . He's not a chronic drunk but when he does get drunk he drinks heavily to the point of passing out." Near the end of the evening when George and I were leaving, Frank asked George if he would be willing to drive Richard home. George said that of course he wouldn't allow his good friend Richard to drive home in his present condition. Richard put up no fight at all. He knew George quite well and gave him the keys. We carried Richard out of the bar, got him in the car and George and he drove back to his place. I followed in my car to pick up George and we left the car there with the keys under the seat so that Richard would not drive off.

Richard's incompetence is displayable to George but similar incompetence is not so readily shown to everyone. (Note how George defines Richard as "my good friend.") One's friends and intimates have also to attempt to preserve the display of competence where possible, as the older man did for the "kid" above. Two incidents at Al's show the complexity of actors operating on different stages at the same time. One occurred at closing time as a couple probably in their late 50s got up to leave. They had been drinking all night and the man was making a lot of noise, laughing and hollering on his way out.

The young bartender hollered over to him to be careful and to take it easy. The man very stoically said that he was okay; he can take care of himself. In hearing this his wife laughed quite loudly and said that her husband was okay because she was doing the driving. The man looked at her kind of sternly as if embarrassed at her statement about his condition. The couple then quietly walked out. His embarrassment and "stern look" is the sign of his wife's breaking her mandate to support, or at least not undermine, his display of competence.

In another incident the temporary bartender acts to preserve the "front" of a regular customer through handling the display of the customer toward other patrons yet intervening in a "backstage" interaction:

> At about 1:30 a.m. Tim actually began mentioning that he should really be getting on, because his wife would start to worry about him at this point. As he was speaking, both Harriet and Amy grabbed onto his arms and told him that he should stick around a little bit longer. Harriet joked about how Tim could not possibly leave the presence of such beautiful women. It was at this point that Dana (the female temporary bartender) bought the last house round for everybody, including myself. Tim actually did sit for another ten minutes or so and finished his house drink quite quickly, but again said that he really had to get going. As Tim staggered up off his bar stool, Harriet hollered out that Tim should call a cab to get him home. Amy and Harriet both started laughing at how Tim was really drunker than he figured. At this point Dana entered into the conversation and laughingly said that Tim was too young of a man to take a cab home. Dana said that Tim would take care of himself but would probably have a better ride home if one of the two ladies would take him home with her. We all laughed at this.

Having saved Tim's face in front of the two fellow-customers, the bartender now treats him in a different fashion, on a different stage:

> When Tim did stand up and began saying his goodbyes to everyone at the bar, Dana did go up to him and quite seriously and quietly asked him if he wanted her to call a cab for him. Tim quite soberly answered that he appreciated the offer but thought that he was really okay. Dana did not pursue the topic further but simply told Tim to be careful and to come back soon.

Tim was not a new or transient customer. Dana knew him well enough to be able to comment on his marital problems after Tim had left.

Peer Intervention: The License to Abuse

In the incident above, where the wife embarrasses the husband by contradicting his "front," she acts abusively. It is a mark of intimate relationships that between the parties there is both love and hate; both help and abuse. Abusive relations did occur among strangers and slight acquaintances during our observations but that always meant trouble, violence, or the threat of violence. Abuse occurs, in the framework of this study, where the "front" of the drinker is directly attacked and his competence impugned. Intimates are people to whom incompetence can be displayed and insult accepted without impairing the self irreparably. Mel, a customer at Al's, tells us that his present girlfriend, Maureen, once locked him in his car and drove off in her car, carrying his car keys. She had tried to keep him from driving because she felt, over his protests, that he was too drunk to drive.

The following scene illustrates how the mix of the mandate to help and license to abuse can operate:

At approximately 1:45 a.m. Fern mentioned to Alex: "Let's go, Alex, I want to get out of here." Alex did not respond immediately to her request, for he was again down with his head on the bar. Fern then shook Alex and told him again that she wanted to go home. I noticed that Alex's keys were sitting on the bar along with his money and his change. The following is a close reconstruction of the rest of their conversation before leaving Al's:

Alex: "Yeah, let's go home now."
Fern: "Oh no, you're not driving. Give me the keys."
Alex: "Bullshit, it's my car, lady, and I'm gonna get us home."
Fern: "I'm not riding with you. If you drive, I swear I'll go home with someone else, and you can bet that it will probably be a long ride home."
Alex: "Why you cheap whore . . ."
Fern: "You fucking drunk! You're the one who forces me to have to take care of myself."

By this time the argument was getting quite loud and the bartender came over to quiet them down. (He talked very quietly to them and what was said could not be heard). In any event, when they got up to leave, Fern grabbed the keys just before they got up, and Alex didn't object.

The observer followed them out to the street and watched Fern lead Alex to the car, although he insisted it was parked elsewhere. She unlocked the passenger side and opened it for Alex. He stumbled getting in and she had to hold the door for him. She got in on the driver's side, they discussed something too faintly for the observer to overhear and then Fern drove the car away.

Wives, Lovers and the Place of Women

We have repeatedly drawn attention to the special significance of the male-female intimacy in defining mandates and licenses around drinking and driving. The woman with whom the man has an intimate relationship is a source of responsibility for the male. He should be competent to drive her home. But the protest against her intervention is often a sham, a display to the bar audience. It is contradicted by the behavior in which she takes the keys and drives. The expectation of the greater sobriety of the female remains a folk belief in this segment of American society.

The case of Dave and Debra will serve as illustrative of the relationship frequently observed. Dave and Debra are regulars at Al's. Dave is a pool player by avocation and spends much of his time at Al's drinking and shooting pool, while Debra, who is with him, usually sits nearby also drinking but neither as much nor as frequently as Dave. Dave also represents Al's as part of the pool team in competition with other bars.

Debra acts as a kind of "mascot" for the pool team, arranging schedules and taking care of equipment. The observer asked her if her duties ever involved her in having to drive the guys around:

Debra said that she often drives home after an evening of shooting pool because the men tend to get carried away with each other, mostly in their post-game celebrations. . . . I later noticed that Dave simply allows Debra to drive him home after leaving Al's, without any apparent negotiation between them.

I asked Debra if she ever felt any responsibility for Dave and his driving home after a date with her. Debra says that Dave is a very strong man and can take care of himself . . . I mentioned that I remembered seeing her drive Dave home on several occasions. She said that sometimes she will drive Dave back to her apartment because he has a long ride after he leaves her. On this particular evening Dave did the driving. He appeared quite sober after drinking only two or three drinks the entire evening. The only times I have seen Debra drive Dave are when he gets drunk, which is never while he is playing competitive pool. I have seen her drive when they stop at Al's after playing pool at another bar.

At all three bars—The Club, Al's, and The Hermitage (the cocktail lounge)—women driving men passengers was by no means unusual. Counts of driving at closing times showed that among couples, women drive anywhere from one-quarter to one-half of the observed occasions. The display of competence and responsibility inside the bar was belied by the behavior inside the automobile.

The peers whom we observed in the bars described above constituted related people for whom the social script provided a set of roles that could be drawn upon in interacting between the drinker and potential interveners in the drinking-driving process. In this arena the inhabitants of the bar, including the bartenders and the regular customers, had developed recurrent patterns which, along with the extra-bar relationships of husband-wife, friends and/or lovers, constituted a small society. It is a stage on which to display the varying layers of acceptance and/or rejection of the self conveyed by the drinker. Although not elaborated on in this paper, the role which the bartender could play as intervener and as supporter of the drinker's displays of competence was an important part of the total picture. Rights of intervention, of obligatory help and of public abuse were embedded in a social organization that governed the actions permitted or constrained by the intermixture of roles and relationships.

Contrasting mixes of scenes and relationships made for distinctive differences in the drinking-driving phenomena. One of the bars studied, That Place, was large, two-storied, crowded, noisy and patronized by young (mostly under twenty-five), single men and women. Characterized both by us and by its patrons as a "singles bar" it was one in which mixed couples (male and female) seldom arrive together. Women arrive, and often leave, in twos and threes and men in groups or alone. Especially among the men, the belief in the normalcy and competence of drinking-driving persisted with little observation of bartenders, women or others intervening, although the "buddy" system was potentially at work. Here, at That Place, the management was conspicuously absent, a cluster of regulars was less observable and the patrons thrown more often onto their own resources than was the case at the two neighborhood bars described. A sense of fluidity, chaos and open space mitigated the physical closeness between the management bartender and the patron. What this meant for the drinking-driving process was an atmosphere of heightened privacy and non-intervention. Patrons came and left encased in the bubble of their own sense of competence. No social world was generated in which new relationships could emerge in the bar or where existent roles could be drawn upon.

One of the bouncers sums up the orientation of the singles bar and its prevailing atmosphere (This is from the observer's account of his conversation.):

> he said that he had never called a cab for a customer. . . . most of the guys who come into That Place pride themselves on being good drivers, even when they're totally loaded . . . you just have to look at their 'wheels.' . . . some of them do a lot of racing, on and off the road . . . it's kind of a tough thing to talk to a customer about his ability to drive home, whether or not he's drunk or sober . . . he thought that even some of the customers who are really drunked up have very little trouble driving home because of their expertise behind the wheel."

SITUATING CONTEXTS: THE BAR AS SCENIC

The dramaturgy of drinking-driving was observed by us to be a play about competence and incompetence. But dramas occur on different stages and the bar is not a single, uniform stage. The discussion of the singles bar, above, suggests what our study found to be the case; different kinds of bars have different impacts on the drinking-driving situation. The bar constitutes a setting within which the relations between intimates is differently displayed and the relation between bar personnel and customers varies from one type to another.

In the context of this paper, we can only summarize some aspects of our observations. They indicate the ways in which the type of bar creates a scenic background for varying forms of control or absence of control. Both economic considerations in managing bars and emergent forms of intimacy between bar personnel and customers interact with the characteristics of patrons and the relationships between them to affect the intimate relations described earlier and the drinking-driving act.

The bar is both an arena for display of competence and a place which generates intimate relations. Friendships are both nurtured among patrons and extramural ones continued within it. The bartender, especially in the neighborhood bar, can use his or her role to bring drinking-driving into the situation and set in motion the norms of mutuality, dependence and welfare which govern intimate relations in connection with drinking-driving. Especially in neighborhood bars, the bartender is also among the circle of intimates. There is a considerable difference between singles bars, where the bartender is distant from customers, transient bars, where this is also the case but couples are more in evidence and the neighborhood bar, where the circle of regulars, couples and the bar constitute a continuing social group. In the latter the drinking-driving situation is more likely to emerge as a situation for control than in these areas in which the norm of the display of competence has least possibility for exceptions and excuses.

Bars sell much more than alcohol. As sites for the pursuit of leisure they create distinctive environments for behavior. Bars differ in the type of environments created. In two of the bars we studied an atmosphere of club and recurrent sociability among regulars is sustained; in one of these the regulars are the major partronizing group and the bartender is one among them. In the other, efforts are made to draw everyone into the ambit of the bartender's control and leadership. In the two others studied, the role of the bartender is minimal. Patrons depend on themselves for the social atmosphere created.

In these different kinds of establishments, the economy of the establishment has different effects for the drinking-driving occurrence. In the neighborhood bars, where circles of regulars have emerged and the bartender observes and interacts with everyone, the maintenance of sociability and social accessibility is a major source of the bar's market position. The bartender needs to sustain his or her relationship to patrons. Maintaining the "front" of the customer is thus important and keeping a "good feeling" about the bar important. The bartender thus has an economic pressure to achieve a sense of intimacy with patrons and to promote their relationship with others. As intimate, he or she is caught in the same complex web of dual pressures to maintain the "front" of competence and to discharge the obligations to care for the patron's safety and welfare. The bartender becomes a major source both of serving drinks and limiting the drinking of patrons; of protecting the front of competence and intervening to aid in alternatives to driving. For example, it is toward regulars that the bartender is most likely to advise using a taxi or to call one without the patron's permission.

Where the bar setting minimizes the practical possibility for bartender controls, the role of management in controlling drinking-driving or in generating its emergence as a topic is lessened. Here again, the neighborhood bar, with its circle of personal relationships and with a bartender capable of utilizing the social rules of drinking-driving, is better able to control both the drinking and the drinking-driving patterns.

Some small "flavor" of the differences between bars can be given in a description of the two non-neighborhood bars we studied. These contrast sharply with the material presented on The Club and Al's described in the paper above. Both That Place, the singles bar, and The Hermitage, a cocktail lounge, illustrate an absence of the close relationships and social control that characterize the presence of a core of "regulars" and bar personnel who have established quasi-intimate relations with them.

At That Place there is an entrance by a group or single person every three or four minutes during the peak of the evening. People congregate and move around through the several rooms and two levels that constitute the premises. The bartenders have little contact, if any at all, with the customers. "Management," in the sense of social control and interaction, is absent.

What does not appear is the informal, social network of relations between the management and the customers observed at The Club and Al's. Much of the area of the bar is not visible to either the bartenders or the bouncers. The entire impression is that of a large warehouse to which people are invited and then left to themselves on condition that they buy drinks when approached by waiters.

The relation between management and customers is marked by the routinization of control. Unlike The Club or Friendly Al's, there is no mass exodus at closing time; That Place is not a club. There are no free drinks.

> That Place is a kind of bar where the bartenders will turn on all the lights, turn off the music and clear the tables at five minutes to two. The bouncer and the bartenders will circulate among the crowd at closing and take the drinks away from them and loudly announce that it's closing time and everybody has to leave. As a matter of fact the call for last drinks at That Place is made over the P.A. system and is made at approximately twenty minutes to two. . . . This is understandable due to the logistics problem of having to clear such a large crowd.

A good deal of interaction occurs in the parking lots adjacent to the bar; men and women continue conversations, arguments occur, men try to get in a last-minute "hustle" with some woman they've met. This "external" life of That Place, however, goes on without either the watchful eyes or intervention of bouncers or bartenders.

The source of control of That Place are the bouncers. Physically they are large and strong-appearing. Stationed at the entrances to the bar, their major activity is the prevention of under-age persons from being customers. They routinely check identification cards for age and refuse permission if identification of legal age cannot be proven to the bouncer's satisfaction. In addition, they do attempt to control situations when they reach the point of visibility. They neither watch for incipient trouble nor intervene until it has reached considerable visibility within the bar. They do not attempt to manage situations nor to act in aid of customers. The following discussion with one of the bouncers is indicative of the detachment of "management":

> Paul said that whenever an incident occurs outside the bar, they always try to call the police first and let the police take care of the incident. He said that they do this because any trouble that occurs outside the bar is really none of the bar's responsibility, but is a police responsibility because it happens outside. . . . Again, as during our first conversation Paul told me that he doesn't feel, nor do the other personnel at That Place feel that it is their responsibility to look out for the customers after they leave the bar. He again told me that the customers who are old enough to drink are old enough to pay the price for what happens after they drink.

The pattern of free drinks, of concern for the "good will" observed in the neighborhood bars is absent between the bartenders or bouncers and customers. The economic basis of That Place is very different from The Club and Friendly Al's. As one customer at That Place put it, in explaining why he drives about twenty miles three or four times a week to That Place and other nearby bars, "It's the best place to go because there aren't too many girls in the other places, especially around National City."

The absence of management also characterizes The Hermitage but it has a distinctively different character. Here the entire bar is open to the observation of the bartender. He is aware of and concerned with possibilities of "trouble." His relation to customers is almost exclusively that of service tinged with control. His job is to mix drinks and occasionally talk to the "loners" at the bar. As compared to the more intimate kind of bar represented by The Club and Friendly Al's, the management of drinking and driving at The Hermitage is almost exclusively a product of the setting and the customers themselves. The bartender has no stable set of social interactions either emergent from his relation to customers nor supported by an economic need to create the setting of a small club. As the regular bartender at The Hermitage put it,

> a bartender can't keep track of what his customers do after they leave the bar. The bartender's only real responsibility to the customers is to cut them off when the bartender feels that the customer has been drinking too much.

In the several observations made at The Hermitage we never saw a group of regulars akin to the groups at The Club and Al's. We never saw any customer on more than one occasion. Nor did we see the bartender cut off any customer or suggest that he not drive, either trying to arrange another ride or suggesting that he call a taxi. More than at any of the three other sites, we were dependent on the bartender for much information about the bar. However, much about the setting and customers was considerably different from the neighborhood bar or the singles bar. For one thing, a number of customers used the bar on the way to something else. Few customers were there for most of the evening. Some customers came to the bar before or after eating in the restaurant which was part of the establishment. There was very little movement from spot to spot within the bar or evidence of people meeting friends in the casual fashion of regulars. Couples stayed to themselves. Even on Saturday night, when The Hermitage became a "night spot" it was one of several places on the circuit. On weekdays it closed early, often before midnight.

The setting of The Hermitage further mitigated against the closeness of a neighborhood bar or the loose, casual disorganization of the singles bar. The upholstered furniture and the paneled wood walls had the mark of taste and age that fitted its name. The dress of many of the men was more formal, more the mark of the suited businessman than the blue-jeaned Californian youth. In age The Hermitage was at least two levels above That Place; in class one or two levels above both The Club and Al's.

These two aspects of setting and clientele at The Hermitage help explain the limited role of the bartender and the absence of management. As the bartender maintained on several occasions, his way of handling trouble is to call the police. His management of drinking is to refuse further service. He gives no recognition of an ability to mobilize the peers of the drinker or to utilize his own personal knowledge or attachment as a device to influence the drinker. But, as he also maintained on two occasions, the kind of people who come into The Hermitage are not likely to give him much trouble. They are "nice people, cool people." "The Hermitage is a nice place attracting nice customers." "This is a real nice place here. Nice customers, nice atmosphere. We don't have a lot of hassles."

> They know when to quit drinking or know when to call a cab for themselves. . . . The 'cool' customers . . . can control their drinking and be aware of their incapacities. They are, in fact, most gracious when he suggests a cab. Again they are the kind of customers attracted by the atmosphere of The Hermitage.

Here the bartender is not the center of interaction nor is he the source of the atmosphere. Like That Place he tries to control but not to manage.

CONCLUSIONS AND COMMENCEMENTS

A decent regard for the opinions of fellow sociologists impels us to a section of this paper labeled "Conclusions." Two considerations make for hesitancy. First, the value of an ethnographic study is largely the result of the depth and richness of the contexts within which actions are described. Summaries and conclusions represent a style of certainty and definiteness which contrast with the grounded character of ethnography. The *genre* of ethnographic reports depends on the embedded quality of the questions suggested and typologies used. Secondly, the data are grounded. Collection and analysis are directed by the problems posed by theory and applied concerns. This study has been directed by intentions to understand the drinking-driving phenomenon. The interactive character of persons playing roles has been an aspect of the study but not the primary one. It is not all uncommon that data collected for one primary purpose provides an occasion to reflect upon their implications for another or an auxiliary problem. Nevertheless, it is an *ad hoc,* after the fact rumination.

We did begin with a body of theory about dramaturgical actions, about the public accessibility of bars and about the situated character of interactions. The concept of "display" was consequentially important. So too was the distinction between competence and incompetence. The display of competence in the context of the bar was thus given priority in understanding how the drinking-driving act was talked about on the stage of the barroom.

A second idea was that of controls over behavior and over display-self-controls, peer controls and the controls of bar personnel. These ideas led us to expect that different contexts, different kinds of bars, would affect the ways in which self-controls and peer controls operate.

What we observed proved more complex in two ways. These might be said to constitute what we learned that is most pertinent to this volume.

The first is that the concept of role is alive and well and at least living in bars in San Diego. We are much attracted by the criticisms of concepts of structure in the work of ethnomethodologists in recent years (Cicourel, 1973, Ch. 1; McHugh, 1968, pp. 42ff). We recognize that the situation is not self-evident and given. The definition of which roles are to be used is itself prior to the occurrence of a situation, part of defining that situation. We recognize the flexibility and situated character of much human interaction. Nevertheless within those understandings, in the public light of the bar, husbands and wives observe different actions toward each other, live by different rules of interaction than do strangers, friends, bartenders—all of whom in turn relate to each other in differing manners. Without knowing the status of persons vis-à-vis each other, the interaction in the bar would be enigmatic. Those patterns are thus generalizable, understood as categories of action relevant to people occupying specific statuses. That is what "role" is all about. So, too, we learned that whole categories of people—men, old men, women, old women, past offenders, "alcoholics"—occupy particular statuses and are cast into particular roles. A competent female drinker is not accorded the same expectancies and obligations as is the competent male drinker. This too is transsituational.

Secondly, there is a reflexive quality to the display of identity. The self needs to display not only competence but self-understanding. There are levels in the display of competence as in the recognition of health and illness. The role of competent drinker demands not only competence but showing that the role-player knows when he is no longer competent. The "true" incompetent cannot recognize that or cannot display such reflexive capacity.

Is it perhaps the case that being human requires us to make our humanity evident to each other, to show that we not only are playing a role but that we understand that it is a role and that an authentic self is watching our act. That is a cynical note on which to end or to commence.

ACKNOWLEDGMENTS

The total ethnographic study was supported by a grant from the National Science Foundation and is reported in NSF Report, *The World of the Drinking Driver* (Gusfield 1979). It, too, is part of a larger project studying drinking-driving from a variety of concerns and interests. A major part of the project is found in the book *The Culture of Public Problems* (Gusfield, 1981). We are grateful to the National Science Foundation for a grant of funds which enabled us to conduct the study from which this paper is drawn. We appreciate the help of H. Laurence Ross, then Director of the National Science Foundation Law and Society Program.

NOTES

1. The fact that the observer as customer has a prescriptive right to interaction with other customers and with bartenders does not mean that differences in levels and types of interaction rights do not exist. Indeed, such differences as those between "regulars" and "transients" are central to the total analysis. Informal rules further limit admission, as an upper-class woman in furs is "out of place" in a workers' bar. Nevertheless, the actual and potential anonymity of bar customers makes it a public situation distinct from privacy of home.

2. The very conditions of being a customer which enable the observer to gain entry to the cultural world of the bar also limit his/her ability to record what he/she observes. Field work has constantly faced this problem (Schatzman and Strauss, 1973, Ch. 6). Efforts to record conversation verbatim, through moment-by-moment note-taking or videotape or auditory recording has two drawbacks: it prevents the observer from himself being accessible to others and thus, secondly, threatens his access to the scene he seeks to enter. It turns the barroom atmosphere into a publicly exposed situation. We assumed any effort to accomplish such a state would make the observer's later interaction so constrained, even were it to have been refused by bartenders, that the natural interaction would be decisively distorted. Put another way, it would have put customers "on guard."

REFERENCES

Brissett, Dennis, and Edgley, Charles.
1975 "Life as theater: a dramaturgical sourcebook." Chicago, Ill.: Aldine Publishing Co.
Cavan, Sherri
1966 Liquor License. Chicago, Ill.: Aldine Press.
Cicourel, Aaron
1973 Cognitive Sociology. London: Penguin Education.
Frake, Charles
1969 "Notes on queries in ethnography." In Stephen Tyler (ed.), Cognitive Anthropology. New York: Holt, Rinehart and Winston.
Goffman, Erving
1956 The Presentation of the Self in Everyday Life. Edinburgh: University of Edinburgh Social Sciences Research Center.
Goffman, Erving
1963 Behavior in Public Places. Glencoe, Ill.: The Free Press.
Gusfield, Joseph
1979 The World of the Drinking-Driver. National Science Foundation Report, May.
Gusfield, Joseph
1981 The Culture of Public Problems: Drinking-Driving and the Symbolic Order. Chicago, Ill.: University of Chicago Press.
Hart, H. L. A.
1968 "Legal responsibility and excuses." Punishment and Responsibility. Oxford: Clarendon Press.
Hughes, Everett
1958 Men and Their Work. Glencoe, Ill.: The Free Press.
McHugh, Peter
1958 Defining the Situation. Indianapolis, Ind.: Bobbs-Merrill.
Manning, Peter
1978 Police Work. Cambridge, Mass.: MIT Press.
Mehan, Hugh
1980 Learning Lessons. Cambridge, Mass.: Harvard University Press.
Parsons, Talcott, and Fox, Renee
1952 "Illness, therapy and the modern urban American family." Journal of Social Issues 8.

COMMUNAL DIFFUSION OF FRIENDSHIP:

THE STRUCTURE OF INTIMATE RELATIONS IN AN ISRAELI KIBBUTZ

Wayne Baker and Rosanna Hertz

One problem that I have done a lot of thinking about is the lack of close friends people have. People have friends here; but what I mean is intimate friends. And if people have one intimate friend, there are few intimate groups of friends. Maybe it is because we live so closely together. We do everything together, and maybe this prevents us from developing (this kind of) intimate relationship.

Unfortunately, (the time) when you really see the community acting as a whole and you really feel the connection and closeness of the people is when a tragedy occurs. Then you feel you're not alone. It is then you feel that there are people to help you and people that really care. You have the community to support you. [An adult member, born in the kibbutz]

"Lack" of friendship is a common self-perception in the kibbutz we studied. Founders recall minimal friendship in the early settlement; in the contemporary kibbutz, nearly a half-century later, members maintain that they have few or no close friends. Friendship, we were told, is less prevalent in the kibbutz than in urban Israeli society, even in American society.

At first we found such perceptions startling: How could a revolutionary society, founded on egalitarian and humanitarian ideals, lack friendship? The answer to this lies in the unique structure of intimate relationships in the kibbutz. Intimate relationships, in general, are characterized by some degree of interpersonal knowledge, trust, mutual caring, shared experiences and interests, and exclusivity. To understand the structure of intimate relationships in the kibbutz, however, we need to make an analytic distinction between "exclusive" and "nonexclusive" intimate relationships. The exclusive type involves a limited number of people sharing a personal sphere of private intimacy apart from other members of the community. Two examples of this are family and friendship. The nonexclusive type, on the other hand, expands intimacy to the boundaries of community, embracing the entire membership. The typical form of this is brotherhood or comradeship, based on communal intimacy rather than private intimacy. Therefore, the distinction between comradeship, on one hand, and family and friendship, on the other, is one of nonexclusivity versus exclusivity.

Comradeship was the idealized form of intimate relationship in the kibbutz. All members were included in the experience of communal intimacy. The characteristics of early kibbutz life were conducive to the maintenance of communal intimacy: small size, homogeneous membership, common cultural origins, high frequency of face-to-face interaction, shared proximate space and time, and an explicit and highly articulated communal ideology. The combined force of these characteristics countered the principles of private intimacy, substituting the intimacy of community for exclusive intimate relations.

However, the growth and differentiation of the kibbutz eroded the situational supports of communal intimacy, making it more difficult to sustain communal intimacy and retard the formation of more traditional forms of exclusive intimacy. Eventually, the social basis of intimacy shifted from community to sub-communal bases. The same processes that eroded communal intimacy recreated intimacy in new locations of interaction, affiliation, and integration.

Intimacy was partitioned into three major social bases: ethnic similarity, second generation cohorts, and family. Each of these, in their own way, duplicated the characteristics of the early kibbutz, communities in miniature, providing face-to-face interaction, proximate space and time, shared experiences, and common identity. But in the context of the larger community, each represents a return of the exclusivity of traditional intimacy. Of course, communal intimacy did not disappear in its struggle with the partition of intimacy. Communal attachment persists as an overarching bond in kibbutz life, a tie far stronger than neighborhood or community attachment in American society.

Friendship primarily emerged in ethnic groups and second generation cohorts; but, for a variety of reasons, friendship did not become a prevalent form of intimate relationship in the contemporary kibbutz. First, many situational constraints still operate to restrict the formation of exclusive intimate relationships. Second, family has become a more-durable and socially-acceptable arena of intimacy than friendship; further, marriage and family foster the division of ethnic groups and cohorts. Third, many of the functions or duties typically performed by friends are either entirely absent or satisfactorily fulfilled through other means in kibbutz life. For example, of the seven major functions of friendship[1] that Cohen (1961) found in a cross-cultural comparison of 65 societies, only one—sociopolitical and emotional support—is applicable to friendship in the kibbutz, and even this function is also met by the family. The most ubiquitous function of friendship, material exchange and/or assistance, is completely fulfilled by community.

Friendship in the kibbutz fits neatly into a proposition Gilmore (1975) forwards relating friendship with community structure and culture. The community Gilmore (1975) studied is "a typically atomistic community in which class hostility eliminates a strategy of seeking patronage and where a lack of emphasis on fictive kinship negates the alliance potential of *compadrazgo* (godparenthood) . . ." (p. 321). Friendship was adapted to mitigate this disintegrative structure, counter individual alienation, and become a major mechanism of alliance and cooperation. Comparing the essential role of friendship in this community to the characterization of friendship as a "residual," Gilmore (1975) offers this proposition:

> The residualness of friendship therefore seems to correlate negatively to the degree of organizational and operational denseness of the society, that is, the degree to which social, economic, and psychological resources are provided by the range of alternative groupings traditionally practiced . . . (p. 321).

From this perspective, friendship will be minimal if most social, economic, and psychological provisions are met by alternative means; in the kibbutz, we contend, most provisions are met by community and family.

COMMUNITY AND THE CONTEXT OF FRIENDSHIP

A central theme in this collection of essays is that friendship is determined by the social context in which it occurs; friendship takes on shape and

meaning in the situations and circumstances which bound the formation
and maintenance of this type of social relationship [see especially, Maines
(this volume)]. Our proposition is a specification of this general theme:
community forms a holistic social context of friendship. The form and
meaning of friendship are circumscribed by the social structure and culture of community.

By using a community perspective, we are implying that the kibbutz
has some characteristics in common with other communities [cf. Hillery
(1968)]. Consequently, friendship in the kibbutz also shares characteristics with friendship in other communities. Therefore, we have reviewed
several community studies to identify general conceptual themes of
friendship in community. These provide a comparative framework for
understanding friendship in the kibbutz.

Two further analytic points about friendship in community need to be
considered. First, we are less concerned with "momentary friendship,"
temporary or passing friendships between pairs of kibbutz members;
rather, we are more concerned with "structural friendship," the more-
enduring friendships that are part of the roles and relationships intrinsic
to the social structure of community [cf. Redfield (1960), pp. 34–35]. For
example, if social relations in a community are segregated by sex and
age, then friendships are likely to emerge in the structural locations of
sex and age homogeneity. Friendships which cross these lines are problematic for the community and the individuals involved; not only is this
type of friendship less probable, but if it occurred, it would also elicit
negative social sanctions.

Second, friendship is embedded in a system of intimate relations.
Friendship, as any specific type of intimate relation, must be viewed as
an interdependent part of a larger whole of intimacy. For example, comradeship is the quintessential form of kibbutz relationship, expressed by
the term for kibbutz member: *chaver* (f., *chavera*), literally "comrade."[2]
This term was also used for "husband" (*chaver;* companion, friend) and
"wife" (*chavera;* companion, friend); this idiomatic usage indicated the
submergence of the dyad in comradeship, the intimate relationship of
community. With the emergence of marriage and family in community,
however, the idiom changed. Today, one may hear the more traditional
terms for "my husband" (*baali;* my husband; my master) and "my wife"
(*eshti;* my wife, my woman). Thus, these changes in idiom indicate a
major rearrangement of the system of intimate relations in the kibbutz
community.

FRIENDSHIP IN COMMUNITY

From our review of various community studies, we have extracted three
general characteristics of friendship in community:

First, friendship formation follows the overall lines of the social organization of community. Friendships in the Addams area most often emerged within the homogeneous groups formed by the "ordered segmentation" of the community [Suttles (1968)]. Many of the West Enders' relationships, including friendships, were restricted to people of the same sex, age, and life-cycle status, reflecting the "peer group society" in which West Enders lived [Gans (1962)]. Friendships which cross lines of social organization are exceptional; however, sharp social divisions may be overcome when primary groups are reconstructed by the organization of work or participation in partisan politics [e.g., Kornblum (1974)].

In communities with low social and geographic mobility, such as Cornerville [Whyte (1943)] and West End [(Gans (1962)], friendships form in childhood and adolescence and persist throughout life. This life-long tenure of friendship contrasts with the pattern of friendship in middle-class communities, such as Crestwood Heights (Seeley, *et al.*, 1967) or Levittown [Gans (1967)] which are characterized by greater social and geographic mobility. As Gans (1967) describes:

> In middle class American society geographical and social mobility often separates people who have grown up together, so that shared interests among childhood friends is rare. Instead, they develop new friends at each stage of the life cycle or as they move up occupationally and develop new social and leisure interests. Closeness is not replaced by superficiality, but permanent friendships give way to new and perhaps shorter ones of similar closeness (p. 164).

Friendships in mobile communities extend beyond the boundaries of the immediate community [e.g., Seeley, *et al.*, (1967, p. 206)]. In East York, only a small minority of the typical respondent's intimates, for instance, live in the same neighborhood as the respondent, though the majority live in the metropolitan area [Wellman (1978, p. 11)]. The separation of work and residence means that men have fewer intimate ties in the community than women have [Seeley, *et al.*, (1967)]. Friendships are less sex-segregated in these communities; typically, friendships are worked out in the cross-sex foursome of two couples [Gans (1967)].

Second, a prominent element of friendship in community is the exchange of goods and services for mutual aid, support, and protection [e.g., Gans (1962, pp. 84–85); Liebow (1967, p. 176); Vidich and Bensman (1968, pp. 33–36); Whyte (1943, pp. 256–257); Bennett (1968), Cohen (1961, p. 373); Gilmore (1975, p. 320)]. Exchanges among friends develop into a system of reciprocal obligations, a pattern of giving and receiving, where expectations to receive are met with obligations to give.

The community (state) provides a variety of goods and services (police and fire protection, education, unemployment compensation) and others are available in the market (consumer goods, life insurance, health care). But the exchange of goods and services in friendship appears to fill the gaps left by the provisions available from other sources. The material reciprocity of friendship thus becomes a form of social insurance [see especially Vidich and Bensman (1968, pp. 33–36)].[3]

Third, communities vary in the social mixture of *emergent* intimate relations and explicitly *regulated* intimate relations. Most communities, including all referenced above, explicitly regulate social relations, but only to a minor degree. For example, communities enforce societal mores of family relations; adjudication is required for the formal severance of marriage, and the minimal responsibilities of parents to children are based on enforceable legal definitions. For the most part, however, intimate relations are unregulated provided they fall within usually wide socially-acceptable limits.

In contrast, utopian communities intentionally regulate most social relations. All communes endeavor to alter conventional economic relations. Many communes abolish private property, substituting communal ownership; others are organized as economic cooperatives. Jobs are rotated, desirable and undesirable work is shared, and a generally more egalitarian organization or work is instituted and maintained [Kanter (1972, pp. 43–44)].

Utopian communities also intentionally regulate intimate relations. The Oneida community, for example, replaced traditional monogamous marriage with a system of "complex marriage" [Carden (1971)]. The early Mormons practiced polygamy, modern groups engage in communal sex, and the Tomales Bay Synanon temporarily banned sex and intimate male-female relationships [Kanter (1972, pp. 44–45)]. Most communal groups introduce a new and "superior" form of intimate relation: communal intimacy, or "brotherhood" as it is typically called [Kanter (1972, pp. 43–49)]. Communal intimacy both supplements and transcends other forms of intimacy. Most utopian communities attempt to control other sources of intimacy that may conflict with "brotherhood." The great threat to the collectivity is what Slater (1963) calls "dyadic withdrawal" and "familial withdrawal," two forms of libidinal contraction, which fall short of the diffusion of cathexis needed for aggregate maintenance. The minimal threshold of diffused cathexis is much higher for communities which try to create true "brotherhood" than for communities in which it is not attempted. To stay above this threshold, utopian communities actively and continually strive to retard both dyadic and familial withdrawal. Kanter (1972, p. 91) notes that successful communes of the past, more than unsuccessful ones, have renounced both dyadic and familial intimacy. Some communities, as we describe later, have even attempted to impede the formation and maintenance of friendships in an effort to foster the spirit of "brotherhood."

RESEARCH METHODS AND SETTING

Our data come from a field study of an Israeli kibbutz that we conducted in 1977–1978 for a total of 14 person-months in the field. Methods included participant-observation, living and working in the community; informal and more-formal interviewing; the collection of oral histories; and the collection of demographic records, economic and accounting records, production reports, and other archival data.

We chose the kibbutz site on the following criteria: founded prior to the formation of the State of Israel (1948); combined agricultural-industrial economic base; median population size; and affiliation with Kibbutz *Artzi* (the National Kibbutz) Federation. These criteria served to locate a settlement that was mature, economically stable, had three generations, a stable population, and a radical Marxist-socialist ideology.

COMMUNITY DESIGN: IDEOLOGICAL AND STRUCTURAL CONSTRAINTS

Our thesis is that the basic intentional design of the kibbutz community forms major situational constraints on friendship. Historical transformations of this basic design rearranged the situational constraints on intimate relationships, altering the types and locations of intimate relationships in community.

The structure of the kibbutz—even today—is largely determined by ideological design. Although the kibbutz has undergone major transformations, this basic design, however modified, is still predominant. Below we outline some of the major ideological precepts which impinge on intimate relations. These ideals were probably most closely approximated in the earliest period of the kibbutz. Thus, the outline also provides brief descriptions of friendship and other intimate relations in the formative period of the community.

1. The Kibbutz as a Conscious Community

Kibbutz members possess a high degree of consciousness and self-awareness about their community's structure and culture, and the various internal and external influences which impinge upon them. As a veteran member stated:

> City people tell me that kibbutzniks are too serious. We think too much. We always question everything we do; we always ask why we are doing something.
>
> But I say: This is our life. We want to know why we do things. We are trying to build a new way of life, a new society. We have to understand what we do . . .

At the center of the conscious community[4] is an explicit and highly articulated ideology. Communal self-analysis is built upon this ideological base, using it as a means to assess past and current practices and guide future action. This does not mean that ideology is static. Rather, ideology is continually under reformulation and reinterpretation: theory and praxis interact in an evolutionary process.

All members were expected to confront ideology in their everyday life. The practice of ideology mandated incessant community-wide debate. Consequently, in contrast with the idyllic image of communal life, the kibbutz was characterized by an intense level of conflict. As a member who joined the settlement in the 1940's recalled:

> I came to the kibbutz after the founders were already here. I was amazed at all the arguing and fighting, how they debated everything, every point. I couldn't believe that they actually got something done out of all of this.

The unique structure and values of kibbutz life combined to generate unremitting tension. Similarly, tension in the kibbutz Spiro studied in 1951 was so intense that he rated it as one of the major crises threatening kibbutz life and its future [Spiro (1963, pp. 201–205)].

The turbulence of the early kibbutz precluded the formation of friendships. As a founder said,

> In the kibbutz, you can't really have friends. For example, my generation used to quarrel about everything. We had terrible fights, terrible quarrels. How could you be friends? How can you have [exclusive] intimate relations? . . .
>
> This thing about friendship is just romanticism, like Goethe or Shakespeare's "Romeo and Juliet." It's fine for you when you're sixteen years old. But it's not like that for an adult. And adults who have it are just adolescents. Let me give you an example. I have lived next door to the same man [also a founder] for years, but we aren't friends, we don't share a thing—there's a long history of it . . .

The founder's contention that "adults who have friendship are just adolescents" exemplifies the kibbutz ideology of intimate relations. Exclusive and special relationships, including friendship, are inferior and underdeveloped compared with the ideal kibbutz intimate relationship—comradeship—where all other relationships are transcended by the ubiquitous spirit of community.

2. Conscious Regulation of Social Relationships

The kibbutz founders wanted to establish a "new way of life," based on principles of Marxism-socialism, jettisoning all traditions and short-comings of their former European life. Once cleared of the shortcomings of other societies, a true "new society" would be founded. However, their ideal was not to establish permanent and rigid alternative social structures; rather, they strived to create a structure*less* community. In practice, this would result in minimal and transitory institutions. For example, communal life would be based on face-to-face interaction, immediacy, and spontaneity. Decision-making would be based on continual negotiation, not governed by rule or precedent; social control would be informal and consensual. Overall, legitimate authority was to reside entirely in the collective, not in individuals, positions, or groups.

Punch (1974) calls this ideology an "anti-institutional and anti-authoritarian ideology," noting its presence in several types of social groups and collectivities. As he defines the "anti-institution":

> [The] desire to escape what is perceived as the deleterious consequence of a per-manent social structure in formal organizations and the attempt to capture the absence of constraint in an association with an anti-institutional and anti-authori-tarian ideology is what we mean by an anti-institution. It is an attempt to live perpetually on the margin, resisting the encroachments of formalization. It is the attempt to retain the spontaneous, immediate, ephemeral joys of 'communitas' against the fate of 'declining' into the norm-governed, institutionalized abstract nature of law and social structure. Something of this anti-institutional ideology is to be found in revolutionary communes, kibbutzim, and various other radical social movements . . . (p. 312).[5]

To enact this radical design of community, kibbutz members con-sciously regulated social relationships in all spheres of life—economic, political, and social. One objective was to eliminate any groups which could intervene between the community and the individual [cf. Spiro (1963, p. 110)]. The elimination of intermediate groups would leave the only ideal relationship: the intimate relationship between the individual and the community-at-large.

Family is a prime example of a major institution and intermediate group that the kibbutz attempted to eliminate. The early anti-family ideology was expressed in several ways: no public displays of dyadic affection; a "free love" ethic and experimentation with a variety of sexual relations; the abolition of marriage; and communal-collective child-rearing. Since the modern kibbutz family still remains stripped of most major "functions" of the Western family model, this bears witness to the pervasive and effective impact of the early kibbutz anti-family ideology [see Hertz/Baker (1980); Talmon (1972); Spiro (1963)].

The regulation of social relationships is not confined to the kibbutz. For example, nowhere is love permitted free reign: all societies develop sociocultural patterns of mate-selection to keep love from disrupting existing social arrangements [Goode (1959)]. But kibbutz regulation is qualitatively different. First, the ideal and desired forms of intimate relations are part of an explicit and highly-articulated ideology. Second, decisions about the ideal structure of relationships, the enforcement of these relations, and the control of undesired relationships, are collective-communal decisions. Third, these decisions become articles of community policy, implemented and enforced in daily life. Fourth, instead of maintaining the status quo, the pre-existing social order, the kibbutz has consciously striven to destroy traditional social relationships and prevent their emergence in the kibbutz. Thus, the kibbutz is characterized by the *conscious* regulation of social relationships in contrast to the emergent, more implicit regulation operating in most other communities.

The early kibbutz ideology of love and marriage is exemplary of this conscious regulation. The "free love" ethic and the abolition of marriage not only undermined the founders' European institution of family, preventing its importation, but also precluded its replacement with any other form of family institution. Thus, the kibbutz's conscious *de*regulation of sociocultural patterns of mate-selection—love's free reign—served to keep the community near its anti-institutional ideal.[6]

3. Comradeship

In the ideal vision, kibbutz members' relationships coalesce into the ubiquitous intimacy of comradeship, the spirit of community in its most exalted sense. Friendship, as all exclusive relationships, would be transcended by the superior bonds of comradeship. This could be interpreted to mean that the kibbutz lacks friendship. Instead, it is more accurate to say that the kibbutz is characterized by what Americans lack—comradeship. This delicate issue was expressed in a conversation with a kibbutz-born member:

[How many friends do you have?] I have some, but then again I don't have any. [Other people in the kibbutz tell us that they don't feel they have close friends. What do you mean when you say you don't have friends?] I want to tell you, I've been thinking about it since I said it. I think it was a reaction to the way you asked the question when you asked "How many friends do you have?"

If you ask a question "Do you have any close friends?" and you use some kind of statistics, then it's easier for you. You can do some mathematics and you find out that everyone says: "No." Then you can write that people in the kibbutz don't have friends. But I think the reality is a little more complicated. Maybe in the kibbutz everyone has friendly relations with everyone, so it is spread out, and you don't focus on any one person.

The ideal of comradeship in the kibbutz is similar to the concept of "brotherhood" in utopian ideologies.[7] As Kanter (1972) describes:

> A . . . utopian value is brotherhood. Just as the social world can be brought into harmony with the natural laws of the universe, according to utopian thought so can people be brought into harmony with one another . . . In order to bring about such harmony, utopians believe that it is necessary to remove the "artificial" barriers between people that cause competition, jealousy, conflict, and tension, and prevent "natural" relationships. Utopian communities attempt to erase these barriers by substituting for individual possession community of property, of work, of lovers, of families. (p. 43).

Many communes have regulated intimate relationships which could potentially impede the development of "brotherhood." The effort to promote "brotherhood" by hampering the emergence of special and exclusive relationships has even extended to friendships:

> Even special friendships may be discouraged, being considered a form of exclusiveness interfering with brotherhood, as in Oneida and Shaker communities, where the composition of work groups was changed frequently to prevent the development of exclusive, close personal relationships. A temporary ban on both sex and intimate male-female relationships at the Tomales Bay Synanon may be another expression of the desire to foster brotherhood rather than exclusive relationships. [Kanter (1972, p. 45)].

> Some communities extended renunciation of the couple from sexual attachments even to close friendships . . . . . . Oneida similarly taught its children not to form exclusive friendships that left out other members of the peer group. Such control of the dyad did not eliminate intimacy in successful utopian communities; rather, it spread intimacy more widely through the group instead of concentrating it only on one other . . . . . . In renouncing the couple, members gained the community. [Kanter (1972, p. 89)].

The kibbutz community, much like other communes, has attempted to encourage the ethos of comradeship, partly by preventing the emergence of anti-communal ties, partly by replacing all other intimate ties with comradeship.

4. Supremacy of the Group

Emphasis on comradeship made the "group" the apotheosis of kibbutz life. This parallels what Spiro (1963) calls the "moral value of the group":

> The group, in kibbutz culture, is not only a means to the happiness of the individual; the group and group processes are moral ends in their own right. This has three aspects. It means, first, that the interests of the individual must be subordinate to the interests of the group . . . (p. 29).

> A second aspect of the emphasis on the ethical value of the group involves the

assumption that the individual's motivations will always be directed to the promotion of the group's interests, as well as of his own (p. 29).

Behavior is expected to be characterized by *ezra hadadit*, or mutual aid. This means that every member of the kibbutz is responsible for the welfare of every other member and for the welfare of the kibbutz as a whole, just as the kibbutz is responsible for the welfare of each individual . . . (p. 30).

[F]inally . . . group living and group experiences are valued more highly than their individual counterparts. Indeed, so important is the value of group experience that those *chaverim* [members] who seek a great degree of privacy are viewed as "queer . . ." (p. 30).

The immersion of the individual in the group severely restricts the possibility of any intimate exclusive relationships, including friendships. Not only is cathexis focused on the entire group, but proper behavior means that one avoids participation in exclusive relationships.

The material element of friendship, so conspicuous in non-utopian communities, is absent in the kibbutz. The community is the sole provider of all goods and services in the short-run and the long-run. Individual welfare is guaranteed by community. For example, the kibbutz has broken the link between consumption and production. The maxim "from each according to ability; to each according to need" still guides economic action in the kibbutz. Although there is strong social pressure to excel in work and sharp social criticism of "parasitism," the material security and overall welfare of even those who don't or cannot work is guaranteed. However, if material expression is a vital element of friendship, then one major support is removed by the basic economic organization of the kibbutz.

5. Informal Social Control

Community design created a kibbutz with "primary group" properties [cf. Schwartz (1964)]. For example, kibbutz life is built around a high frequency and intensity of face-to-face interaction; interaction involves the totality of self, rather than a segmental self; and interaction is characterized by intimacy and expressiveness. Unlike a more conventional primary group, however, these properties are not emergent; rather, they were consciously chosen and exalted virtues of communal life.

Social control in the kibbutz is almost entirely informal, a feature of kibbutz life which persists throughout its history. Schwartz (1964) has concluded that the effectiveness of informal social control in the kibbutz made internal legal institutions unnecessary. The second major type of collective settlement in Israel, the semi-private property, family-based *moshav*, lacks the high level of face-to-face interaction, communication, and public observation present in the kibbutz. Thus, the relative ineffectiveness of informal social control in the *moshav* has led to the establishment of a formal, legal institution, the Judicial Committee.

"Gossip," as one founder put it, "is part of the life here, and it's different than in the city. Here they talk about something and in 24 hours, everyone knows." Each bit of gossip about members becomes part of the cradle-to-grave biographies known by each member about every member. Gossip ensures that all pertinent information, facts, figures, and extenuating circumstances are known. It enables members to know about the situations of fellow members, and to be able to aid and abet one another, apart from any information relating to issues coming before the General Meeting.

Powerful informal social control also has negative consequences. Unfair and irrelevant accusations are transmitted through the gossip machinery as easily as valid and needed information. Members can be negatively labeled, deservedly or not, and acquire an enduring stigma in the community. The possibility of social criticism looms over all actions; some members report that this makes them reluctant to assume risks or try new ventures. In general, members watch their words and deeds. Since a great deal of time is spent under the eyes of the community, members must wear "public faces" with few havens for "private faces." In Goffman's (1958) terms, most of kibbutz life is spent on "front stage"; indeed, very little "backstage" exists.

CHANGES IN THE SOCIAL BASIS OF INTIMACY

Major historical transformations of the kibbutz altered the situational constraints on friendship. Three social rearrangements that directly affected friendship were increased ethnic differentiation, the emergence of a second generation, and the evolution of family structures. Each of these social changes eroded the ideological basis of communal intimacy and undermined the social mechanisms which supported it. Simultaneously, new bases of intimacy were created, each providing an arena of face-to-face interaction, affiliation, and cohesion. The divisions of community were offset with new reintegrative mechanisms on a subcommunal level.

1. Ethnic Differentiation[8]

The original kibbutz founders, thirty teenagers from Polish Galicia, arrived in Palestine in 1930. These youth were members of the Young Guardians Youth Movement (*Hashomer Hatsair*), a European Zionist movement, and had trained as a "nucleus" (*garin*) intent on emigrating to Palestine to found a kibbutz. Over the next decade, other "nuclei" and a few unaffiliated individuals from Galicia, Latvia, Lithuania, and Estonia emigrated to Palestine and joined this settlement.

These founding groups, although conscious of the order of immigration, formed a relatively homogeneous group. The major ethnic split occurred with the arrival of a German-Austrian group in 1941, the last group to arrive before WW II. The "German group," as it is called, was intent on founding its own kibbutz, but the movement wanted them to help populate the Polish settlement. From the start, the German group and the founders were at odds. The Germans felt they were more cultured, learned, and cosmopolitan than the Poles. Even today they analyze their differences in terms of the "mentality" of people from small towns and rural areas with their "mentality" of large urban centers, like Vienna and Berlin. The stereotypical Galician is provincial, frugal, and "uncultured." The Germans contend that the Galicians set the dominant tone of the community, and this is largely responsible for the economic success and supremacy of economics in the kibbutz earned at the expense of an inferior and deficient "cultural" side.

The German group represented the first major internal division of the community. They established their own Secretariat (*meskiroot*) parallel to the pre-existing Galician dominated collective-administration apparatus. While this was antithetical to the democratic ideal of a kibbutz, the separate political organization represents the Germans' desire to retain their own identity and maintain an obvious exclusivity from the rest of the community.

The Germans lived in the same area, interacted face-to-face frequently and intensely, and met as a group several times a week. These members told us that they always did things "as a group"—they visited together informally, celebrated holidays and birthdays, and met to discuss the myriad issues of kibbutz life. They developed a distinctive subculture and maintained a cohesive, well-integrated exclusive group within the community. In a sense, the Germans recreated the original kibbutz in their own group.

For the Germans, the main source of intimacy and identification was their ethnic group. A durable set of intimate friendships emerged, excluding most of the non-German membership. Even though the German group gets together less frequently today, and the separate Secretariat no longer exists, these ethnic-based friendships persist in contemporary kibbutz life.

Two other groups joined the kibbutz after WW II, a mixed Polish-German group of concentration camp survivors and a group from Egypt. Neither group came as a cohesive "nucleus." The survivors were an aggregate of individuals searching for a home in Israel; they were sent to this settlement under the direction of Jewish national agencies. The

"Egyptians" were a small collection of mature families, wealthy elites, predominantly Italian nationals who had lived in an "Italian colony" for a few generations. They immigrated to "find a Jewish home" on the eve of Egyptian nationalism. Neither group rivaled the prior German group in developing a distinctive subculture or intimate friendships. The Polish-German group assimilated into the community. Most of the Egyptians, unaccustomed to the hardships of kibbutz life, anxious about communal child-care, and faced with an unempathetic community, eventually left the kibbutz. Only a few remain today.

The ethnic division of community persists mainly for the original immigrants and their eldest children. The deep rift still underlies many contemporary conflicts between ethnic groups. However, the second generation, born in the kibbutz, does not carry these ethnic divisions and loyalties. As a result, ethnic attachments, especially as sources of friendship and intimacy, peaked with the immigrants and subsided in the kibbutz-born generation.

2. The Second Generation: From Cohort to Community

After the major absorption of immigrant groups, the birth of kibbutz children became the main source of demographic growth. Today about one-half of the total adult membership is kibbutz-born.

Kibbutz children are placed in age-cohorts from infancy onward; as an integral "group," they pass through the system of children's houses. One purpose of this system, as mentioned above, was to minimize the institution of family. A second purpose, equally important, was the primary socialization of future kibbutz members, the first to be "comrades" from birth to death.

Growing up in cohorts simulated the collective way of life in the larger kibbutz community, instilling this way of life as natural and self-evident. The older children's cohorts, for example, were expected to confront and debate ideological issues, such as the "inequality" caused when one child received a gift from the outside, internalizing kibbutz ideology and preparing for full membership in the community. "Strength" in ideological conviction and personal fortitude was a value to instill in kibbutz children. As a kibbutz-born adult recalled:

> We were taught to be strong and to know everything. Not to know something was considered a sign of weakness. We were always forced to defend the kibbutz to outsiders, so we had to be strong. We were made to believe that we were superior
> . . .

The totality of life in kibbutz cohorts is difficult to comprehend. Kibbutz cohorts start with the demographer's definition of cohort and add a high intensity and frequency of interaction, daily common proximate space and time, and full knowledge of cradle-to-present biographies. Growing up in this context is best captured in a comment made by a thirty-year old member as he put his arm around the shoulders of a member of his cohort: "We pissed together."

Cohorts have become a major organizational principle in the community. Integration is based on ties among peers. Cross-age or cross-generation ties are problematical in the community [cf. Talmon (1972, p. 28)]. Cohorts remain socially significant units throughout the lives of their members. For example, contiguous cohorts are clustered into residential neighborhoods, resulting in neighborhoods segregated by age and generation. Further, members of a cohort pass through the stages of the life-cycle in common space and time; thus, they share many experiences and problems.

Neighborhood groups can act as political interest groups in the kibbutz. For example, the eldest cohorts felt they were "entitled" to new housing because in the past they had lived in the most primitive conditions. Also, they complained about lack of space for their larger families.[9] Several active members of the eldest cohorts were the principal movers behind the construction of new apartments, raising the standard of housing, and pushing for their group to occupy the neighborhood of new apartments.[10]

Cohorts and neighborhoods are twin sources of friendship formation and maintenance. Throughout the life of a member, the cohort of birth remains an intimate group. As one kibbutz-born member said:

> You have to realize that most of the friends you have on the kibbutz, you have since you were children. With few exceptions, people are friendly with the people they were friendly with as children . . .

Another member expressed the persistence and felt-presence of the cohort:

> I have some friends in my "group," but I really don't do much with them. But I can say that they are there as a potential in case I want them. They are always there if I need them. I may not visit them for a long time, but I can. . . .

Residential proximity serves to maintain a high level of interaction among members of the same cohort. Neighbors visit spontaneously; their children play together when they come to visit in the afternoon. The minutiae of neighboring activities, such as borrowing small food items, occur to a degree. However, since the community is the main provider of goods and services, borrowing is merely a convenience that saves a walk to the communal dining hall. Many holidays are celebrated by neighborhoods. For instance, in the years prior to our fieldwork, *Sukkot* (harvest festival) was celebrated in each neighborhood.

The separation of neighborhoods is perceived as a barrier to the maintenance of friendships. One couple, who declined to move to a new neighborhood with their cohort, felt isolated:

> My husband and I are regretting that we didn't move into the new neighborhood with all the people our age. Now we are living here and there will be a lot of younger people living here. We won't be in the center of things here. But we never thought about it like that. All we thought about was that this is an end-house and they would make it larger than the new houses and we would have more space here for the children.
>
> [I don't understand. You make it seem like you and your friends live at opposite ends of a large city.] But it's so far to go. It's hard not to live near your friends, near people your own age. I sometimes visit my friends in the other neighborhood, but it's far. And, I didn't realize that my children's friends would be visiting their parents over there. While my children try to make me feel better and say, "So what if our friends are over there, we don't care," my children are always over there playing with their friends . . .

The physical distance between the two neighborhoods farthest apart is not great, about a ten-to-fifteen minute walk. The "barrier" of distance indicates a cultural difference in perception of distance, the time constraint of distance, and social distance created by isolation from cohort.

While cohorts are maintained by residential propinquity, the typical pattern of marriage and residence has a divisive impact on the composition of cohorts. Upon marriage, choice of cohort is necessary. In general, women move into their husbands' cohorts. Thus, if two members born in this kibbutz marry (about 20 percent of all second generation marriages),[11] the wife enters her husband's "group." This male orientation also occurs when one spouse, either the wife (39 percent) or the husband (28 percent), comes from outside the community, or when both immigrate to the kibbutz (13 percent). Residence is established by the husband's cohort, if he is a member, or by the husband's age,[12] if he comes from the outside.[13]

This would not be problematic if spouses were close in age; however, members of the same cohort never marry [cf. Talmon (1972); Shepher (1972)] and kibbutz women typically marry men several years older. Almost half of all kibbutz-born women who are married have moved from cohorts of birth, entering older kibbutz cohorts, and shifting into different stages of the life-cycle and sets of interests and concerns.

This pattern separates women from their childhood cohorts and friends. Women from one cohort may be dispersed across the kibbutz, each living in quite separate neighborhoods. New friends are acquired from the husband's cohort. A conversation with a kibbutz-born woman married to an older kibbutz-born man pinpoints this changeover:

> [(At a kibbutz party) Who are you and your husband sitting with?] They are our friends. [Are all of them close friends?] No, not all, but most of them. They grew up with my husband. [Where is your group?] Not many are on the kibbutz. But when I joined with my husband, I passed into his group of friends . . .

Although cohort is a source of friendship for men and women, men are better able to maintain friendships formed in cohorts of origin. This does not mean that women are unable to keep old friends. Rather, the marital division of cohort creates an asymmetrical structure of intimate relations. This in turn diminishes the level of interaction and shared experiences for women of the same cohort, undermining the foundation of enduring friendships.

People who marry into the kibbutz rely upon their spouse for community entry and acculturation, a process of community acceptance and adjustment that typically takes years. This process is especially problematic for those who were not born and raised in another kibbutz. Coupled with the traditional problems of an outsider status in any community, a foreign life-style must be learned.

The husband from the outside has less adjustment and acceptance difficulties than the wife from the outside since he moves into a cohort of age-peers, but she typically moves into an older cohort. While the female spouses within a cohort may become friendly, it is the male who is the major determinant of friendship patterns. Reliance on the husband for friendship and companionship was expressed by a woman from an Israeli city, who had married a kibbutz-born member:

> The first two years when I was seeing my husband I came to the kibbutz slowly. At first I would go with him to his friends. They were people from his "group." He had people from his "group" and he had friends; I didn't have any. At the beginning when I came to live here I wouldn't go to the members' club or the dining room or a movie myself because I didn't know anyone and I felt strange. I have been living here seven years now and I go where I want by myself. My husband is gone a lot and I am not going to sit home myself like many women do, for example, when their husbands are in the army.

3. Emergence of Family

In a fifty-year period, the kibbutz community grew from a complete absence of kinship to a full three-generational kinship structure. Ninety-five percent of the total adult membership is part of some kinship structure; the largest kinship structures, the kibbutz's "clans" (*hamula*), are comprised of 20 to 40 adult members each. The early proscriptions against family have shifted to the acceptance and promotion of family as a central pillar of community. A founder summarized the place of family in the contemporary kibbutz as follows:

> Today the family is very important. We think that the family is the first important cell of the kibbutz. If the family is not exhibited, or is not living at a high level, the kibbutz cannot be stabilized and developed . . .

Even though the family has become a salient unit in the community, its functions are still circumscribed in many important ways. Communal childrearing, for example, has never been radically altered, though its continuation has been debated. Our contention is that family and kinship have partly superseded and replaced earlier mechanisms of communal integration and solidarity. Family has become a "community surrogate," providing the main basis of personal attachment and the principal source of intimacy; it is through family that community is integrated.[14]

Family is perceived to be the main source of intimacy in the community. As one founder stated:

> . . . there is a need for intimate relations and you find it in the family. This is one reason in many societies the family is undergoing rapid change but in the kibbutz— there is a strengthening of the family. People have a need to belong. And they belong to family . . .

Family is the main haven of exclusive intimacy in the contemporary kibbutz. From marriage through early family life, the couple retracts into itself, withdrawing from community, and builds a private sphere—the first prolonged experience of dyadic privacy in either of their lives. It is a socially recognized problem that those who are "building their families" tend to reduce their participation in community. The danger of "familial withdrawal" [Slater (1963)] to collective maintenance is also recognized, as one veteran member observed:

> . . . The kibbutz is also in danger if the family closes itself up. The family should be open to the demand of the kibbutz. How to build the synthesis of these two points is the key: family as a cell and keeping the family together as a builder of the kibbutz.

The "temporary" withdrawal of young families is expected; however, various families have permanently retracted from community. The "closed family" (*mishpachah sgorah*), whose members "put in their time at work" and then retreat into family life, are a growing threat to communal life. The "open family" (*mishpachah pituchah*), whose members sit on committees, accept offices, volunteer for various duties, and so forth, is heralded as the mainstay of the community.

Family has disrupted older intimate relations. The ethnic solidarity of the German group, for example, has diminished in favor of family. Once members of this group interacted frequently, visiting several times a week, but now more and more time is spent with their individual families. Many of them express nostalgia about their younger days when they "did things as a group."

In the earlier periods of the kibbutz, if a member had to travel outside for a few days, their "friends" would take care of the children in the afternoon. Today, kin care for the children whenever the parents travel outside the community.

In general, family has become the single most important haven of intimacy in the kibbutz. Family eroded the supports of comradeship and transmuted communal intimacy into exclusive familial intimacy.

At this point, we need to summarize the separate and joint effects of these transformations. First, the ideal of comradeship, a nonexclusive intimate relationship, was most closely approximated in the early kibbutz. Second, ethnic differentiation precipitated the initial erosion of communal intimacy. Friendship within ethnic groups was the first major form of exclusive intimate relationships. From an overview of the structure of intimate relations, however, friendship via ethnicity decreased in importance as the second generation emerged. Third, friendship within cohorts increased with the rise of the second generation to become a major location of friendship today. However, friendship in cohort is restricted by the divisive impact of marriage and family. Fourth, family evolved to become the single most important source of intimacy in contemporary kibbutz life. Last, communal intimacy was eroded by each of these single transformations; the joint effect is a continual diminution of comradeship.

SOCIAL ORDER OF INTIMATE RELATIONS

We now return to the three general characteristics of friendship in community which we outlined in the beginning of this paper and compare them with friendship in the kibbutz.

The transformations of the kibbutz spread the fabric of community, creating new structural locations for exclusive intimate relationships. Friendship formation followed the overall lines of kibbutz social organization. The initial emergence of friendship was produced by the first major division of community, created by ethnic differentiation. Later, friendship emerged within the homogeneous locations of second generation cohorts.

Like some communities, the kibbutz is characterized by low social and geographic mobility. Membership in the community is a cradle-to-grave affair. Prolonged interaction with the outside, such as working in an outside job, is restricted. Significant interaction with the outside only occurs at certain narrow periods of the life-cycle: obligatory military service after high school, periodic reserve duty, higher education, and occasional service in the kibbutz federation or regional enterprises. Social mobility is also restricted. Virtually no internal "upward" mobility is possible within the community. The rare career outside the kibbutz almost always incurs social ostracism within the kibbutz. Thus, friendship is bounded by community.

The growth and differentiation of the kibbutz can be viewed as a move from a single set of primordial ties to a multiplicity of intermediate groups enmeshed in social networks. Each member is no longer directly linked to every other member; rather, each member is directly linked to a subset of the total membership and indirectly linked to the remainder. This has two effects: first, although the community remains an overarching locus of attachment,[15] members' primary attachments are diffused into intermediate groups; second, some of the mechanisms of informal social control have weakened. For example, there is a socially-recognized "weakness of reactions to public opinion . . . in working arrangements and in the social and cultural order."[16] These changes indicate a shift in the mix of emergent and consciously regulated social relationships; overall, there is a relative increase in the proportion of emergent social relationships.

The net effect was the creation of more *potential* for exclusive intimate relationships. However, friendship has not become a prevalent form of exclusive intimate relationships. The creation of more potential for friendship was not matched with a creation of a role for friendship in kibbutz life. Most significantly, the basic economic organization of the kibbutz eliminated the one nearly-ubiquitous role of friendship, material exchange and assistance. Further, family evolved to become the most enduring provider of intimacy and sociopolitical/emotional support in the contemporary kibbutz.

The transformation of intimate relations in the kibbutz can be viewed as a shift towards a more traditional structure of intimate relations. The relative importance of kibbutz intimate relationships roughly parallels the rank order of informal affiliations in some American urban communities. In these communities, the order of informal relations, from most important to least important, is family, friends, neighbors, and co-workers [Axelrod (1956), Bell and Boat (1957)]. Similarly, family in the contemporary kibbutz is the most important location of intimate relationships. Friends through cohorts, coterminous with neighbors, is second. Last, co-workers are a minor source of informal attachment in the kibbutz.[17] However, the typical American community lacks a type of intimate relationship present in the kibbutz: comradeship. Even in its residual state, comradeship still pervades kibbutz life and sets the kibbutz community apart from most others.

ACKNOWLEDGMENT

We gratefully acknowledge the helpful comments and suggestions of Bernard Beck, Richard Fritz, Albert Hunter, Janet Lever, and Allan Schnaiberg. Partial support for this project was provided by NIMH Training Grant #MH-10497.

NOTES

1. The seven major functions that Cohen (1961) identifies are: material exchange and/or economic assistance; sociopolitical and emotional support; go-between in love affairs and marriage arrangements; homosexuality; sponsorship in rites of passage; mourning obligations; and exchange of children. Some of these are inapplicable to kibbutz life, others are fulfilled through a variety of nonfriendship means.

2. The term *chaver* cannot be understood out of context. For instance, a member of the Israeli parliament is called *chaver knesset*, "member of parliament" (MP). In this context, of course, *chaver* does not represent the communal intimacy of comradeship; the parliament has been anything but "kibbutz-like."

3. We are not implying that material needs cause friendship, nor that friendship is entered into solely for exploitation. Rather, friendship in community exemplifies what is a near-maxim in economic anthropology: enduring social relationships have some material expression. Family and kin, of course, also provide a wide variety of goods and services. Familial "social insurance" is prevalent especially in "stateless" societies [e.g., Strathern (1971)]. Several social relationships, including "friendship reciprocity," provided labor to work the land in traditional Bantu society [Dalton (1967, p. 67)]. See also Schnaiberg and Goldenberg (1975) for an examination of family economic exchanges.

4. For a fuller elaboration of the concept of "conscious community" and its use in the analysis of social change, see Baker/Hertz (1979).

5. Punch's study mainly concerns a radical-progressive school. He adds emphasis to this with comparisons to Bettelheim's (1969) study of kibbutz children and communal education.

6. Note that this is similar to the courtly model of romantic love—a love relationship separated from marriage; that is, love was encapsulated in temporary relationships with no enduring social unions to threaten existing structure.

7. We are using "comradeship" instead of "brotherhood" although the meanings are very similar. Comradeship, implied in the term for members, *chaverim* or "comrades," better represents the "brotherhood" of the kibbutz.

8. Apart from Kressel's (1977) study of ethnic duality in a kibbutz, there is a dearth of research on ethnicity in kibbutzim. Talmon [(1972, p. 35)] briefly mentions the ethnic differences of kibbutzim. Weintraub (1971) and Weintraub and associates (1971) have explicitly studied ethnicity and community development in a different type of Israeli cooperative settlement, the *moshavim*.

9. Parents and children visit in the afternoon in the parents' "rooms." Each couple lives in a small 2 1/2 room apartment. The eldest of the second generation, in their late thirties to forties, are in the life stage where they have a large number of children and thus are cramped during afternoon visitations.

10. Since these new apartments were above the standard of housing in other neighborhoods, *all* other apartments were remodeled to expand the floor area until it equaled the floor area of the new apartments. This attempt to maintain material equality was a major undertaking which took over two years to complete.

11. Percentages are the number of marriages of specified type over total second generation marriages. Out of 238 second generation members, 188 are married (94 couples).

12. This is determined by the system of *vedik*, age and seniority (length of membership). Lately, the trend is to use age only.

13. This is similar to the rule of patrilocal residence described by anthropologists [e.g., Bohannan and Middleton (1968)]. Unlike patrilocal residence, we find preference for residence with the husband's cohort, not the husband's family; indeed, familial residence does not exist in the kibbutz. The divisive effect on woman's solidarity is the same in the kibbutz as in true patrilocal residence.

14. For an elaboration of these issues, see Hertz/Baker 1980; alongside the integrative role of family in the community, divisive elements, especially the potential power of the "clans," also exist.

15. Although attachment to community may be a weak tie, it should not be compared to "weak ties" [cf. Granovetter (1973)] in American communities; our opinion is that the "weak" tie of comradeship is stronger than many "strong" ties in our American culture.

16. This is an excerpt from a kibbutz-newspaper report. On *Yom Kippur* the community divided into neighborhood-based groups and discussed the problems of kibbutz life in the past year. The written reports of each group were compiled and reported in the newspaper.

17. The majority of work branches are not significant locations of friendship. The two exceptions are the cotton branch and the fishery branch. In these branches, the organization of work demands cooperation and team work; each set of workers develops into a cohesive group with a strong team spirit. However, since the workers in these branches are close in age, often from the same cohort or contiguous cohorts, it is difficult to separate intimacy derived from cohort affiliation from intimacy created through close working conditions.

REFERENCES

Axelrod, Morris
    1956   "Urban structure and social participation," American Sociological Review XXI (February): 13–18.
Baker, Wayne/Hertz, Rosanna
    1979   "The conscious community and its transformation: a community study of a kibbutz." Candidacy Research Paper, Department of Sociology, Northwestern University, Evanston, Illinois.
Bell, Wendell, and Boat, Marion D.
    1957   "Urban neighborhoods and informal relations." American Journal of Sociology Vol. LXII, No. 4 (January): 391–398.
Bennett, John W.
    1968   "Reciprocal economic exchanges among North American agricultural operators." Southwestern Journal of Anthropology 24, No. 3 (Autumn): 276–309.
Bettelheim, Bruno
    1969   Children of the Dream. New York: Macmillan.
Bohannan, Paul J., and Middleton, John (eds.)
    1968   Kinship and Social Organization. Garden City, New York: Natural History Press.
Carden, Maren Lockwood
    1971   Oneida: Utopian Community to Modern Corporation. New York: Harper and Row Publishers.

Cohen, Yehudi A.
1961 "Patterns of friendship." Pp. 351–386 in Yehudi A. Cohen (ed.), Social Structure and Personality: a Casebook. Holt, Rinehart and Winston.
Dalton, George
1967 "Traditional production in primitive African economics." Pp. 61–80 in George Dalton (ed.), Tribal and Peasant Economies, Austin, Texas: Texas Press.
Gans, Herbert
1967 The Levittowners. New York: Vintage Books.
Gans, Herbert
1962 The Urban Villagers. New York: The Free Press.
Gilmore, David
1975 "Friendship in Fuenmayor: patterns of friendship in an atomistic society." Ethnology Vol. XIV, No. 4 (October): 311–324.
Goffman, Erving
1958 The Presentation of Self in Everyday Life. Social Sciences Research Center, Edinburgh: The University of Edinburgh.
Goode, William J.
1959 "The theoretical importance of love." American Sociological Review 24, No. 1 (February): 38–47.
Granovetter, Mark S.
1973 "Strength of weak ties." American Journal of Sociology 78 (May): 1360–80.
Hertz, Rosanna/Baker, Wayne
1980 "Kinship in an Israeli Kibbutz: community continuity and division." Paper presented at the Annual Meetings of the Midwest Sociological Society, Milwaukee, Wisc.: April.
Hillery, George A.
1968 Communal Organizations: A Study of Local Societies. Chicago, Ill.: University of Chicago Press.
Kanter, Rosabeth Moss
1972 Commitment and Community; Communes and Utopias in Sociological Perspective. Cambridge, Mass.: Harvard University Press.
Kornblum, William
1974 Blue Collar Community. Chicago, Ill.: University of Chicago Press.
Kressel, Gideon M.
1977 "Ethnic duality in a kibbutz." Ethnic Groups 1: 241–262.
Liebow, Elliot
1967 Tally's Corner: A Study of Negro Streetcorner Men. Boston: Little, Brown and Company.
Punch, Maurice
1974 "Sociology of the anti-institution." British Journal of Sociology 25 (September): 312–325.
Redfield, Robert
1960 The Little Community and Peasant Society. Chicago, Ill.: University of Chicago Press.
Schnaiberg, Allan, and Goldberg, Sheldon
1975 "Closing the circle: the impact of children on parental status." Journal of Marriage and the Family (November): 937–953.
Schwartz, Richard D.
1964 Social factors in the development of legal control: a case study of two Israeli settlements." Yale Law Journal 63.

Seeley, John R., Sim, Alexander R., and Loosley, Elizabeth W.
  1967   Crestwood Heights. New York: Science Editions.
Shepher, Joseph
  1971   "Self imposed incest avoidance and exogamy in second generation kibbutz adults." Ann Arbor, Mich.: Xerox Mimeograph Nos. 72–871.
Slater, Philip E.
  1963   "On social regression." American Sociological Review 28 (June): 339–364.
Spiro, Medford E.
  1963   Kibbutz: Venture in Utopia. New York: Schocken Books.
Strathern, Andrew
  1971   The Rope of Moka. Cambridge, Mass.: Cambridge University Press.
Suttles, Gerald D.
  1968   The Social Order of the Slum. Chicago, Ill.: University of Chicago Press.
Talmon, Yonina
  1972   Family and Community in the Kibbutz. Cambridge, Mass.: University of Chicago Press.
Vidich, Arthur J., and Bensman, Joseph
  1968   Small Town in Mass Society. Princeton, N.J.: Princeton University Press.
Weintraub, Dov
  1971   "Rural cooperation, local government and social structure: a comparative study of village organization in different types of communities in Israel." Pp. 83–136 in Peter Worsley (ed.), Two Blades of Grass. Manchester: Manchester University Press.
Weintraub, Dov and associates
  1971   Immigration and Social Change. Manchester: Manchester University Press.
Wellman, Barry
  1978   "The community question: the intimate networks of East Yorkers." Manuscript, Centre for Urban and Community Studies, Canada. (April) University of Toronto.
Whyte, William F.
  1943   Street Corner Society. Chicago, Ill.: University of Chicago Press.

BIOGRAPHICAL SKETCH OF THE CONTRIBUTORS

Joan Acker is Professor of Sociology at the University of Oregon. Her most recent publication is *Doing Comparative Worth* with Temple University Press. She has written on women and stratification, women and work, and women in organizations. She is the 1989 winner of the Jessie Bernard Lifetime Award of the American Sociological Association.

Wayne Baker is Associate Professor at the University of Chicago. The research on which this manuscript is based is part of a larger community study of the kibbutz, conducted with Rosanna Hertz. He has presented two co-authored papers on kinship and family in the kibbutz, both of which are being adapted for publication. Other forthcoming works about the kibbutz include an article on the professional structure of work and a general review of family literature to appear in *Marriage and Family*

Review. He received a B.S. in Finance (1974) and a M.A. in Sociology (1976) at Northern Illinois University, Dekalb, Illinois.

Elizabeth A. Bankoff was an instructor of the Masters of Arts Program in the Social Sciences at the University of Chicago at the time her chapter was written. As a doctoral candidate in the Committee on Human Development, Department of Behavioral Sciences, at the University of Chicago, Ms. Bankoff's research focused on social support systems and adaptation to major life crises. In addition to her current study of the ways in which friends can facilitate or hinder adaptation to widowhood, Ms. Bankoff has also explored the role self-help groups play in effecting adaptation to widowhood and heart surgery [cf. Bankoff, E.A.(1979), Widow groups as an alternative to informal social support. In M.A. Lieberman and L.D. Borman (Eds.), *Self-Help Groups for Coping with Crisis*. San Francisco: Jossey-Bass; Bond, G.R., Borman, L., Bankoff, E.A., Daiter, S., Lieberman, M., and Videka, L. (1979), Mended hearts: A self-help case study. *Social Policy*, 9(4)].

Kate Barry is Director of the Women's Program at Lane Community College, Eugene, Oregon. She is a graduate of the University of Newcastle in England and the University of Oregon.

B. Bradford Brown is an Assistant Professor of Human Development in the Department of Educational Psychology at the University of Wisconsin-Madison. He received his Ph.D. from the University of Chicago. His research has focused on the role of social support systems in personality development and adaptation to stress, and on the determinants of personality change across adulthood. Currently, he is investigating the role of peer groups on adolescence, social development, and school achievement.

Joke Esseveld is teaching sociology at Lund University of Sweden. She is a graduate of the Nederlandse Economische Hogenschool in Rotterdam and studied at the University of Oregon.

Thomas M. Gannon, S.J., former Professor and Chairman of the Department of Sociology at Loyola University of Chicago, is currently Director of Research for the Heartland Center in East Chicago. He received his Ph.D. in Sociology from the University of Chicago and also holds graduate degrees in philosophy (Ph.L.) and theology (S.T.L.). His main publications include *The Desert and the City* (Macmillan, 1968); *The Society of Jesus in the United States: A Sociological Survey* (5 vols., Argus Publications, 1971); articles and reviews in the *American Journal of Sociology*, *Sociology and Social Research*, *Sociological Analysis*, *So-*

cial Compass, Review of Religious Research, Journal for the Scientific Study of Religion, and several sociology readers and popular journals. His major interests are social organization theory, sociology of religion, urban policy, and deviance.

Joseph R. Gusfield obtained his Ph.D. in Sociology from the University of Chicago (1954) and is Professor of Sociology at the University of California, San Diego. He has published in the areas of social movements, development theory, sociology of law, and political sociology. Among his books are *Symbolic Crusade, Protest, Reform and Revolt: Academic Values and Mass Education* (with David Riesman and Zelda Gamson); and *Community: A Critical Response.* His most recent book is *The Culture of Public Problems: Drinking-Driving and the Symbolic Order.* He has been a Fellow at the Center for Advanced Studies of Behavioral Science and a Guggenheim Fellow.

Rosanna Hertz was a doctoral student at Northwestern University when this chapter was written. She obtained her Ph.D. there in 1983 and is presently an Associate Professor of Sociology at Wellsley College and a Fellow in Sociology in the Department of Psychiatry at the Harvard Medical School. She is author of *More Equal Than Others: Women and Men in Dual Career Marriages,* and is currently at work on a study of the financial arrangements among dual earner couples.

Joseph Kotarba is currently Associate Professor in the Department of Sociology, University of Houston, Texas. He has his Ph.D. from the University of California, San Diego (1979). He has published in the areas of deviance and medical sociology. He has been especially interested in the institutional systems dealing with treatment of pain.

Judith A. Levy is Assistant Professor of Health Resources Management, School of Public Health, University of Illinois, Chicago. She obtained her Ph.D. from Northwestern University and has conducted research on the American hospice movement, AIDS, and various aspects of the medical professions. She edited *Current Research on Occupations and Professions,* which appeared as volume 6 of the JAI series *Research in the Interweave of Social Roles.*

Roger Little is Professor Emeritus of Sociology, University of Illinois at Chicago Circle. He has conducted research on role performance in a variety of military settings. His doctoral dissertation was based on a participant-observer study of an infantry platoon in combat during the Korean Conflict. After receiving his Ph.D. at Michigan State University

(1956), he was a sociologist with the Army Medical Service until 1966. He has since conducted studies of the medical aidmen and fatal casualties in Vietnam. He is the editor of *Selective Service and American Society* (1969) and *Handbook of Military Institutions* (1971).

Helena Znaniecka Lopata is Professor of Sociology and Director, Center for the Comparative Study of Social Roles, Loyola University of Chicago. She received her Ph.D. from the University of Chicago (1954). She is author of *Occupation: Housewife, Widowhood in an American City, Polish American: Status Competition in an Ethnic Community*, and *Women as Widows: Support Systems*. She has edited *Marriage and Families*, and a series, *Research in the Interweave of Social Roles*. Her newest book, forthcoming in 1991, is *Circles and Settings: Changing Roles of American Women*.

David R. Maines, Associate Professor of Sociology at Pennsylvania State University, has worked to articulate an interactionist approach to the study of social organization as well as the fundamental relevance of temporality and communication for sociological analysis. He is Editor of *Symbolic Interaction*, a co-author of *Chronic Illness and Quality of Life* (1984), co-editor (with Carl Couch) of *Communication and Social Structure* (1988), and author of *Time and Social Process* (in press).

Paul Rasmussen has his Ph.D. from the University of California, San Diego (1978), and was a post-doctoral fellow at the University of Southern California at the time his chapter was written. He has published in the areas of deviance and human sexuality. He is the author (with Jack Douglas) of *Nude Beach*.

Marijean Ferguson (Suelzle) is Associate Professor, LaRoche College, Pittsburgh, Pennsylvania. She obtained her Ph.D. in Sociology from the University of California, Berkeley, in 1977, and moved to Northwestern University. After setting up a consultation firm in the Chicago area, she returned to teaching, now developing interests in social gerontology.